CIVIL WAR

YOUNG AVENGERS & RUNAWAYS

After discovering they were the children of a group of super-villains known as the Pride, Nico Minoru and her friends stole weapons and resources from the criminals before running away from home and eventually defeating their parents. Together, the teenage RUNAWAYS now hope to atone for their parents' crimes by taking on the new threats trying to fill the Pride's void.

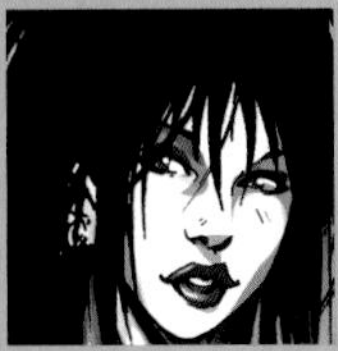
NICO MINORU
Daughter of Dark Wizards

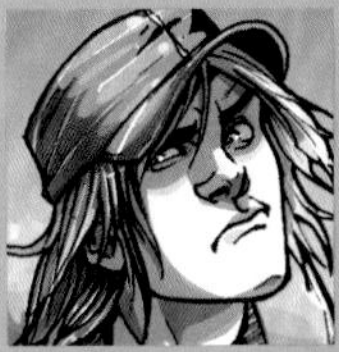
CHASE STEIN
Son of Mad Scientists

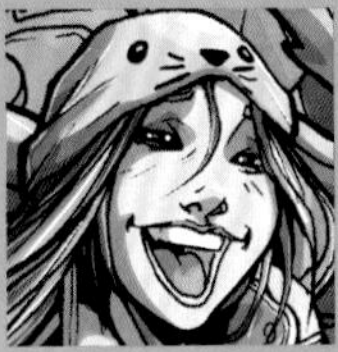
MOLLY HAYES
Daughter of Evil Mutants

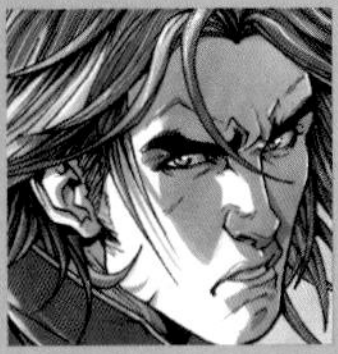
VICTOR MANCHA
Son of a Killer Robot

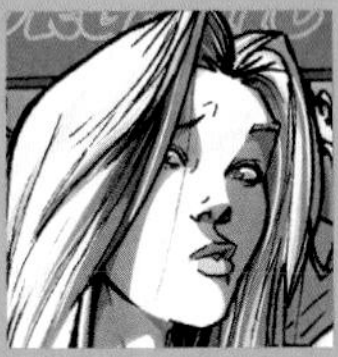
KAROLINA DEAN
Daughter of Alien Invaders

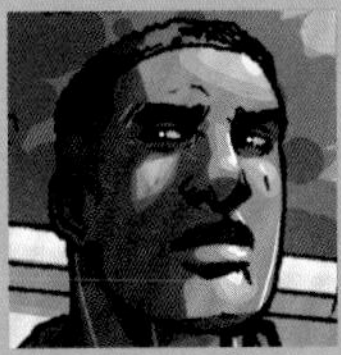
XAVIN
Child of Shape-Shifting Skrull Warlords

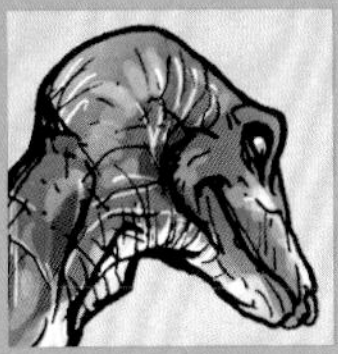
OLD LACE
Genetically Engineered Dinosaur

United by the Avengers Failsafe Program, a protocol designed to assemble the next wave of Earth's Mightiest Heroes, the Young Avengers have faced their fair share of devastating opponents. None, however, as potentially dangerous as the Superhuman Registration Act.

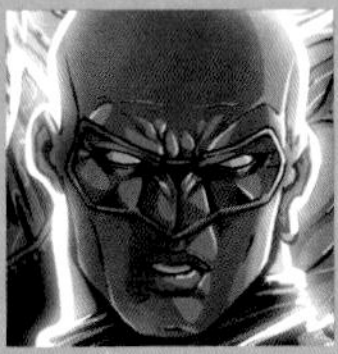
PATRIOT
Eli Bradley

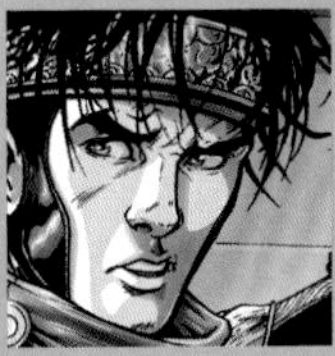
WICCAN
Billy Kaplan

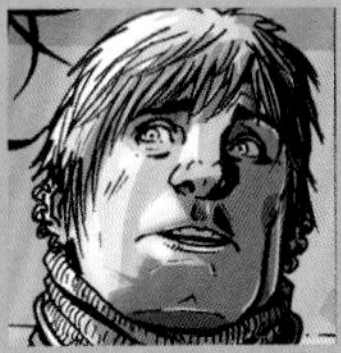
HULKLING
Teddy Altman

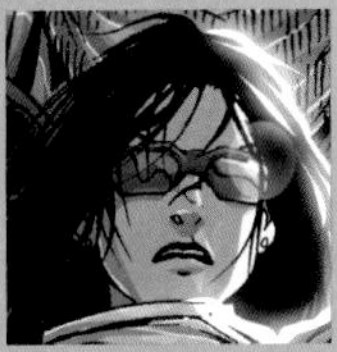
HAWKEYE
Kate Bishop

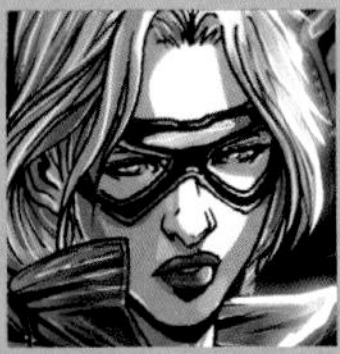
STATURE
Cassie Lang

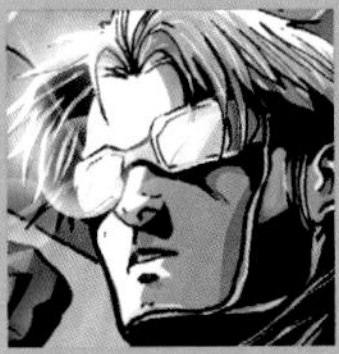
SPEED
Tommy Shepherd

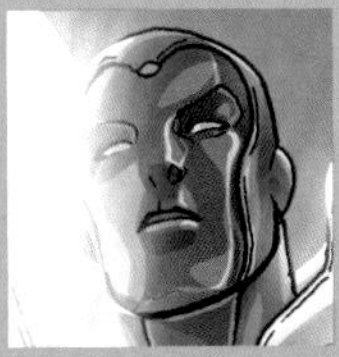
VISION

After Stamford, Connecticut is destroyed during a televised fight between the New Warriors and a group of dangerous villains, public sentiment turns against super heroes. Advocates call for reform, and a Superhuman Registration Act is passed which will require all those possessing paranormal abilities to register with the government, divulge their true identities to the authorities and submit to training and sanctioning in the manner of federal agents. Anyone with super-powers who refuses to register is now a criminal.

Some heroes, such as Iron Man, see this as a natural evolution of the role of superhumans in society and a reasonable request. Others view the Act as an assault on their civil liberties. After being called upon to hunt down heroes in defiance of the Registration Act, Captain America goes underground and begins to form a resistance movement. The Young Avengers are quickly recruited by Cap and his allies.

In California, the Runaways maintain a stance of studied indifference…

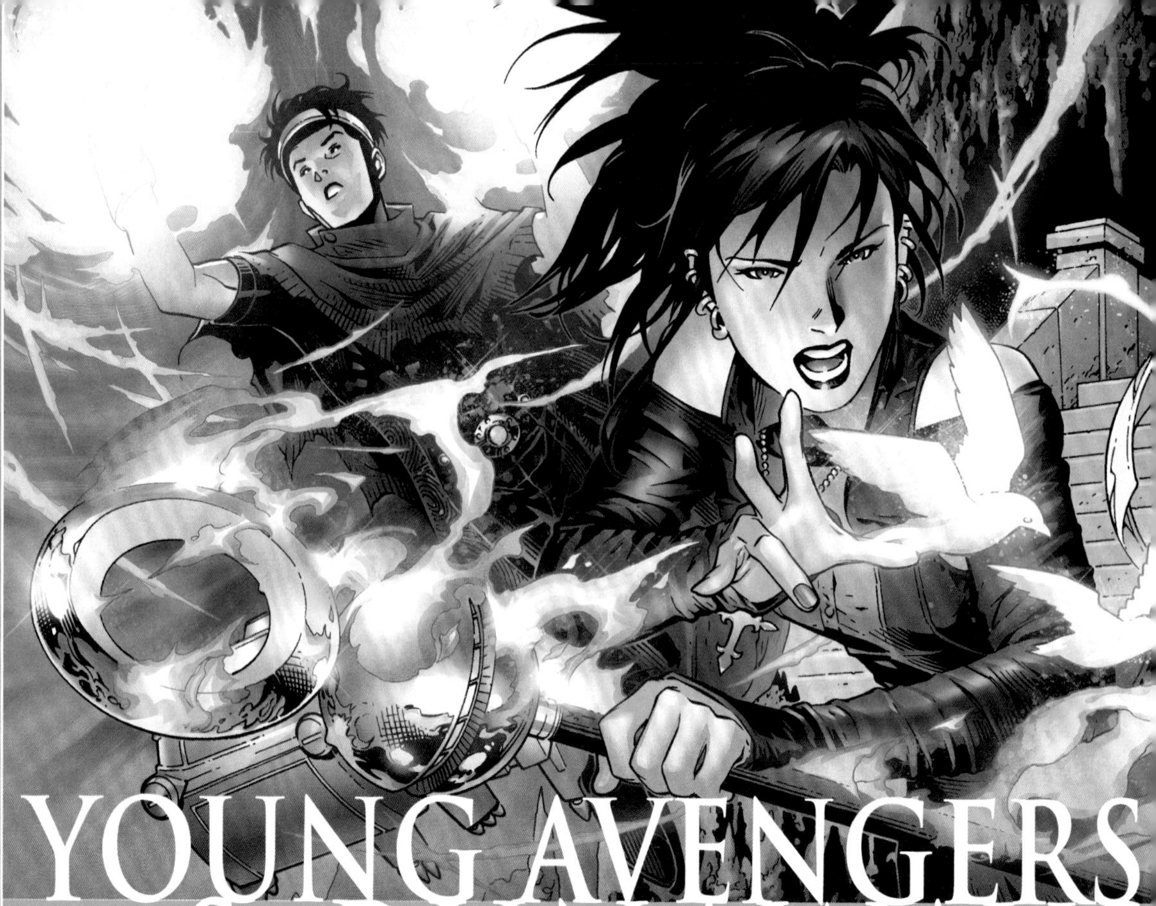

YOUNG AVENGERS & RUNAWAYS

A MARVEL COMICS EVENT

CIVIL WAR

CIVIL WAR: YOUNG AVENGERS & RUNAWAYS #1

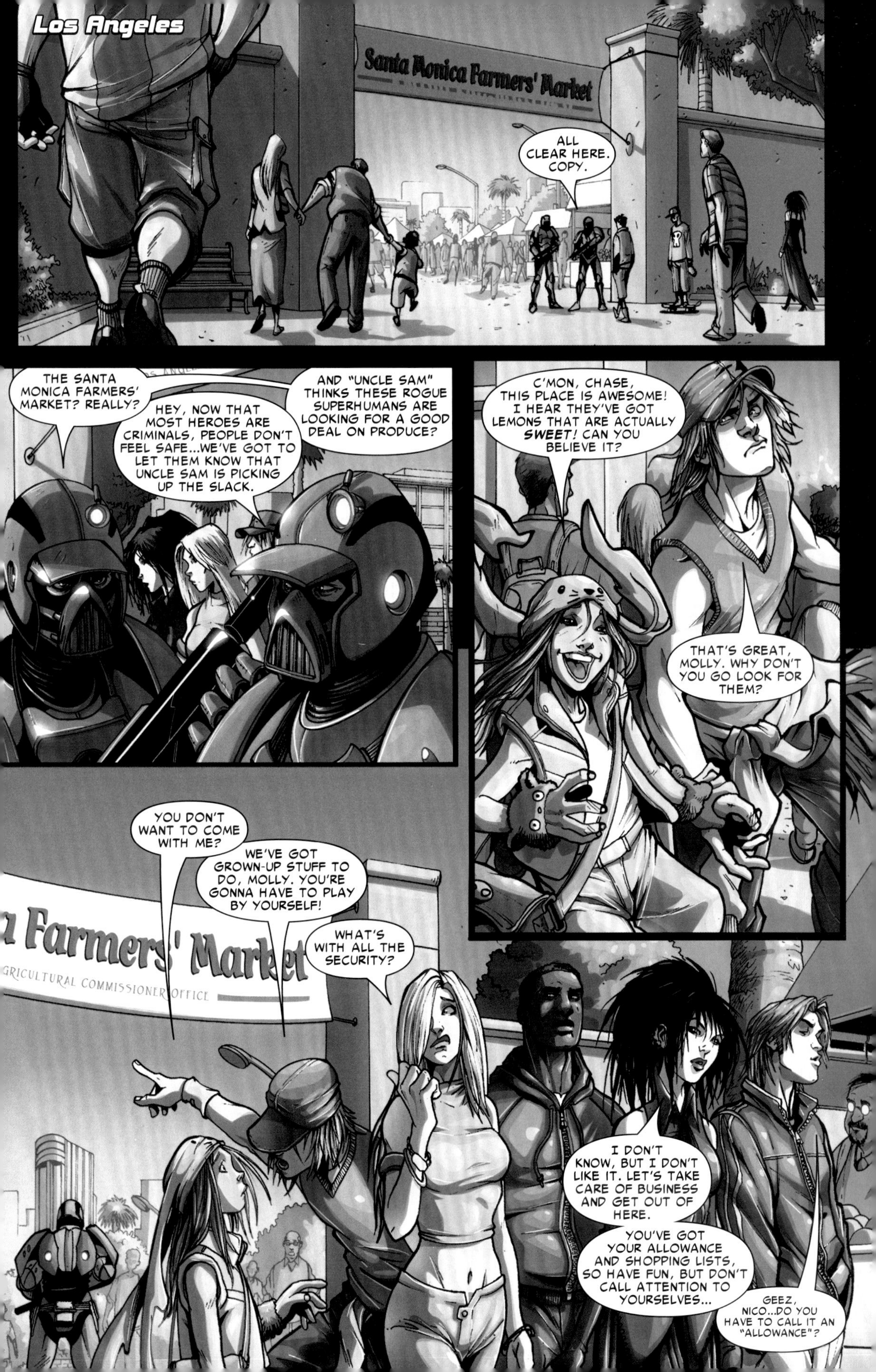
Los Angeles
Santa Monica Farmers' Market
ALL CLEAR HERE. COPY.
THE SANTA MONICA FARMERS' MARKET? REALLY?
AND "UNCLE SAM" THINKS THESE ROGUE SUPERHUMANS ARE LOOKING FOR A GOOD DEAL ON PRODUCE?
HEY, NOW THAT MOST HEROES ARE CRIMINALS, PEOPLE DON'T FEEL SAFE...WE'VE GOT TO LET THEM KNOW THAT UNCLE SAM IS PICKING UP THE SLACK.
C'MON, CHASE, THIS PLACE IS AWESOME! I HEAR THEY'VE GOT LEMONS THAT ARE ACTUALLY ***SWEET!*** CAN YOU BELIEVE IT?
THAT'S GREAT, MOLLY. WHY DON'T YOU GO LOOK FOR THEM?
YOU DON'T WANT TO COME WITH ME?
WE'VE GOT GROWN-UP STUFF TO DO, MOLLY. YOU'RE GONNA HAVE TO PLAY BY YOURSELF!
WHAT'S WITH ALL THE SECURITY?
a Farmers' Market
GRICULTURAL COMMISSIONER OFFICE
I DON'T KNOW, BUT I DON'T LIKE IT. LET'S TAKE CARE OF BUSINESS AND GET OUT OF HERE.
YOU'VE GOT YOUR ALLOWANCE AND SHOPPING LISTS, SO HAVE FUN, BUT DON'T CALL ATTENTION TO YOURSELVES...
GEEZ, NICO...DO YOU HAVE TO CALL IT AN "ALLOWANCE"?

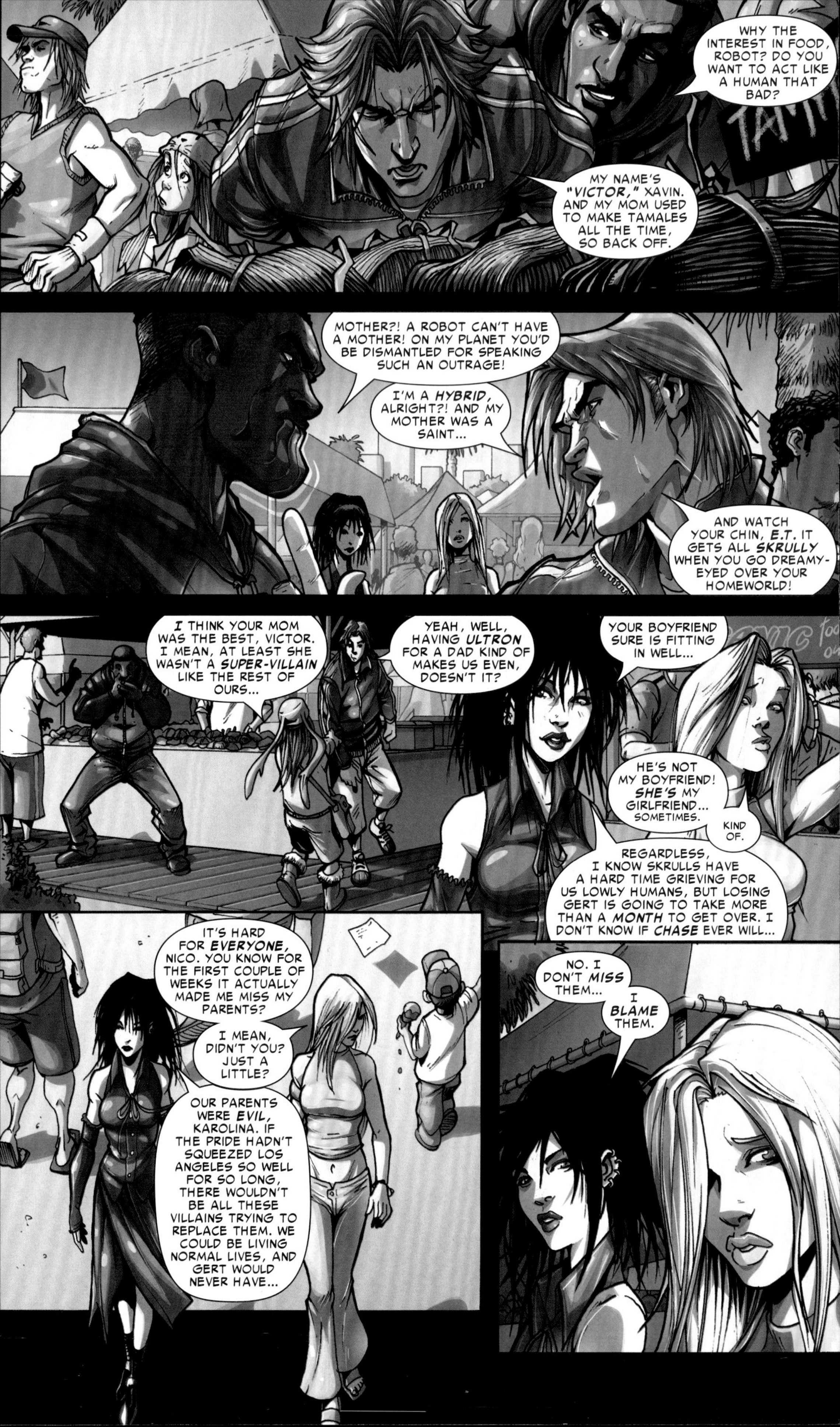
WHY THE INTEREST IN FOOD, ROBOT? DO YOU WANT TO ACT LIKE A HUMAN THAT BAD?
MY NAME'S "VICTOR," XAVIN. AND MY MOM USED TO MAKE TAMALES ALL THE TIME, SO BACK OFF.
MOTHER?! A ROBOT CAN'T HAVE A MOTHER! ON MY PLANET YOU'D BE DISMANTLED FOR SPEAKING SUCH AN OUTRAGE!
I'M A HYBRID, ALRIGHT?! AND MY MOTHER WAS A SAINT...
AND WATCH YOUR CHIN, E.T. IT GETS ALL SKRULLY WHEN YOU GO DREAMY-EYED OVER YOUR HOMEWORLD!
I THINK YOUR MOM WAS THE BEST, VICTOR. I MEAN, AT LEAST SHE WASN'T A SUPER-VILLAIN LIKE THE REST OF OURS...
YEAH, WELL, HAVING ULTRON FOR A DAD KIND OF MAKES US EVEN, DOESN'T IT?
YOUR BOYFRIEND SURE IS FITTING IN WELL...
HE'S NOT MY BOYFRIEND! SHE'S MY GIRLFRIEND... SOMETIMES.
KIND OF.
REGARDLESS, I KNOW SKRULLS HAVE A HARD TIME GRIEVING FOR US LOWLY HUMANS, BUT LOSING GERT IS GOING TO TAKE MORE THAN A MONTH TO GET OVER. I DON'T KNOW IF CHASE EVER WILL...
IT'S HARD FOR EVERYONE, NICO. YOU KNOW FOR THE FIRST COUPLE OF WEEKS IT ACTUALLY MADE ME MISS MY PARENTS?
I MEAN, DIDN'T YOU? JUST A LITTLE?
OUR PARENTS WERE EVIL, KAROLINA. IF THE PRIDE HADN'T SQUEEZED LOS ANGELES SO WELL FOR SO LONG, THERE WOULDN'T BE ALL THESE VILLAINS TRYING TO REPLACE THEM. WE COULD BE LIVING NORMAL LIVES, AND GERT WOULD NEVER HAVE...
NO. I DON'T MISS THEM...
I BLAME THEM.

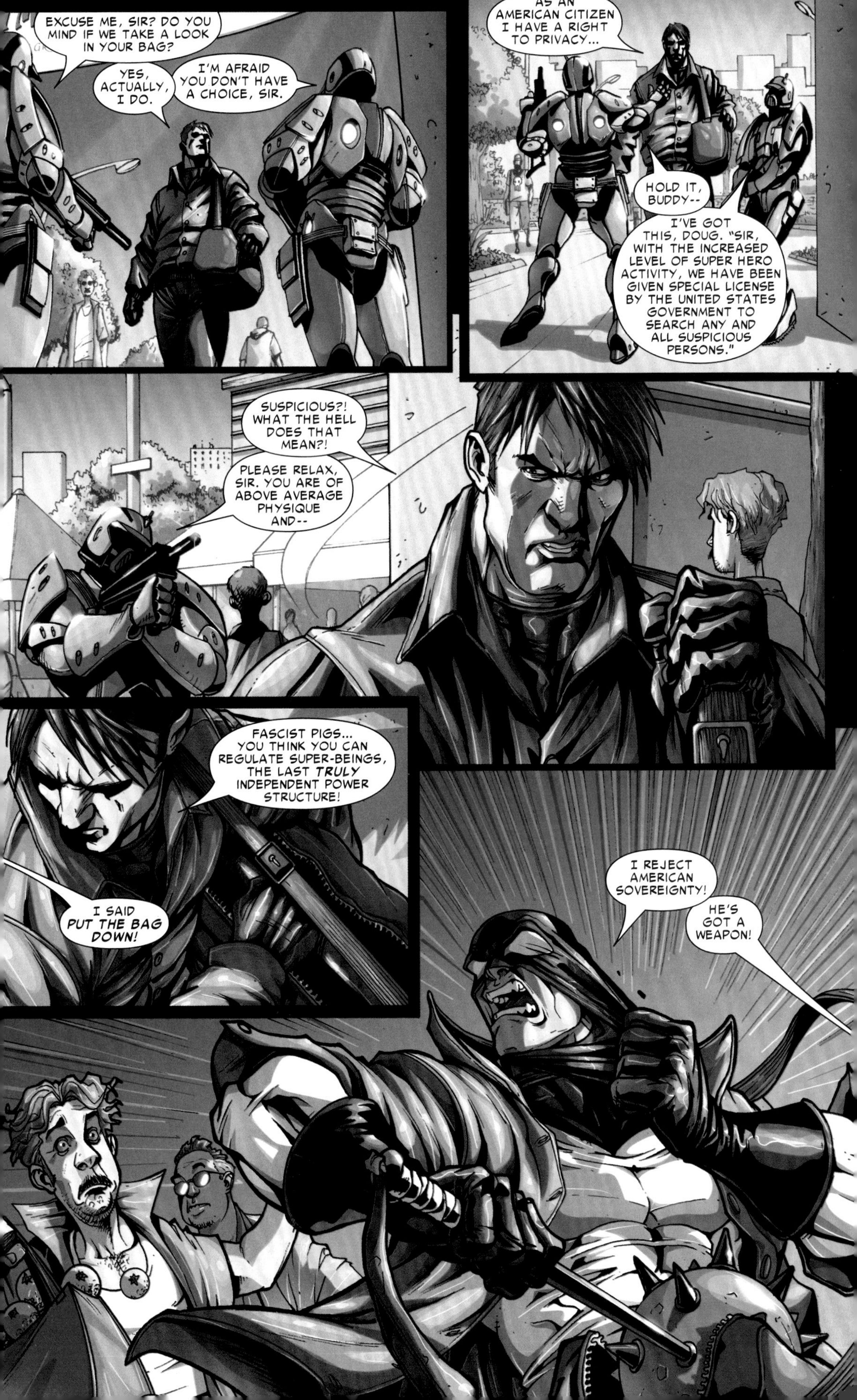
EXCUSE ME, SIR? DO YOU MIND IF WE TAKE A LOOK IN YOUR BAG?
YES, ACTUALLY, I DO.
I'M AFRAID YOU DON'T HAVE A CHOICE, SIR.
AS AN AMERICAN CITIZEN I HAVE A RIGHT TO PRIVACY...
HOLD IT, BUDDY--
I'VE GOT THIS, DOUG. "SIR, WITH THE INCREASED LEVEL OF SUPER HERO ACTIVITY, WE HAVE BEEN GIVEN SPECIAL LICENSE BY THE UNITED STATES GOVERNMENT TO SEARCH ANY AND ALL SUSPICIOUS PERSONS."
SUSPICIOUS?! WHAT THE HELL DOES THAT MEAN?!
PLEASE RELAX, SIR. YOU ARE OF ABOVE AVERAGE PHYSIQUE AND--
FASCIST PIGS... YOU THINK YOU CAN REGULATE SUPER-BEINGS, THE LAST *TRULY* INDEPENDENT POWER STRUCTURE!
I SAID *PUT THE BAG DOWN!*
I REJECT AMERICAN SOVEREIGNTY!
HE'S GOT A WEAPON!

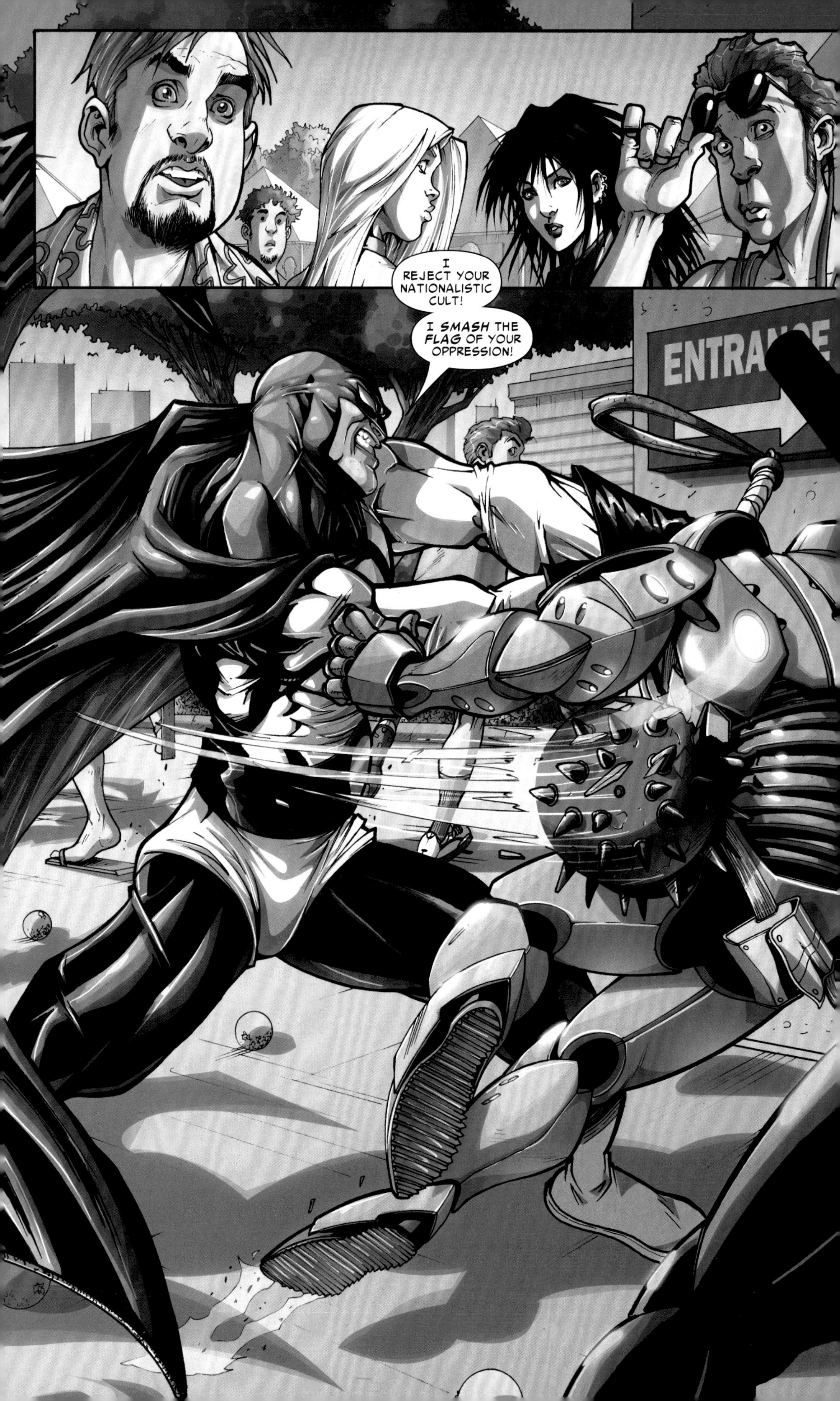
I REJECT YOUR NATIONALISTIC CULT!
I SMASH THE FLAG OF YOUR OPPRESSION!
ENTRANCE

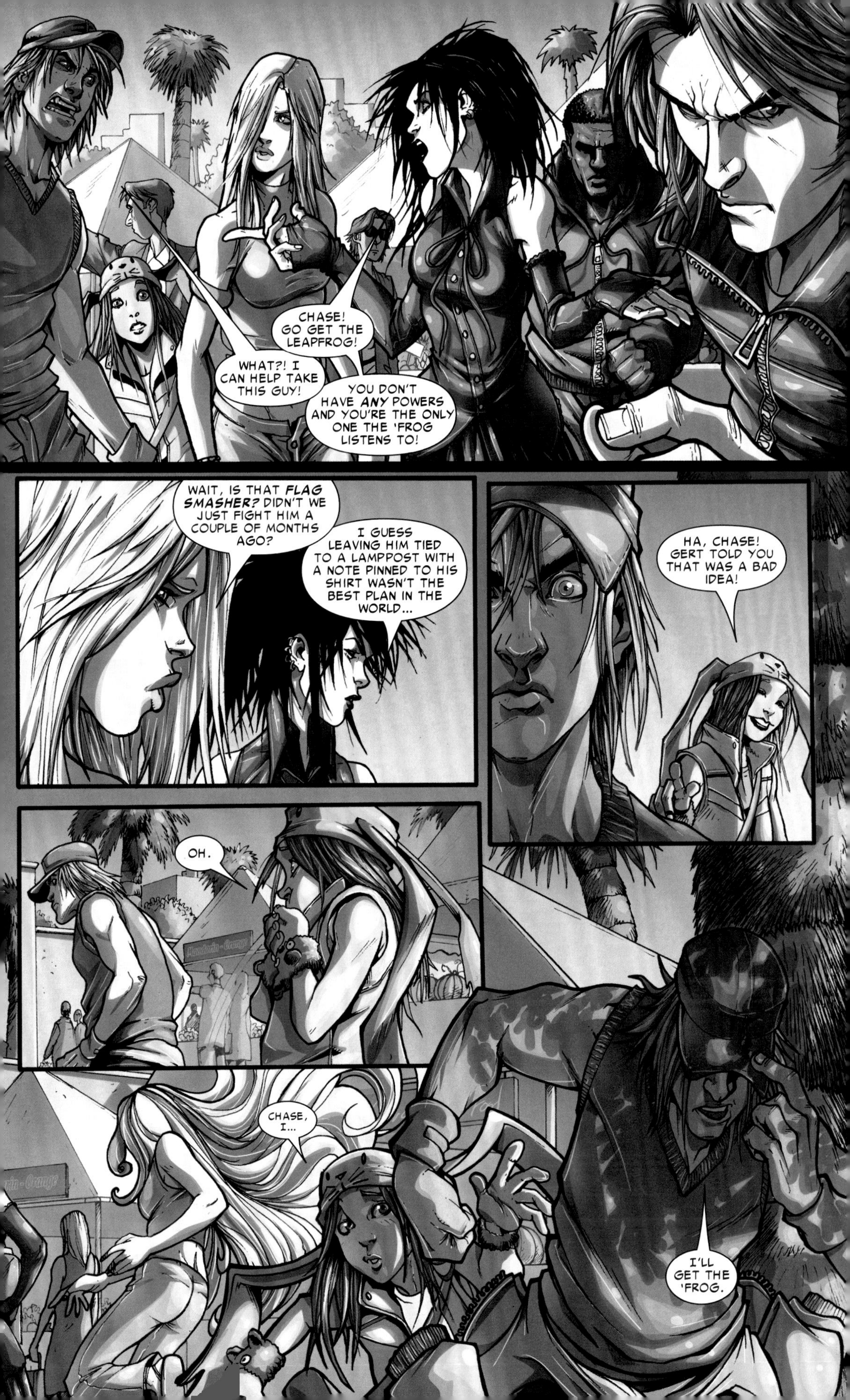
CHASE! GO GET THE LEAPFROG!
WHAT?! I CAN HELP TAKE THIS GUY!
YOU DON'T HAVE *ANY* POWERS AND YOU'RE THE ONLY ONE THE 'FROG LISTENS TO!
WAIT, IS THAT *FLAG SMASHER?* DIDN'T WE JUST FIGHT HIM A COUPLE OF MONTHS AGO?
I GUESS LEAVING HIM TIED TO A LAMPPOST WITH A NOTE PINNED TO HIS SHIRT WASN'T THE BEST PLAN IN THE WORLD...
HA, CHASE! GERT TOLD YOU THAT WAS A BAD IDEA!
OH.
CHASE, I...
I'LL GET THE 'FROG.

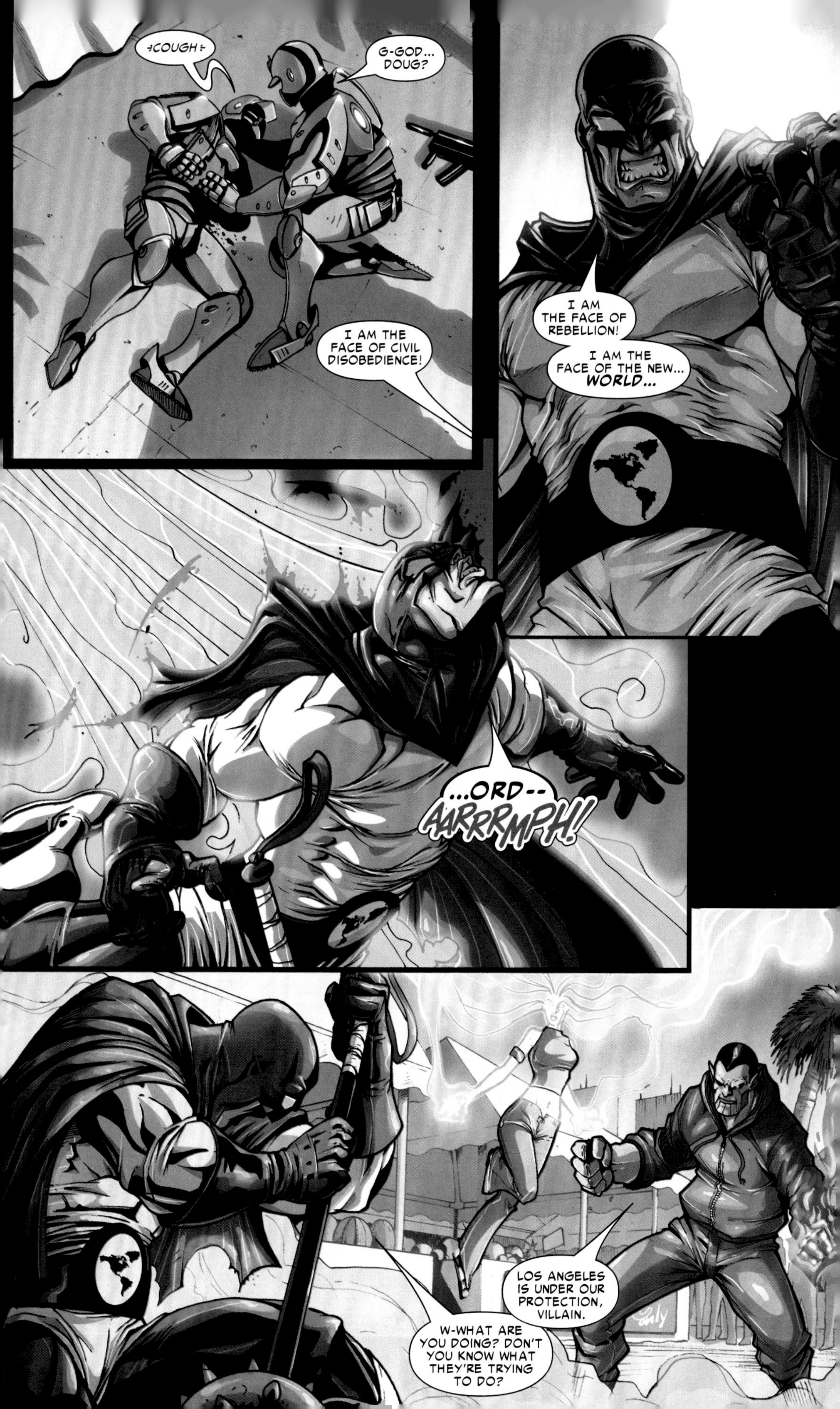

COUGH
G-GOD... DOUG?
I AM THE FACE OF CIVIL DISOBEDIENCE!
I AM THE FACE OF REBELLION!
I AM THE FACE OF THE NEW... WORLD...
...ORD--
AARRRMPH!
LOS ANGELES IS UNDER OUR PROTECTION, VILLAIN.
W-WHAT ARE YOU DOING? DON'T YOU KNOW WHAT THEY'RE TRYING TO DO?

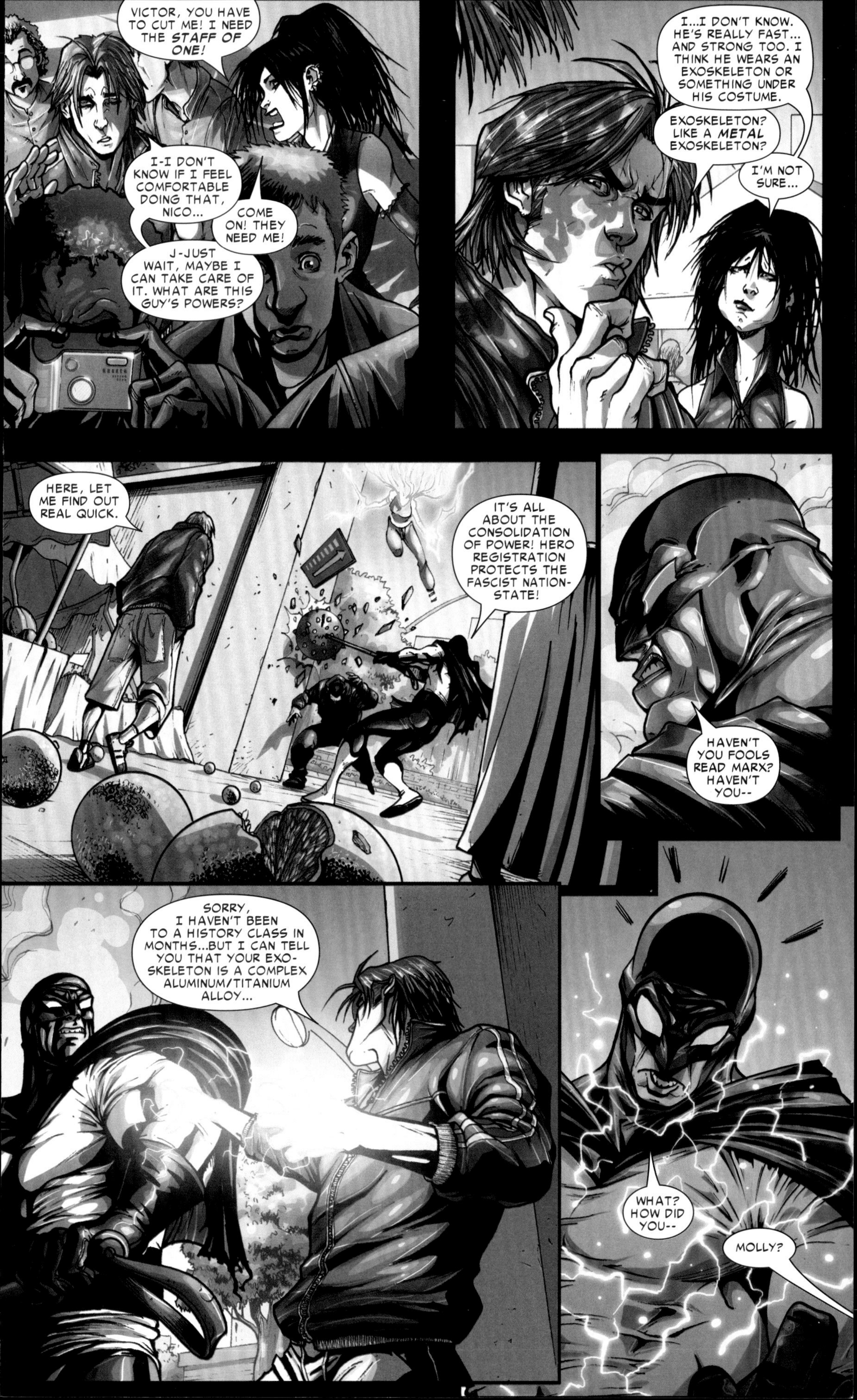
VICTOR, YOU HAVE TO CUT ME! I NEED THE STAFF OF ONE!
I-I DON'T KNOW IF I FEEL COMFORTABLE DOING THAT, NICO...
COME ON! THEY NEED ME!
J-JUST WAIT, MAYBE I CAN TAKE CARE OF IT. WHAT ARE THIS GUY'S POWERS?
I...I DON'T KNOW. HE'S REALLY FAST... AND STRONG TOO. I THINK HE WEARS AN EXOSKELETON OR SOMETHING UNDER HIS COSTUME.
EXOSKELETON? LIKE A METAL EXOSKELETON?
I'M NOT SURE...
HERE, LET ME FIND OUT REAL QUICK.
IT'S ALL ABOUT THE CONSOLIDATION OF POWER! HERO REGISTRATION PROTECTS THE FASCIST NATION-STATE!
HAVEN'T YOU FOOLS READ MARX? HAVEN'T YOU--
SORRY, I HAVEN'T BEEN TO A HISTORY CLASS IN MONTHS...BUT I CAN TELL YOU THAT YOUR EXO-SKELETON IS A COMPLEX ALUMINUM/TITANIUM ALLOY...
WHAT? HOW DID YOU--
MOLLY?

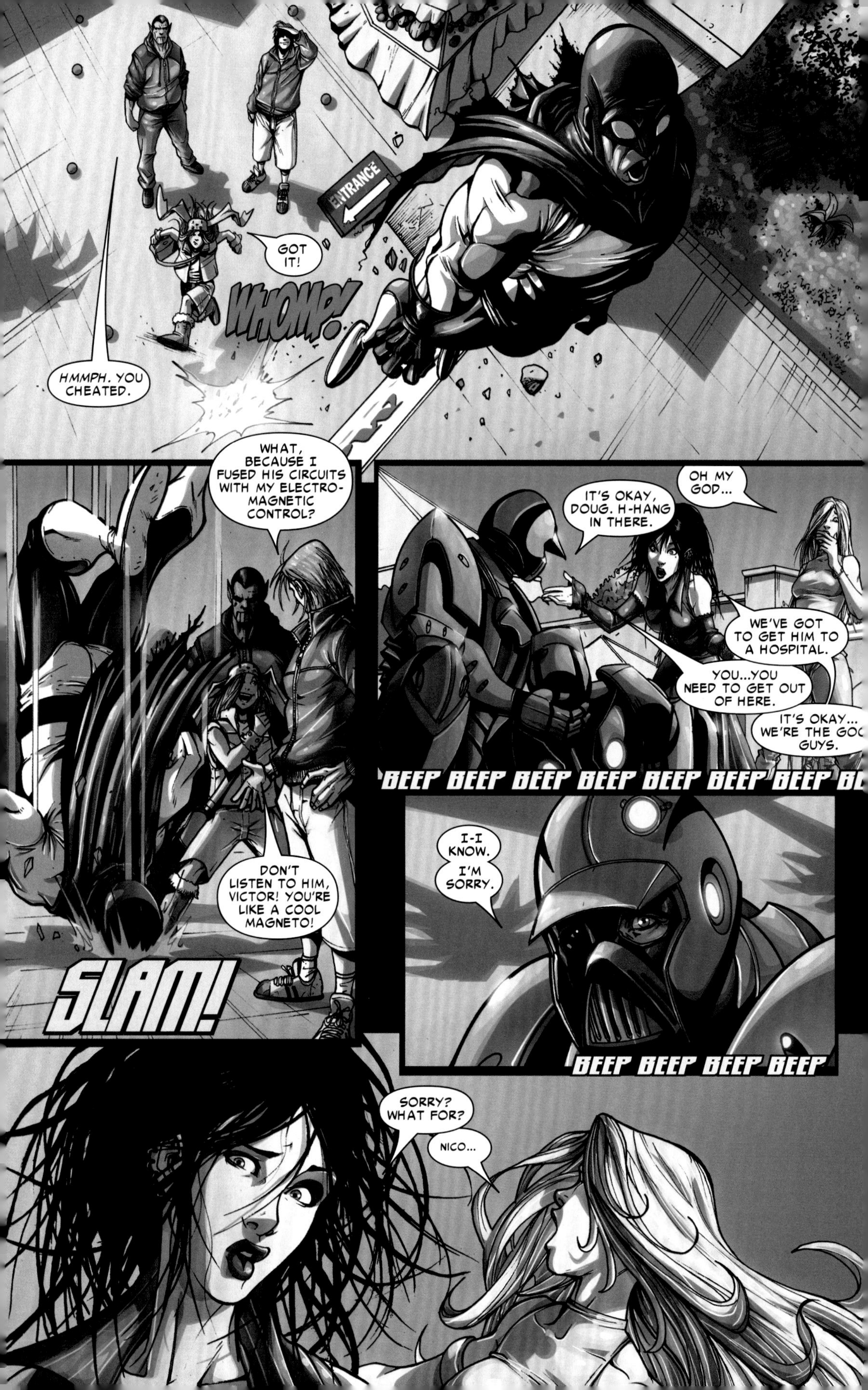
GOT IT!
ENTRANCE
WHOMP!
HMMPH. YOU CHEATED.
WHAT, BECAUSE I FUSED HIS CIRCUITS WITH MY ELECTRO-MAGNETIC CONTROL?
DON'T LISTEN TO HIM, VICTOR! YOU'RE LIKE A COOL MAGNETO!
SLAM!
IT'S OKAY, DOUG. H-HANG IN THERE.
OH MY GOD...
WE'VE GOT TO GET HIM TO A HOSPITAL.
YOU...YOU NEED TO GET OUT OF HERE.
IT'S OKAY... WE'RE THE GOO GUYS.
BEEP BEEP BEEP BEEP BEEP BEEP BEEP
I-I KNOW. I'M SORRY.
BEEP BEEP BEEP BEEP
SORRY? WHAT FOR?
NICO...

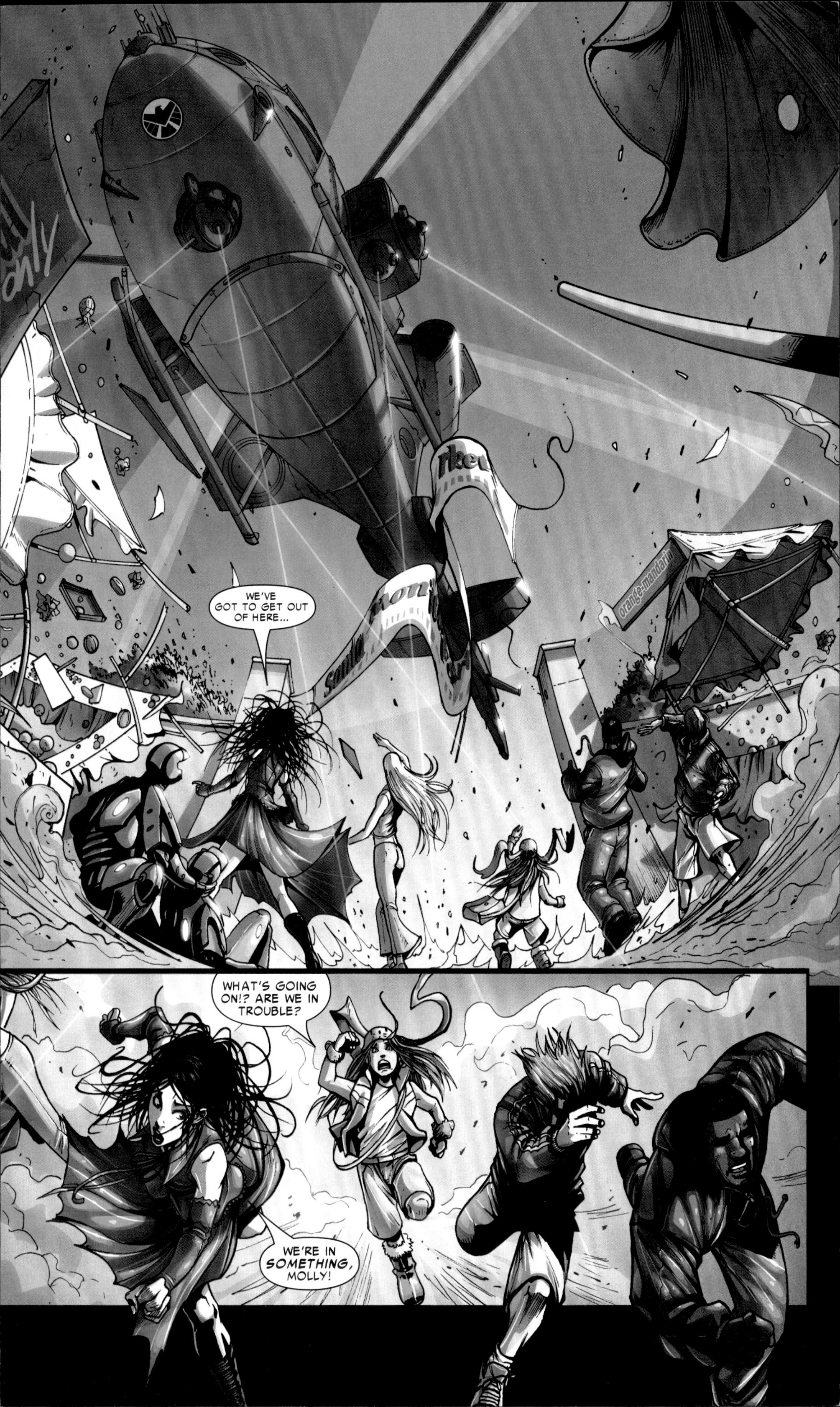
only
orange-mandarin
WE'VE GOT TO GET OUT OF HERE...
WHAT'S GOING ON!? ARE WE IN TROUBLE?
WE'RE IN *SOMETHING*, MOLLY!

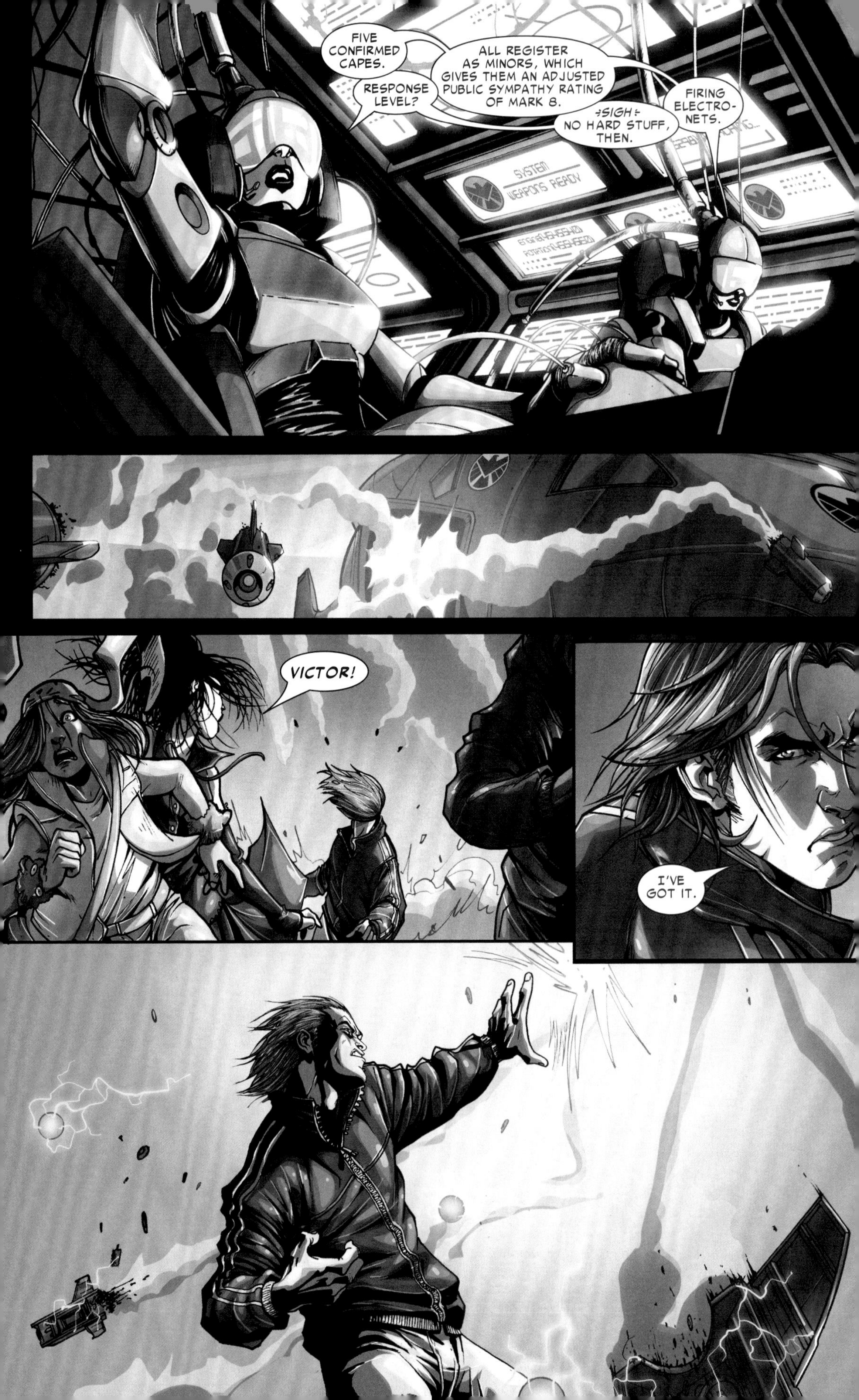
FIVE CONFIRMED CAPES.
ALL REGISTER AS MINORS, WHICH GIVES THEM AN ADJUSTED PUBLIC SYMPATHY RATING OF MARK 8.
RESPONSE LEVEL?
FIRING ELECTRO-NETS.
=SIGH= NO HARD STUFF, THEN.
SYSTEM WEAPONS READY
VICTOR!
I'VE GOT IT.

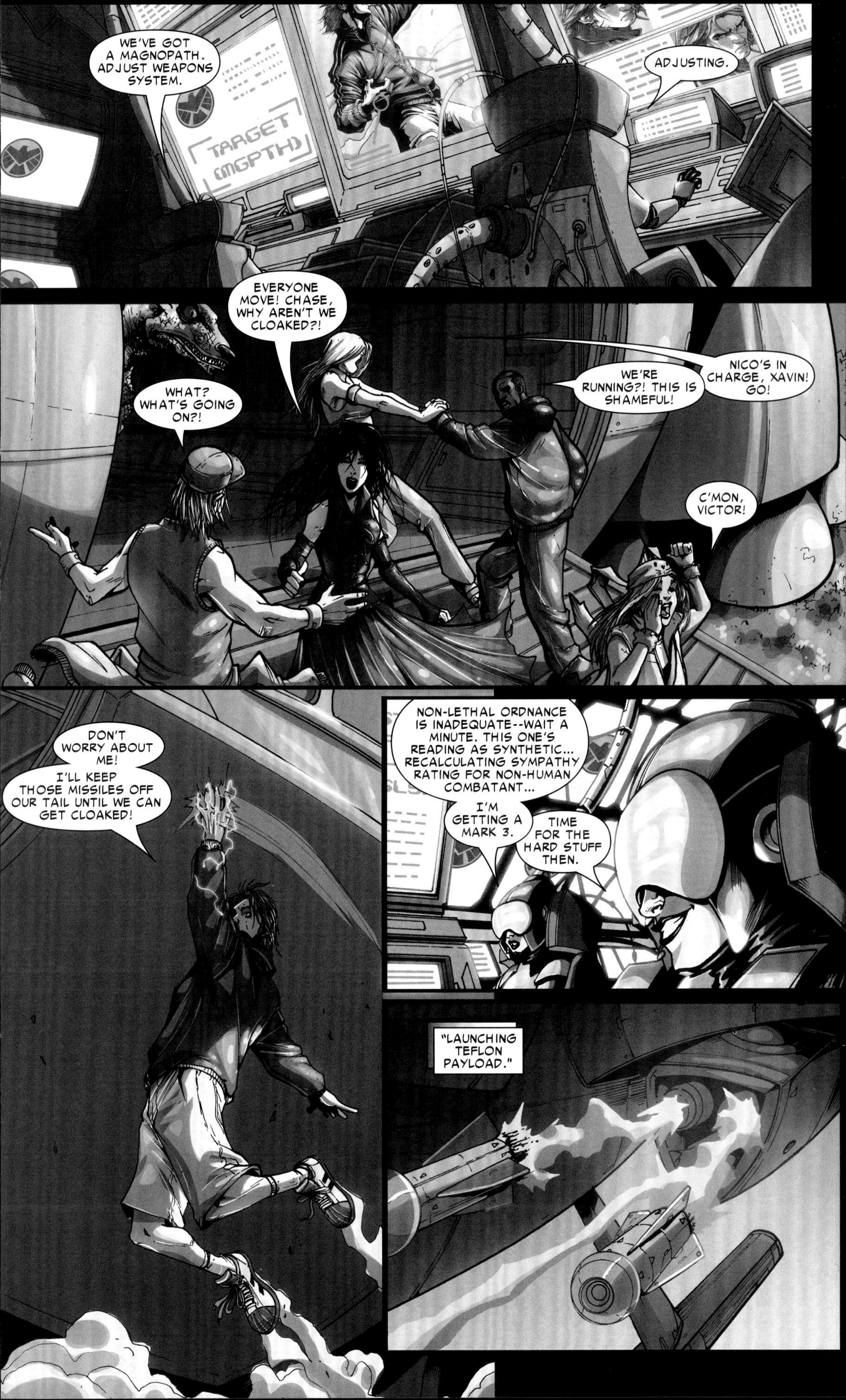
WE'VE GOT A MAGNOPATH. ADJUST WEAPONS SYSTEM.
TARGET (MGPTH)
ADJUSTING.
EVERYONE MOVE! CHASE, WHY AREN'T WE CLOAKED?!
WHAT? WHAT'S GOING ON?!
WE'RE RUNNING?! THIS IS SHAMEFUL!
NICO'S IN CHARGE, XAVIN! GO!
C'MON, VICTOR!
DON'T WORRY ABOUT ME!
I'LL KEEP THOSE MISSILES OFF OUR TAIL UNTIL WE CAN GET CLOAKED!
NON-LETHAL ORDNANCE IS INADEQUATE--WAIT A MINUTE. THIS ONE'S READING AS SYNTHETIC... RECALCULATING SYMPATHY RATING FOR NON-HUMAN COMBATANT...
I'M GETTING A MARK 3.
TIME FOR THE HARD STUFF THEN.
"LAUNCHING TEFLON PAYLOAD."

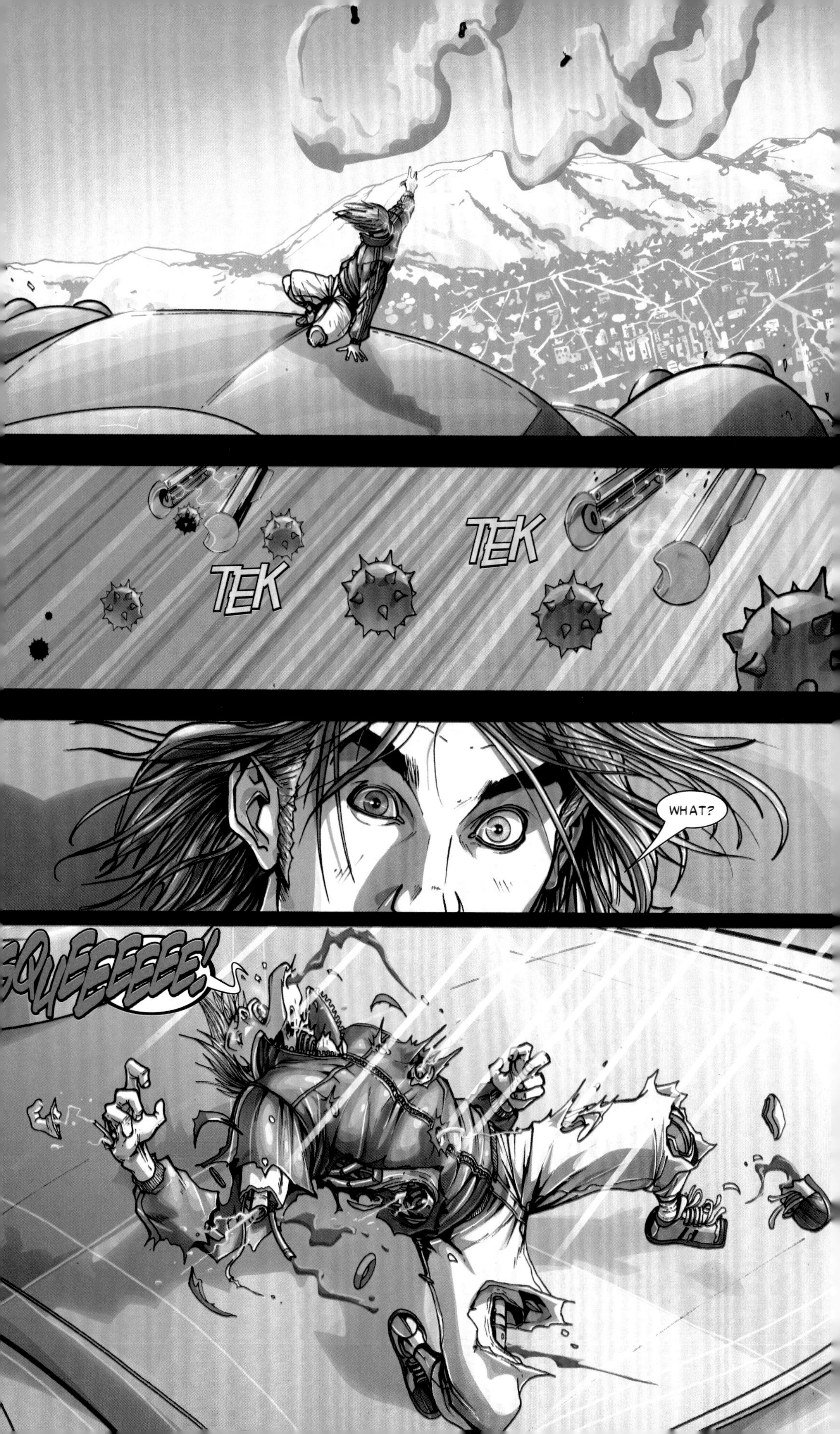
TEK
TEK
WHAT?
SQUEEEEEEE!

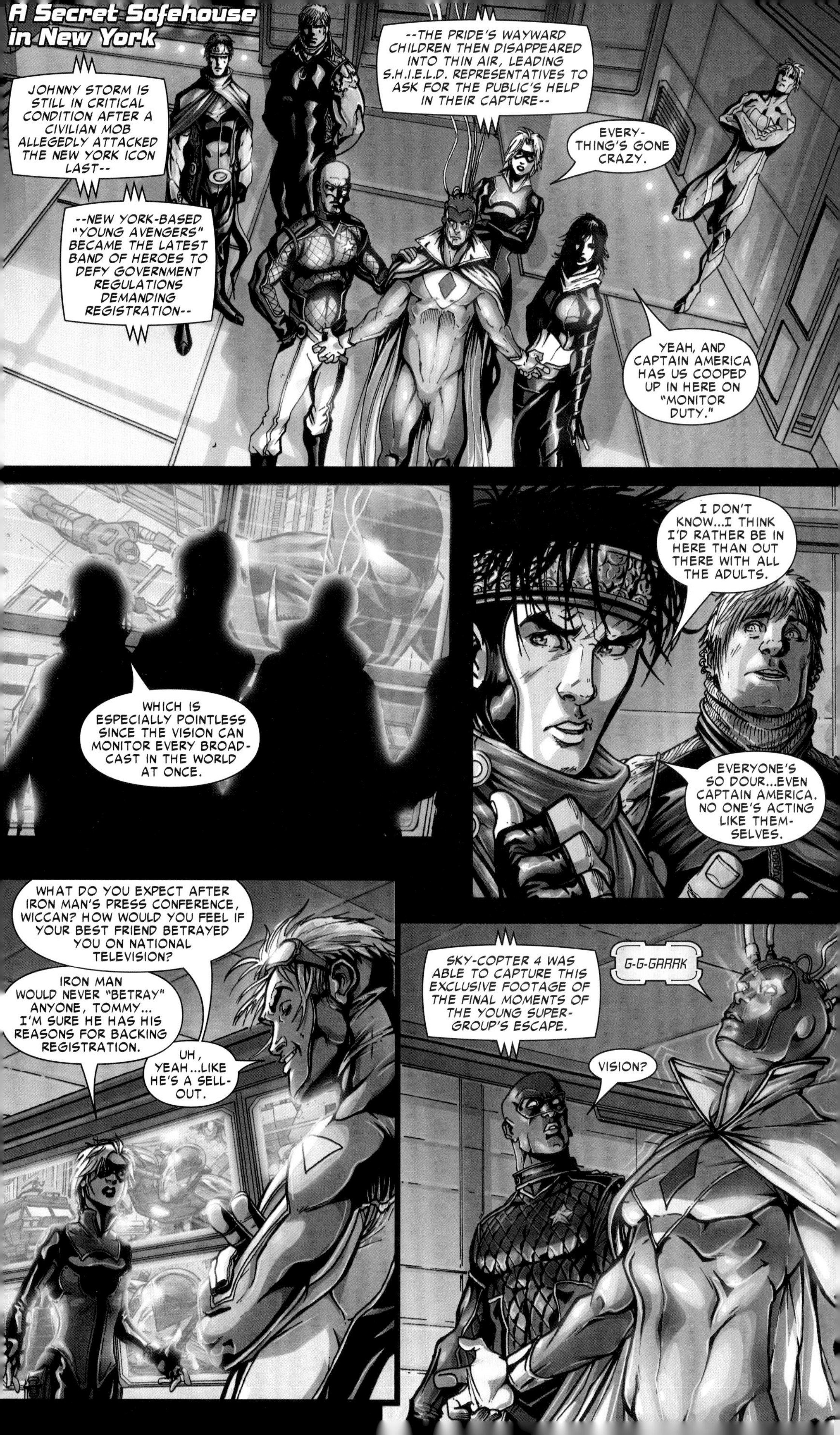
A Secret Safehouse in New York
JOHNNY STORM IS STILL IN CRITICAL CONDITION AFTER A CIVILIAN MOB ALLEGEDLY ATTACKED THE NEW YORK ICON LAST--
--NEW YORK-BASED "YOUNG AVENGERS" BECAME THE LATEST BAND OF HEROES TO DEFY GOVERNMENT REGULATIONS DEMANDING REGISTRATION--
--THE PRIDE'S WAYWARD CHILDREN THEN DISAPPEARED INTO THIN AIR, LEADING S.H.I.E.L.D. REPRESENTATIVES TO ASK FOR THE PUBLIC'S HELP IN THEIR CAPTURE--
EVERY-THING'S GONE CRAZY.
YEAH, AND CAPTAIN AMERICA HAS US COOPED UP IN HERE ON "MONITOR DUTY."
WHICH IS ESPECIALLY POINTLESS SINCE THE VISION CAN MONITOR EVERY BROAD-CAST IN THE WORLD AT ONCE.
I DON'T KNOW...I THINK I'D RATHER BE IN HERE THAN OUT THERE WITH ALL THE ADULTS.
EVERYONE'S SO DOUR...EVEN CAPTAIN AMERICA. NO ONE'S ACTING LIKE THEM-SELVES.
WHAT DO YOU EXPECT AFTER IRON MAN'S PRESS CONFERENCE, WICCAN? HOW WOULD YOU FEEL IF YOUR BEST FRIEND BETRAYED YOU ON NATIONAL TELEVISION?
IRON MAN WOULD NEVER "BETRAY" ANYONE, TOMMY... I'M SURE HE HAS HIS REASONS FOR BACKING REGISTRATION.
UH, YEAH...LIKE HE'S A SELL-OUT.
SKY-COPTER 4 WAS ABLE TO CAPTURE THIS EXCLUSIVE FOOTAGE OF THE FINAL MOMENTS OF THE YOUNG SUPER-GROUP'S ESCAPE.
G-G-GARAK
VISION?

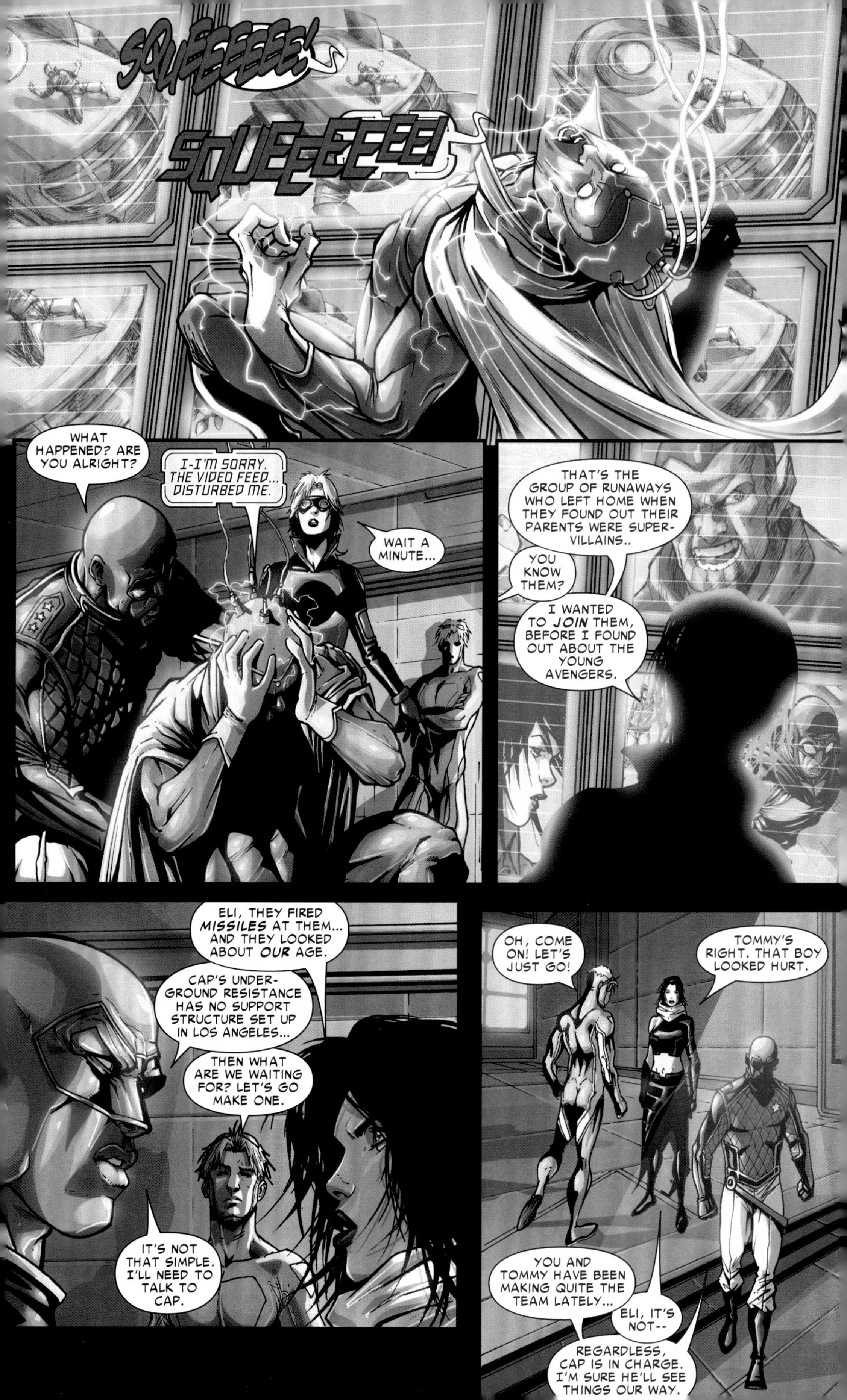
SQUEEEEEE!
SQUEEEEEE!
WHAT HAPPENED? ARE YOU ALRIGHT?
I-I'M SORRY. THE VIDEO FEED... DISTURBED ME.
WAIT A MINUTE...
THAT'S THE GROUP OF RUNAWAYS WHO LEFT HOME WHEN THEY FOUND OUT THEIR PARENTS WERE SUPER-VILLAINS..
YOU KNOW THEM?
I WANTED TO JOIN THEM, BEFORE I FOUND OUT ABOUT THE YOUNG AVENGERS.
ELI, THEY FIRED MISSILES AT THEM... AND THEY LOOKED ABOUT OUR AGE.
CAP'S UNDER-GROUND RESISTANCE HAS NO SUPPORT STRUCTURE SET UP IN LOS ANGELES...
THEN WHAT ARE WE WAITING FOR? LET'S GO MAKE ONE.
IT'S NOT THAT SIMPLE. I'LL NEED TO TALK TO CAP.
OH, COME ON! LET'S JUST GO!
TOMMY'S RIGHT. THAT BOY LOOKED HURT.
YOU AND TOMMY HAVE BEEN MAKING QUITE THE TEAM LATELY...
ELI, IT'S NOT--
REGARDLESS, CAP IS IN CHARGE. I'M SURE HE'LL SEE THINGS OUR WAY.

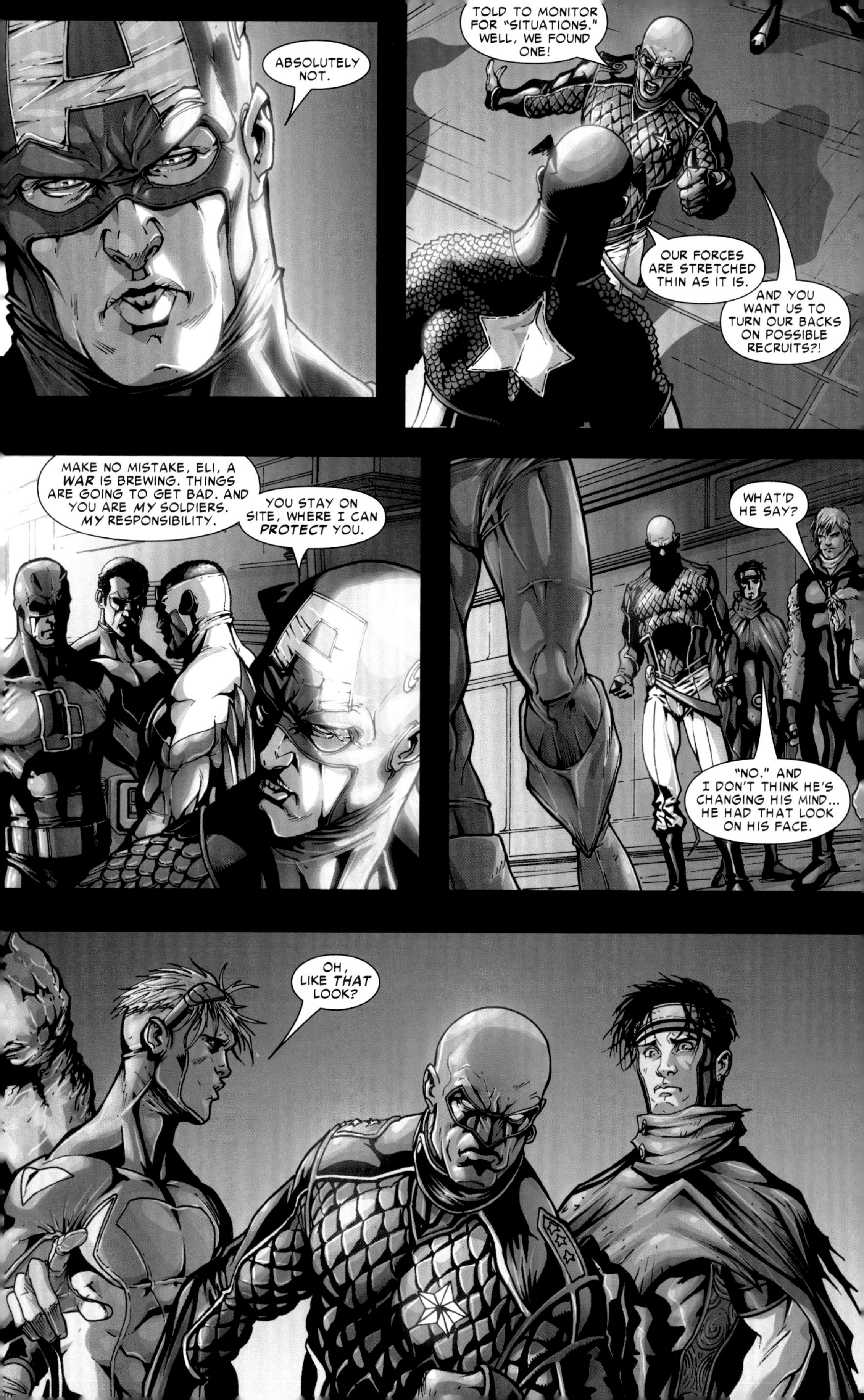
ABSOLUTELY NOT.
TOLD TO MONITOR FOR "SITUATIONS." WELL, WE FOUND ONE!
OUR FORCES ARE STRETCHED THIN AS IT IS.
AND YOU WANT US TO TURN OUR BACKS ON POSSIBLE RECRUITS?!
MAKE NO MISTAKE, ELI, A WAR IS BREWING. THINGS ARE GOING TO GET BAD. AND YOU ARE MY SOLDIERS. MY RESPONSIBILITY.
YOU STAY ON SITE, WHERE I CAN PROTECT YOU.
WHAT'D HE SAY?
"NO." AND I DON'T THINK HE'S CHANGING HIS MIND... HE HAD THAT LOOK ON HIS FACE.
OH, LIKE THAT LOOK?

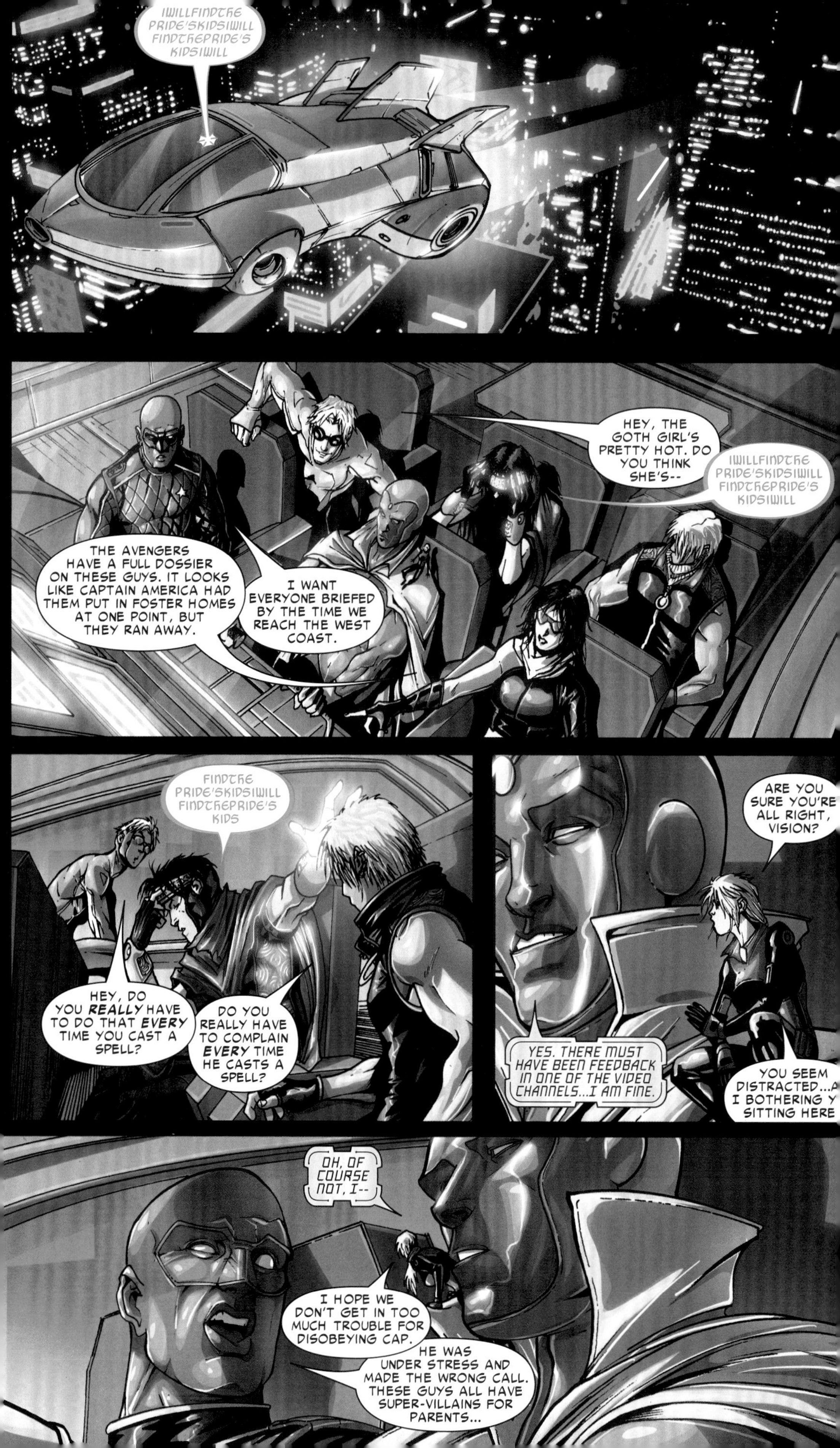
IWILLFINDTHE PRIDE'SKIDSIWILL FINDTHEPRIDE'S KIDSIWILL
HEY, THE GOTH GIRL'S PRETTY HOT. DO YOU THINK SHE'S--
IWILLFINDTHE PRIDE'SKIDSIWILL FINDTHEPRIDE'S KIDSIWILL
THE AVENGERS HAVE A FULL DOSSIER ON THESE GUYS. IT LOOKS LIKE CAPTAIN AMERICA HAD THEM PUT IN FOSTER HOMES AT ONE POINT, BUT THEY RAN AWAY.
I WANT EVERYONE BRIEFED BY THE TIME WE REACH THE WEST COAST.
FINDTHE PRIDE'SKIDSIWILL FINDTHEPRIDE'S KIDS
HEY, DO YOU **REALLY** HAVE TO DO THAT **EVERY** TIME YOU CAST A SPELL?
DO YOU REALLY HAVE TO COMPLAIN **EVERY** TIME HE CASTS A SPELL?
ARE YOU SURE YOU'RE ALL RIGHT, VISION?
YES. THERE MUST HAVE BEEN FEEDBACK IN ONE OF THE VIDEO CHANNELS...I AM FINE.
YOU SEEM DISTRACTED...A I BOTHERING Y SITTING HERE
OH, OF COURSE NOT, I--
I HOPE WE DON'T GET IN TOO MUCH TROUBLE FOR DISOBEYING CAP.
HE WAS UNDER STRESS AND MADE THE WRONG CALL. THESE GUYS ALL HAVE SUPER-VILLAINS FOR PARENTS...

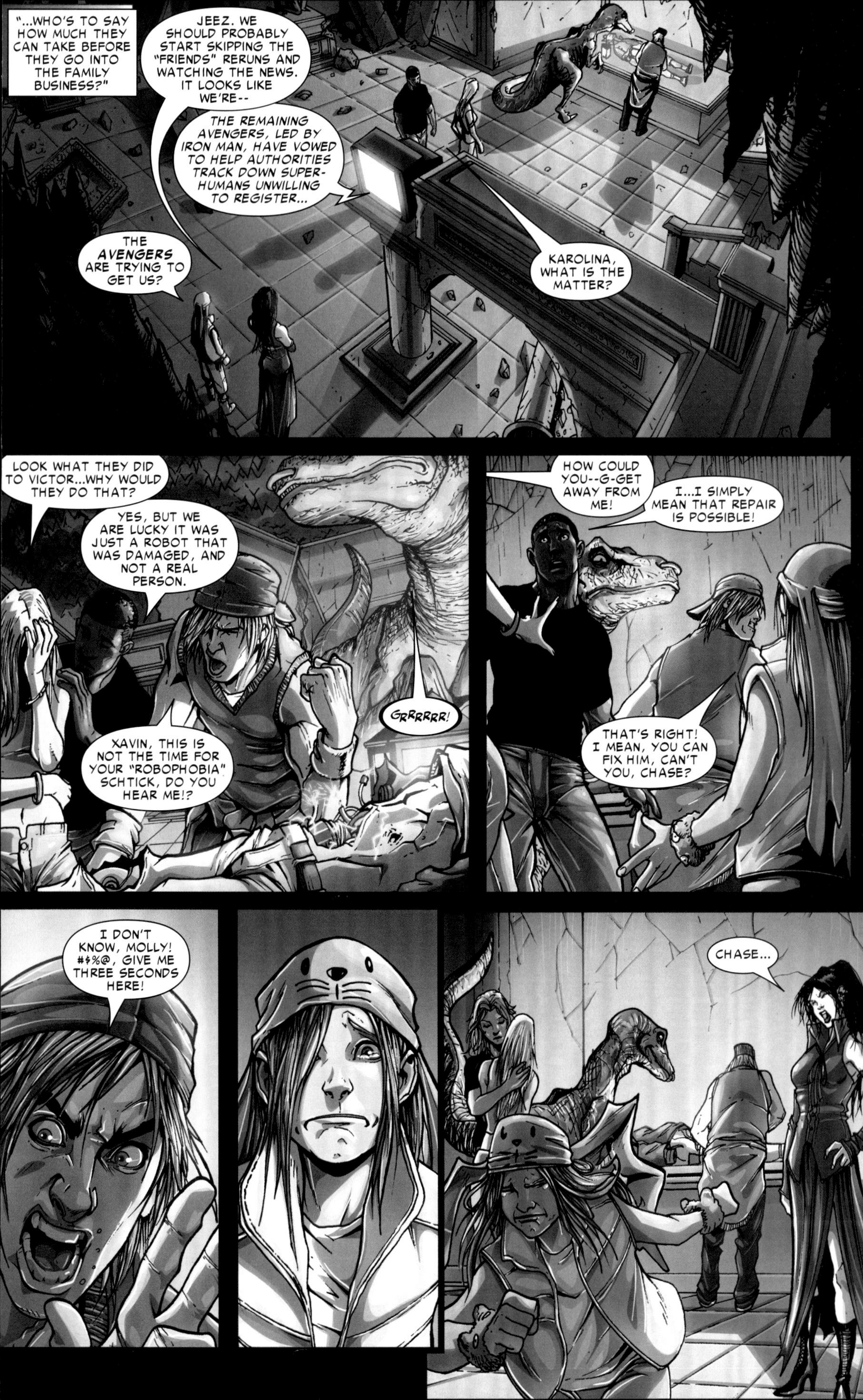
"...WHO'S TO SAY HOW MUCH THEY CAN TAKE BEFORE THEY GO INTO THE FAMILY BUSINESS?"
JEEZ. WE SHOULD PROBABLY START SKIPPING THE "FRIENDS" RERUNS AND WATCHING THE NEWS. IT LOOKS LIKE WE'RE--
THE REMAINING AVENGERS, LED BY IRON MAN, HAVE VOWED TO HELP AUTHORITIES TRACK DOWN SUPER-HUMANS UNWILLING TO REGISTER...
THE AVENGERS ARE TRYING TO GET US?
KAROLINA, WHAT IS THE MATTER?
LOOK WHAT THEY DID TO VICTOR...WHY WOULD THEY DO THAT?
YES, BUT WE ARE LUCKY IT WAS JUST A ROBOT THAT WAS DAMAGED, AND NOT A REAL PERSON.
GRRRRRR!
XAVIN, THIS IS NOT THE TIME FOR YOUR "ROBOPHOBIA" SCHTICK, DO YOU HEAR ME!?
HOW COULD YOU--G-GET AWAY FROM ME!
I...I SIMPLY MEAN THAT REPAIR IS POSSIBLE!
THAT'S RIGHT! I MEAN, YOU CAN FIX HIM, CAN'T YOU, CHASE?
I DON'T KNOW, MOLLY! #$%@, GIVE ME THREE SECONDS HERE!
CHASE...

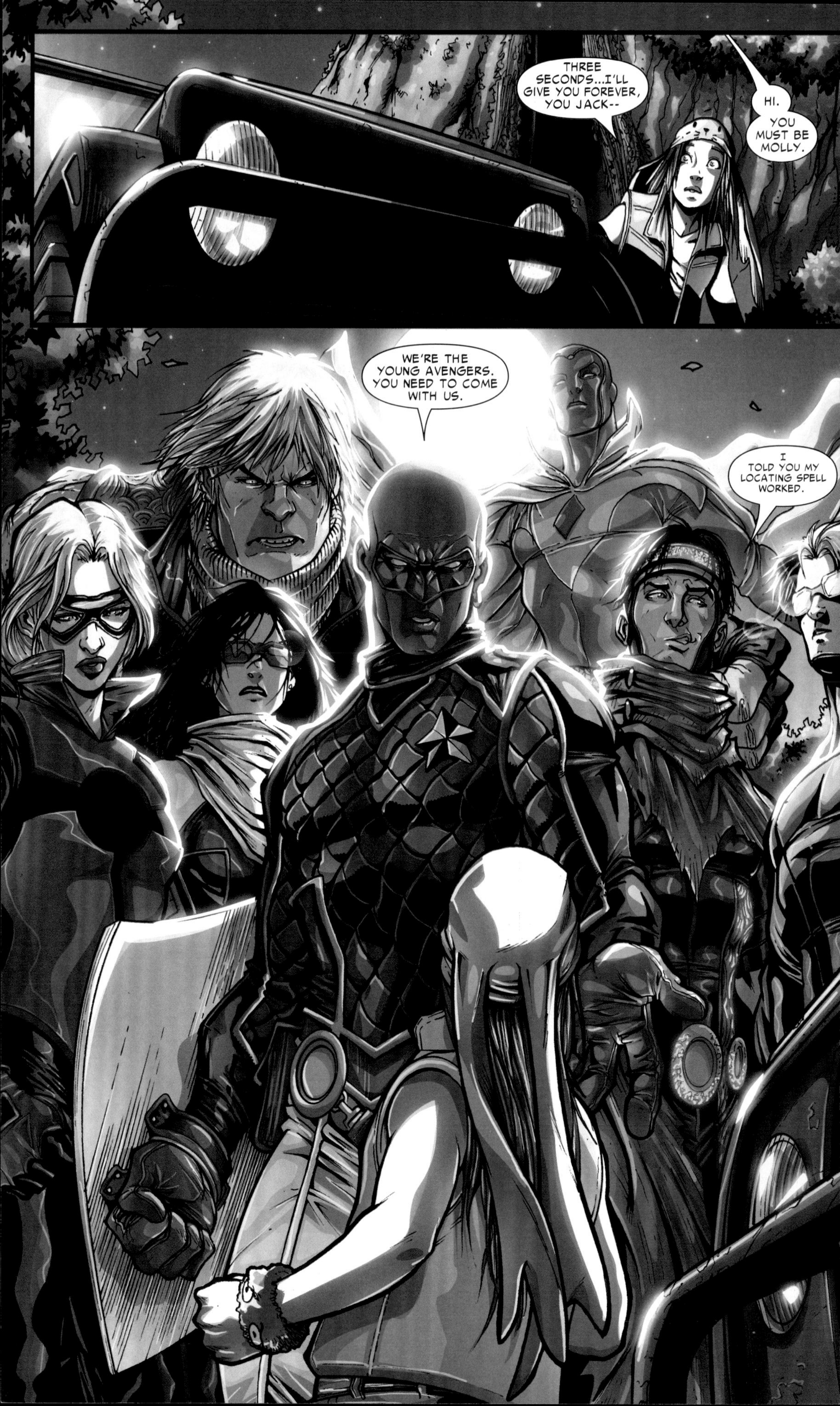
THREE SECONDS...I'LL GIVE YOU FOREVER, YOU JACK--
HI.
YOU MUST BE MOLLY.
WE'RE THE YOUNG AVENGERS. YOU NEED TO COME WITH US.
I TOLD YOU MY LOCATING SPELL WORKED.

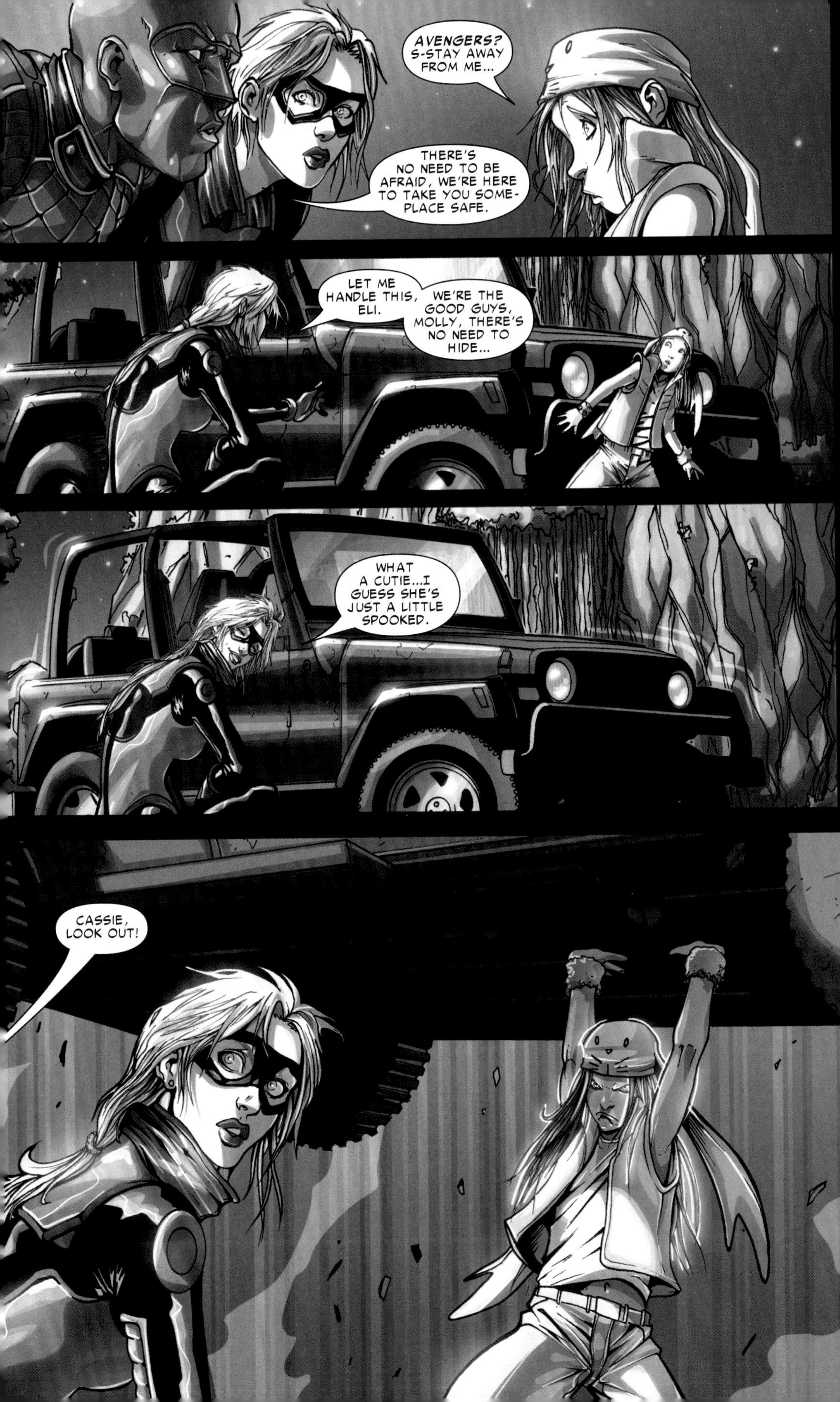
AVENGERS? S-STAY AWAY FROM ME...
THERE'S NO NEED TO BE AFRAID, WE'RE HERE TO TAKE YOU SOME-PLACE SAFE.
LET ME HANDLE THIS, ELI.
WE'RE THE GOOD GUYS, MOLLY, THERE'S NO NEED TO HIDE...
WHAT A CUTIE...I GUESS SHE'S JUST A LITTLE SPOOKED.
CASSIE, LOOK OUT!

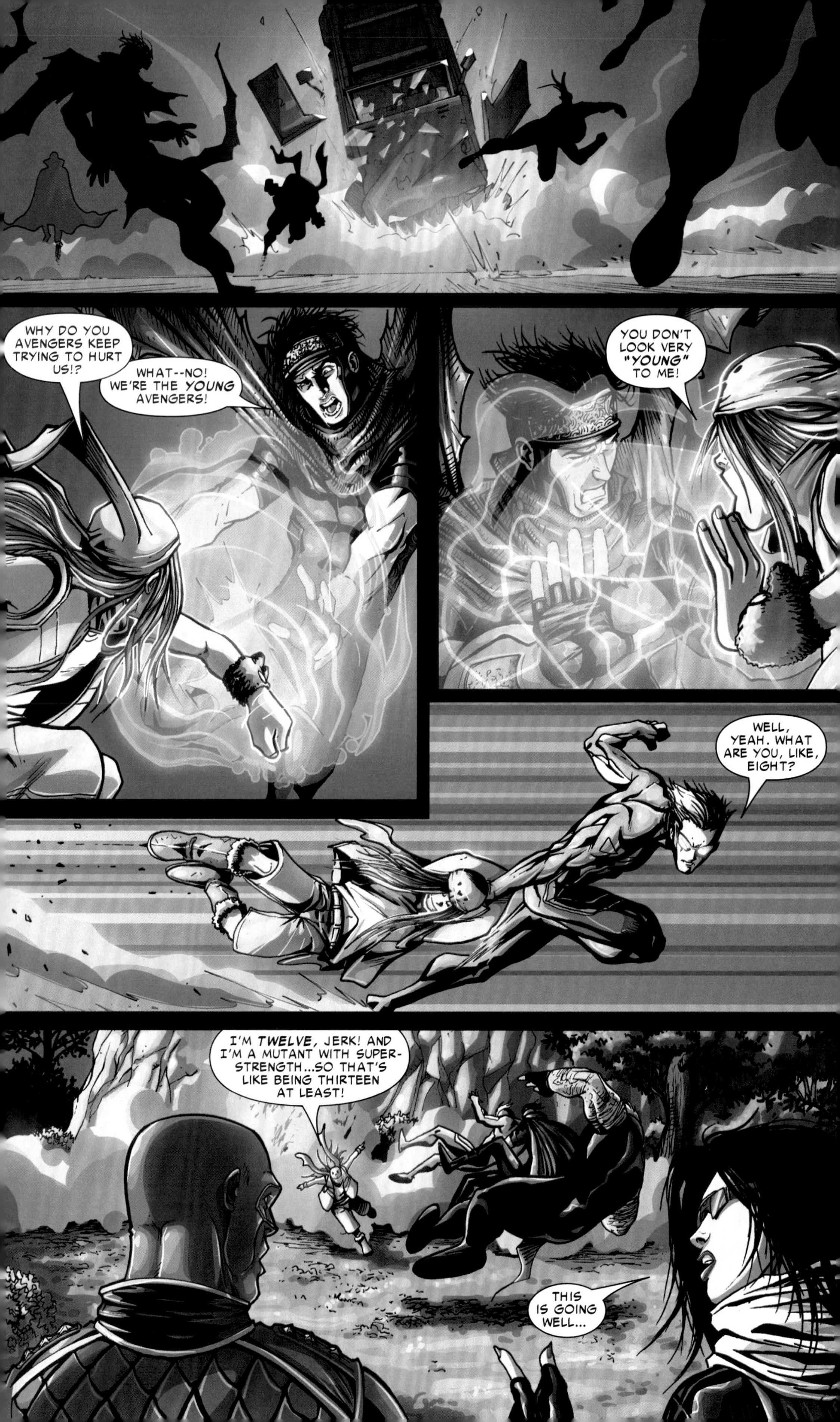
WHY DO YOU AVENGERS KEEP TRYING TO HURT US!?
WHAT--NO! WE'RE THE YOUNG AVENGERS!
YOU DON'T LOOK VERY "YOUNG" TO ME!
WELL, YEAH. WHAT ARE YOU, LIKE, EIGHT?
I'M TWELVE, JERK! AND I'M A MUTANT WITH SUPER-STRENGTH...SO THAT'S LIKE BEING THIRTEEN AT LEAST!
THIS IS GOING WELL...

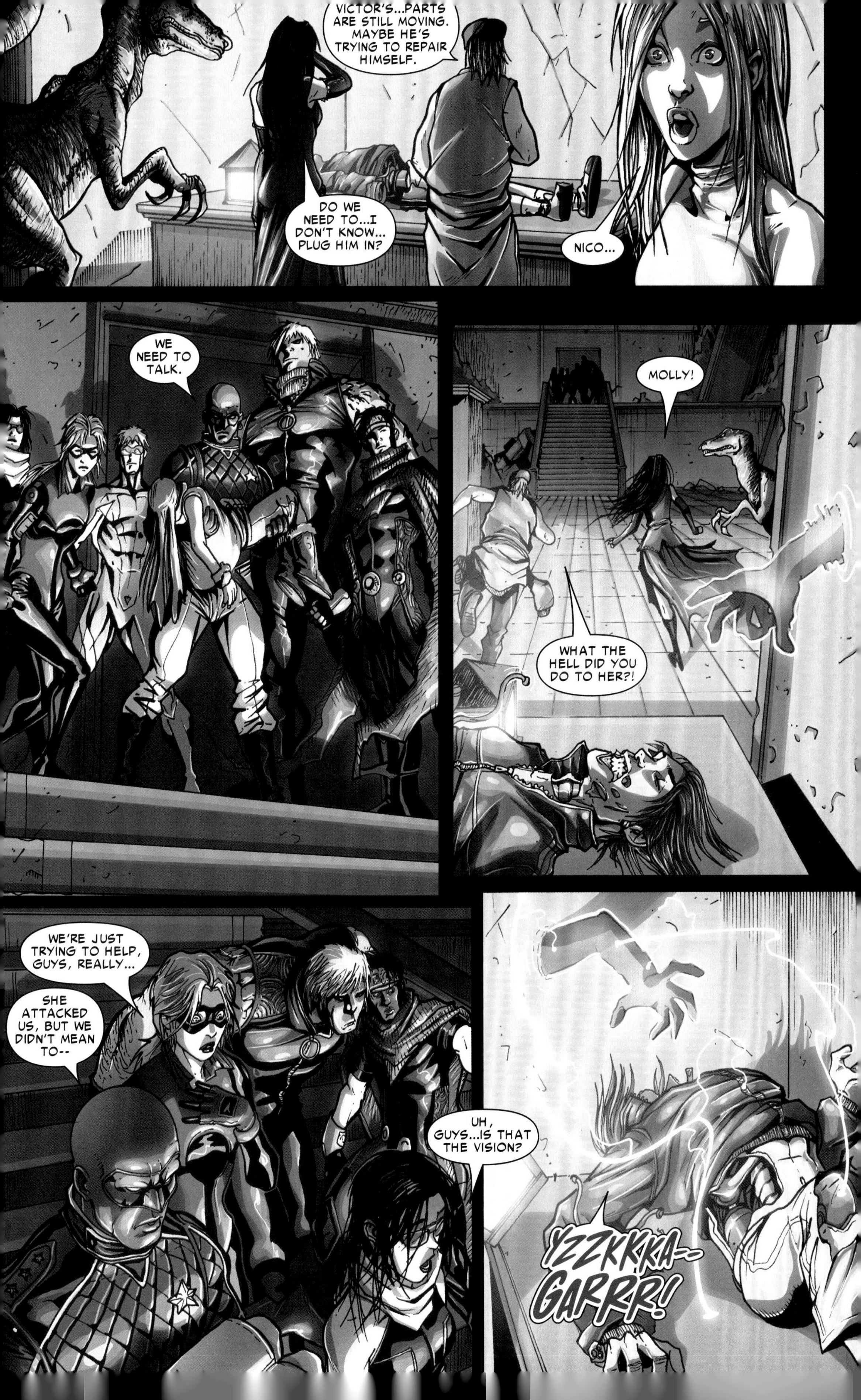
VICTOR'S...PARTS ARE STILL MOVING. MAYBE HE'S TRYING TO REPAIR HIMSELF.
DO WE NEED TO...I DON'T KNOW... PLUG HIM IN?
NICO...
WE NEED TO TALK.
MOLLY!
WHAT THE HELL DID YOU DO TO HER?!
WE'RE JUST TRYING TO HELP, GUYS, REALLY...
SHE ATTACKED US, BUT WE DIDN'T MEAN TO--
UH, GUYS...IS THAT THE VISION?
YZZKKKA-GARRR!

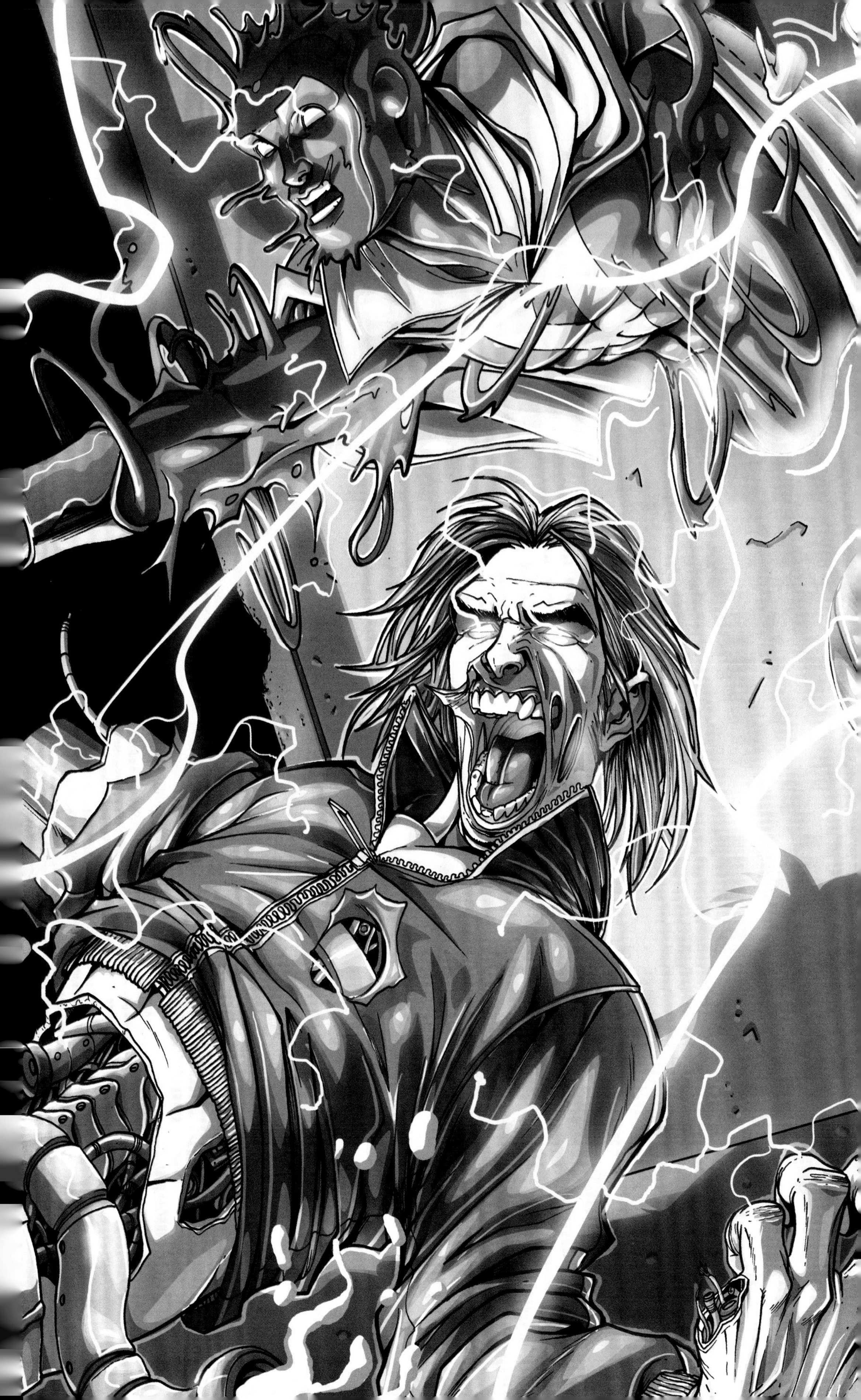

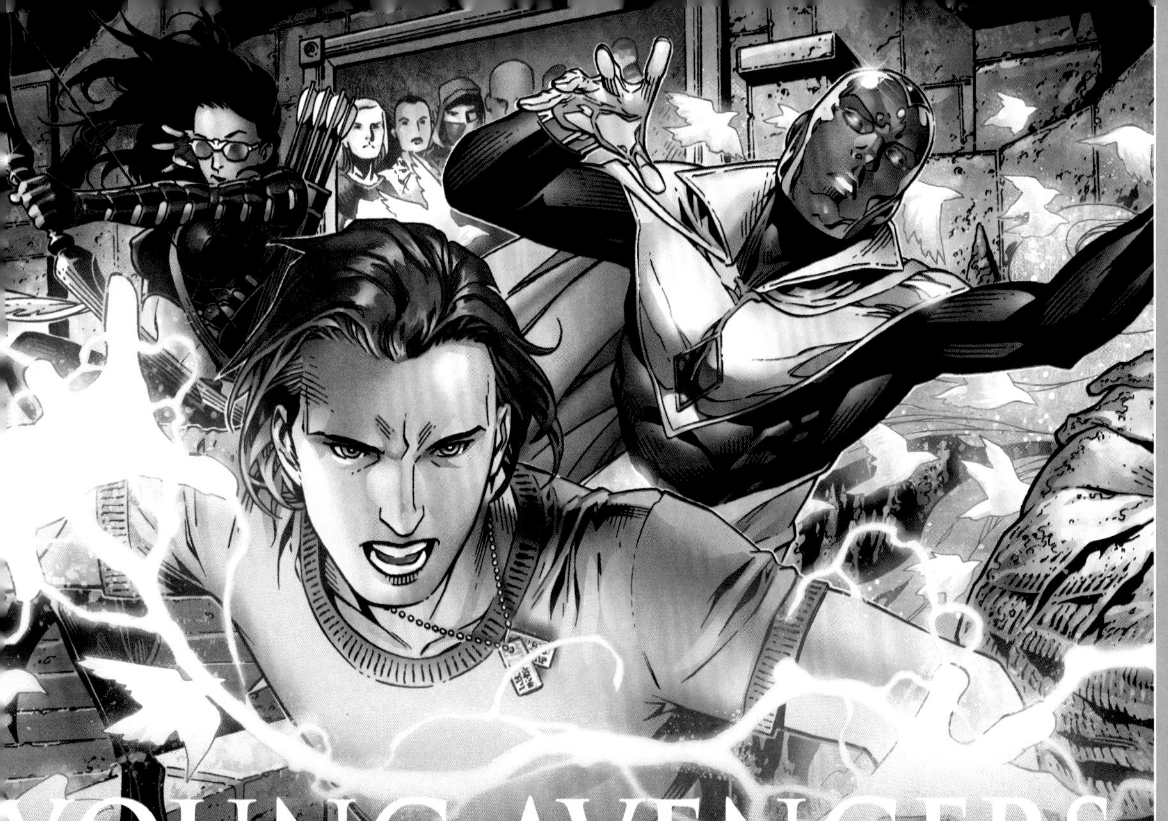

YOUNG AVENGERS & RUNAWAYS

A MARVEL COMICS EVENT

CIVIL WAR

CIVIL WAR: YOUNG AVENGERS & RUNAWAYS #2

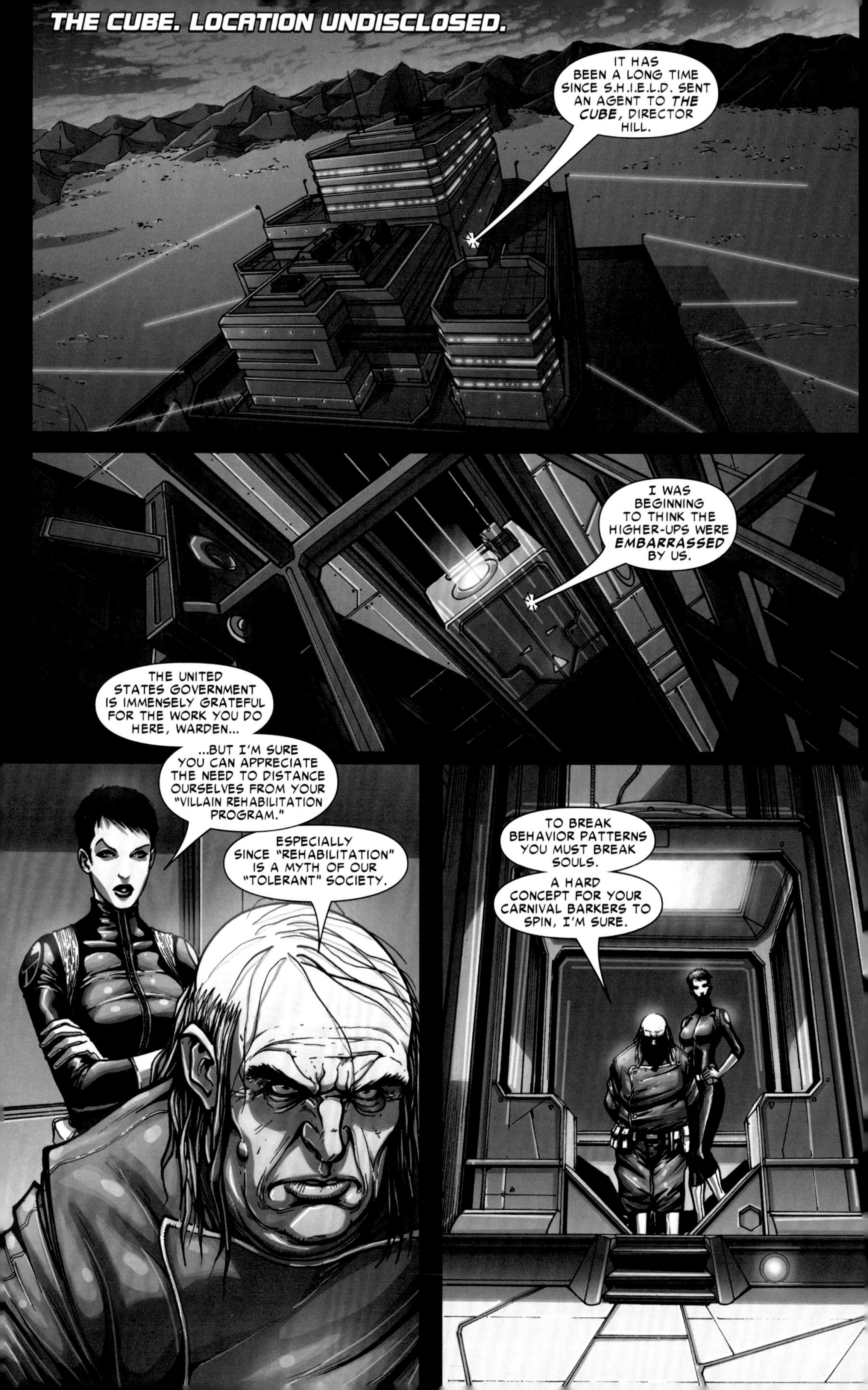
THE CUBE. LOCATION UNDISCLOSED.
IT HAS BEEN A LONG TIME SINCE S.H.I.E.L.D. SENT AN AGENT TO *THE CUBE*, DIRECTOR HILL.
I WAS BEGINNING TO THINK THE HIGHER-UPS WERE *EMBARRASSED* BY US.
THE UNITED STATES GOVERNMENT IS IMMENSELY GRATEFUL FOR THE WORK YOU DO HERE, WARDEN...
...BUT I'M SURE YOU CAN APPRECIATE THE NEED TO DISTANCE OURSELVES FROM YOUR "VILLAIN REHABILITATION PROGRAM."
ESPECIALLY SINCE "REHABILITATION" IS A MYTH OF OUR "TOLERANT" SOCIETY.
TO BREAK BEHAVIOR PATTERNS YOU MUST BREAK SOULS.
A HARD CONCEPT FOR YOUR CARNIVAL BARKERS TO SPIN, I'M SURE.

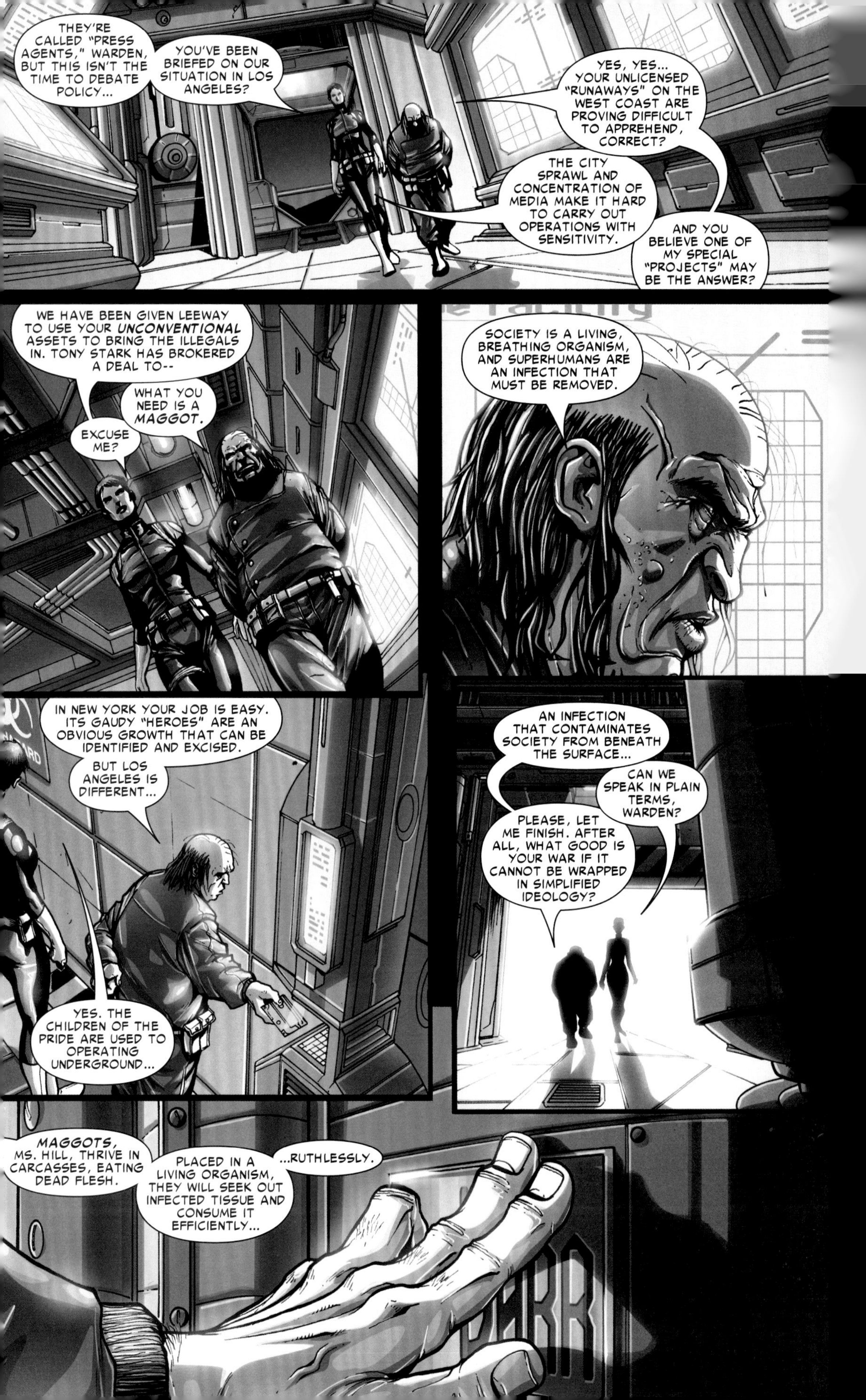
THEY'RE CALLED "PRESS AGENTS," WARDEN, BUT THIS ISN'T THE TIME TO DEBATE POLICY...
YOU'VE BEEN BRIEFED ON OUR SITUATION IN LOS ANGELES?
YES, YES... YOUR UNLICENSED "RUNAWAYS" ON THE WEST COAST ARE PROVING DIFFICULT TO APPREHEND, CORRECT?
THE CITY SPRAWL AND CONCENTRATION OF MEDIA MAKE IT HARD TO CARRY OUT OPERATIONS WITH SENSITIVITY.
AND YOU BELIEVE ONE OF MY SPECIAL "PROJECTS" MAY BE THE ANSWER?
WE HAVE BEEN GIVEN LEEWAY TO USE YOUR *UNCONVENTIONAL* ASSETS TO BRING THE ILLEGALS IN. TONY STARK HAS BROKERED A DEAL TO--
WHAT YOU NEED IS A *MAGGOT*.
EXCUSE ME?
SOCIETY IS A LIVING, BREATHING ORGANISM, AND SUPERHUMANS ARE AN INFECTION THAT MUST BE REMOVED.
IN NEW YORK YOUR JOB IS EASY. ITS GAUDY "HEROES" ARE AN OBVIOUS GROWTH THAT CAN BE IDENTIFIED AND EXCISED.
BUT LOS ANGELES IS DIFFERENT...
YES. THE CHILDREN OF THE PRIDE ARE USED TO OPERATING UNDERGROUND...
AN INFECTION THAT CONTAMINATES SOCIETY FROM BENEATH THE SURFACE...
CAN WE SPEAK IN PLAIN TERMS, WARDEN?
PLEASE, LET ME FINISH. AFTER ALL, WHAT GOOD IS YOUR WAR IF IT CANNOT BE WRAPPED IN SIMPLIFIED IDEOLOGY?
MAGGOTS, MS. HILL, THRIVE IN CARCASSES, EATING DEAD FLESH.
PLACED IN A LIVING ORGANISM, THEY WILL SEEK OUT INFECTED TISSUE AND CONSUME IT EFFICIENTLY...
...RUTHLESSLY.

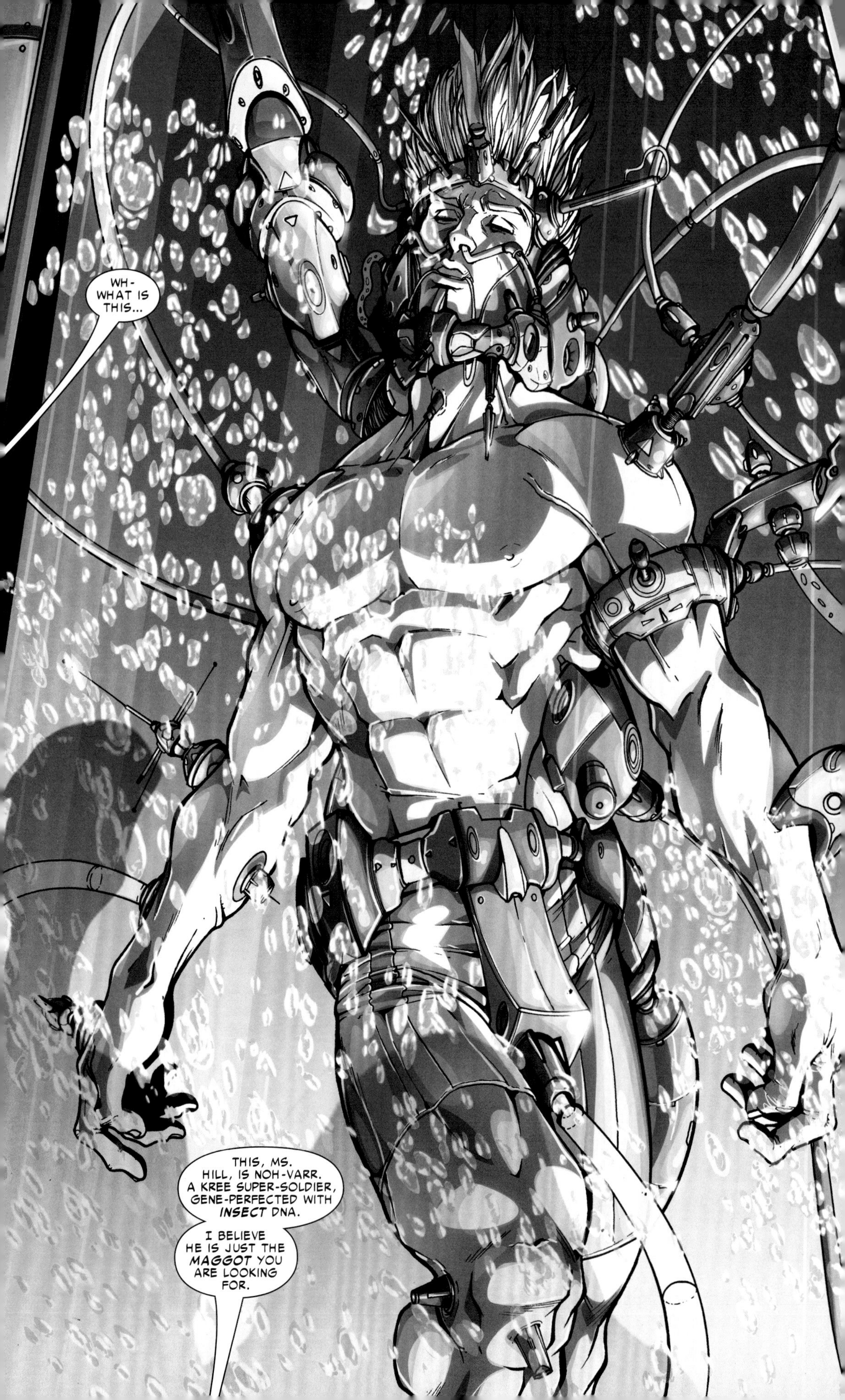
WH- WHAT IS THIS...
THIS, MS. HILL, IS NOH-VARR. A KREE SUPER-SOLDIER, GENE-PERFECTED WITH *INSECT* DNA.
I BELIEVE HE IS JUST THE *MAGGOT* YOU ARE LOOKING FOR.

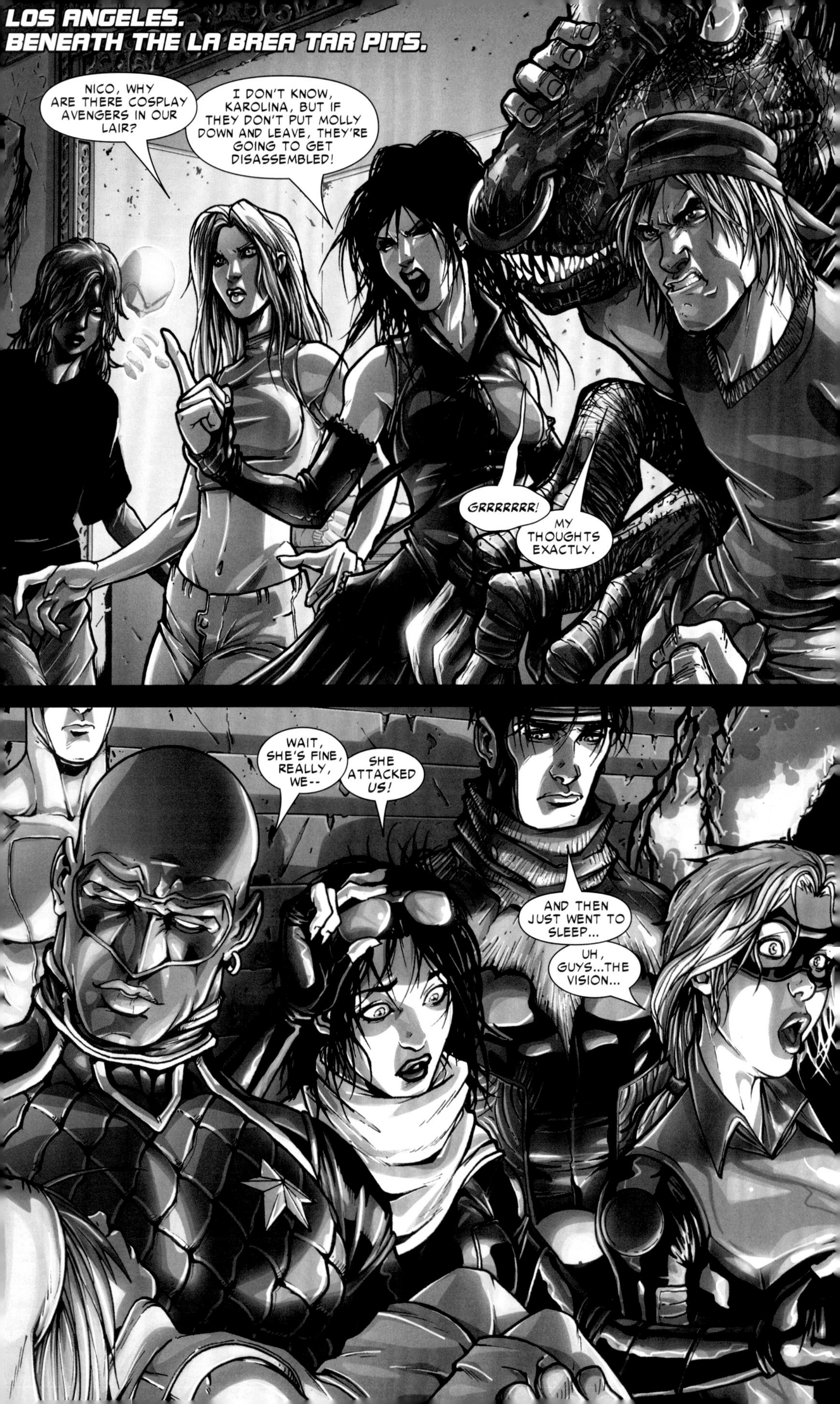
LOS ANGELES.
BENEATH THE LA BREA TAR PITS.
NICO, WHY ARE THERE COSPLAY AVENGERS IN OUR LAIR?
I DON'T KNOW, KAROLINA, BUT IF THEY DON'T PUT MOLLY DOWN AND LEAVE, THEY'RE GOING TO GET DISASSEMBLED!
GRRRRRRR!
MY THOUGHTS EXACTLY.
WAIT, SHE'S FINE, REALLY, WE--
SHE ATTACKED US!
AND THEN JUST WENT TO SLEEP...
UH, GUYS...THE VISION...

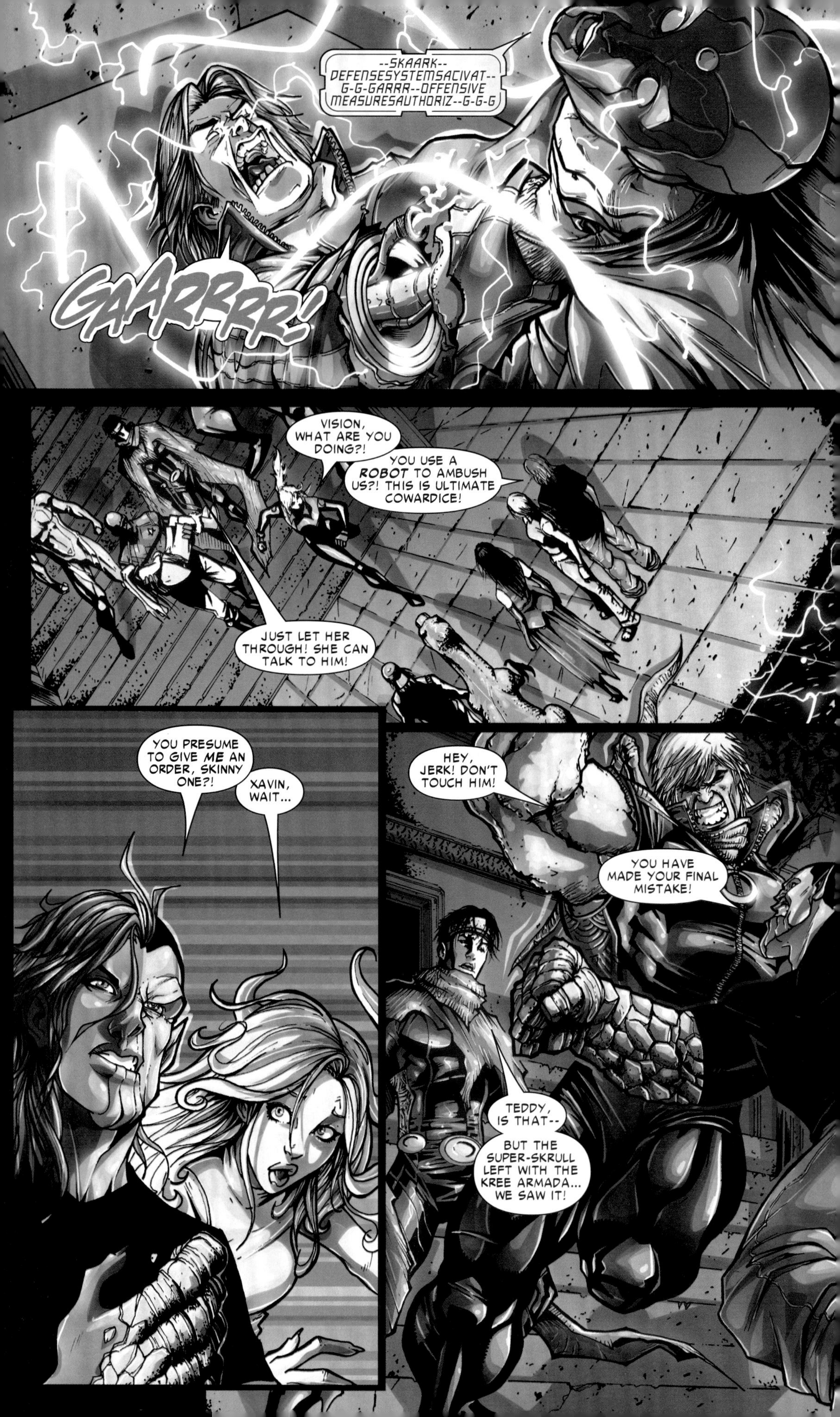
--SKAARK--
DEFENSESYSTEMSACIVAT--
G-G-GARRR--OFFENSIVE
MEASURESAUTHORIZ--G-G-G
GAARRRR!
VISION, WHAT ARE YOU DOING?!
YOU USE A ROBOT TO AMBUSH US?! THIS IS ULTIMATE COWARDICE!
JUST LET HER THROUGH! SHE CAN TALK TO HIM!
YOU PRESUME TO GIVE ME AN ORDER, SKINNY ONE?!
XAVIN, WAIT...
HEY, JERK! DON'T TOUCH HIM!
YOU HAVE MADE YOUR FINAL MISTAKE!
TEDDY, IS THAT--
BUT THE SUPER-SKRULL LEFT WITH THE KREE ARMADA... WE SAW IT!

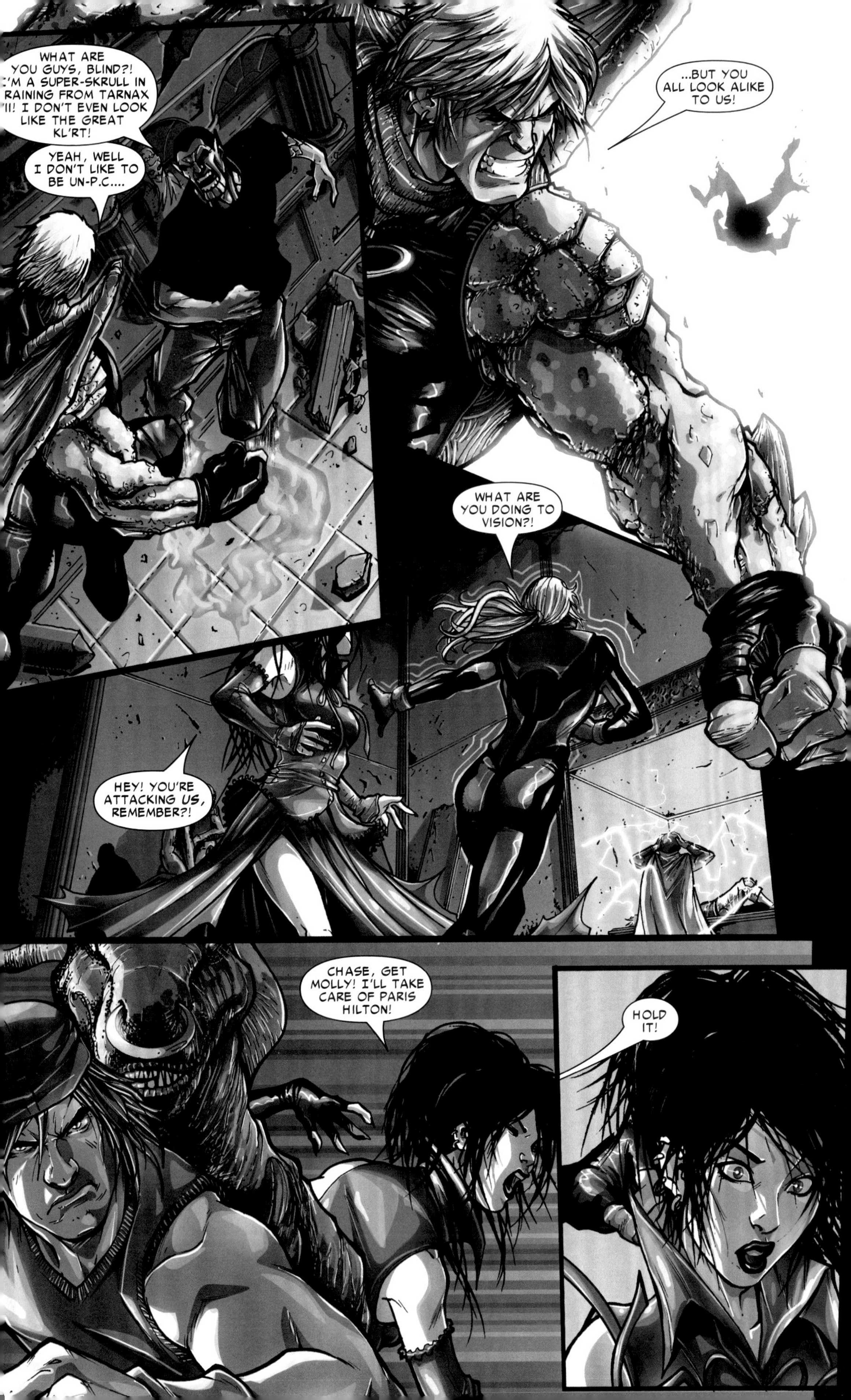
WHAT ARE YOU GUYS, BLIND?! I'M A SUPER-SKRULL IN TRAINING FROM TARNAX II! I DON'T EVEN LOOK LIKE THE GREAT KL'RT!
YEAH, WELL I DON'T LIKE TO BE UN-P.C....
...BUT YOU ALL LOOK ALIKE TO US!
WHAT ARE YOU DOING TO VISION?!
HEY! YOU'RE ATTACKING *US*, REMEMBER?!
CHASE, GET MOLLY! I'LL TAKE CARE OF PARIS HILTON!
HOLD IT!

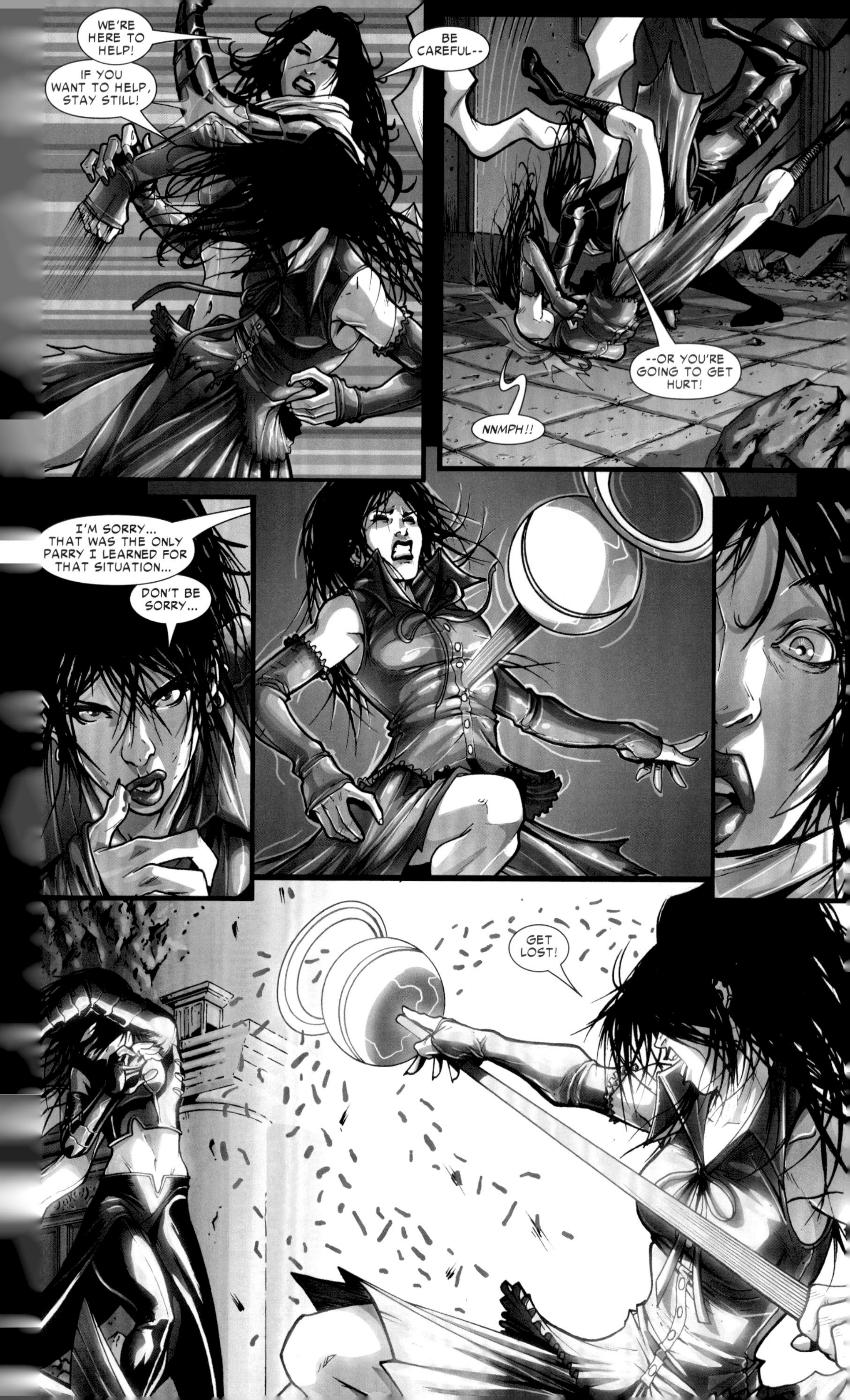
WE'RE HERE TO HELP!
IF YOU WANT TO HELP, STAY STILL!
BE CAREFUL--
--OR YOU'RE GOING TO GET HURT!
NNMPH!!
I'M SORRY... THAT WAS THE ONLY PARRY I LEARNED FOR THAT SITUATION...
DON'T BE SORRY...
GET LOST!

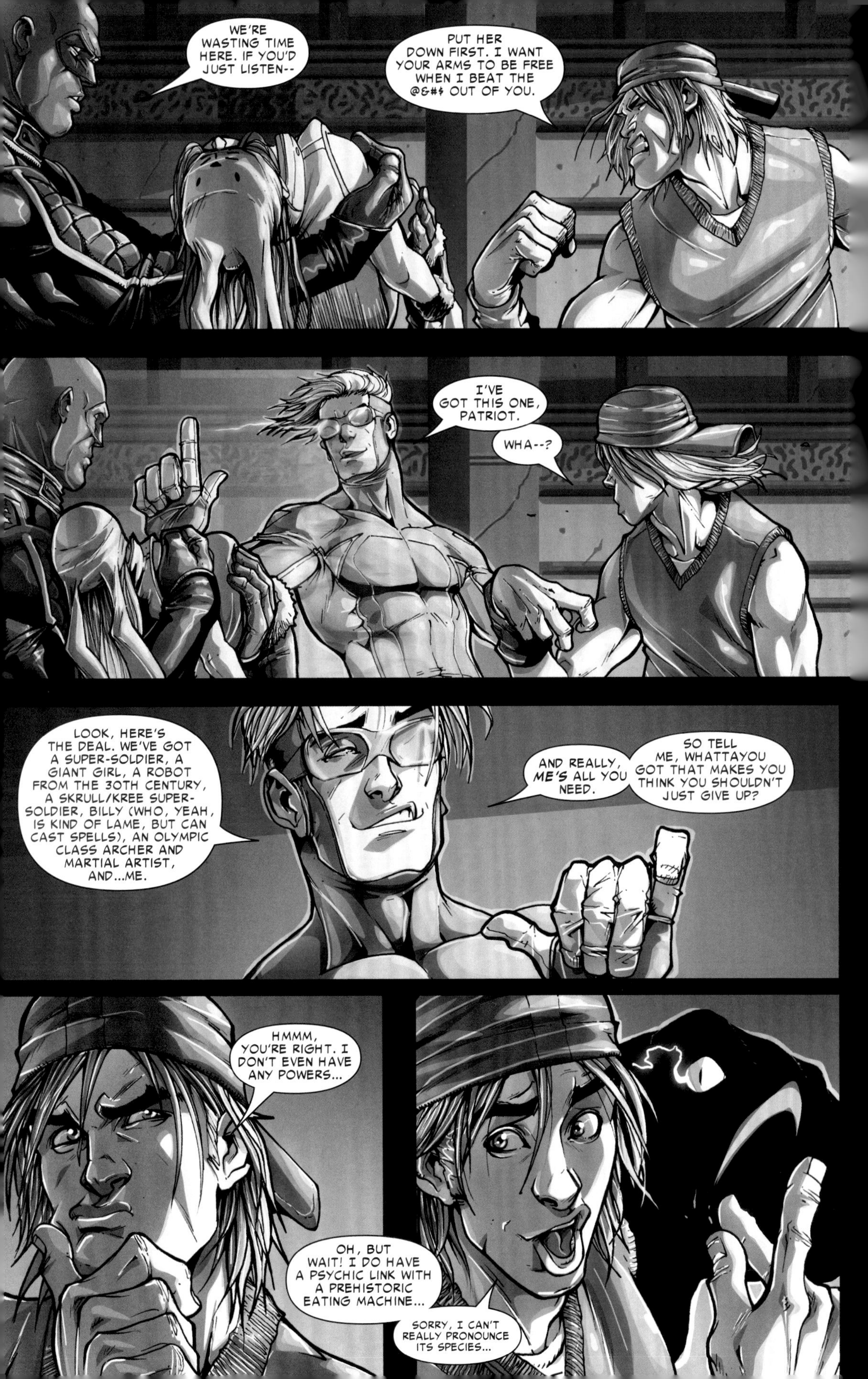
WE'RE WASTING TIME HERE. IF YOU'D JUST LISTEN--
PUT HER DOWN FIRST. I WANT YOUR ARMS TO BE FREE WHEN I BEAT THE @&#$ OUT OF YOU.
I'VE GOT THIS ONE, PATRIOT.
WHA--?
LOOK, HERE'S THE DEAL. WE'VE GOT A SUPER-SOLDIER, A GIANT GIRL, A ROBOT FROM THE 30TH CENTURY, A SKRULL/KREE SUPER-SOLDIER, BILLY (WHO, YEAH, IS KIND OF LAME, BUT CAN CAST SPELLS), AN OLYMPIC CLASS ARCHER AND MARTIAL ARTIST, AND...ME.
AND REALLY, ME'S ALL YOU NEED.
SO TELL ME, WHATTAYOU GOT THAT MAKES YOU THINK YOU SHOULDN'T JUST GIVE UP?
HMMM, YOU'RE RIGHT. I DON'T EVEN HAVE ANY POWERS...
OH, BUT WAIT! I DO HAVE A PSYCHIC LINK WITH A PREHISTORIC EATING MACHINE...
SORRY, I CAN'T REALLY PRONOUNCE ITS SPECIES...

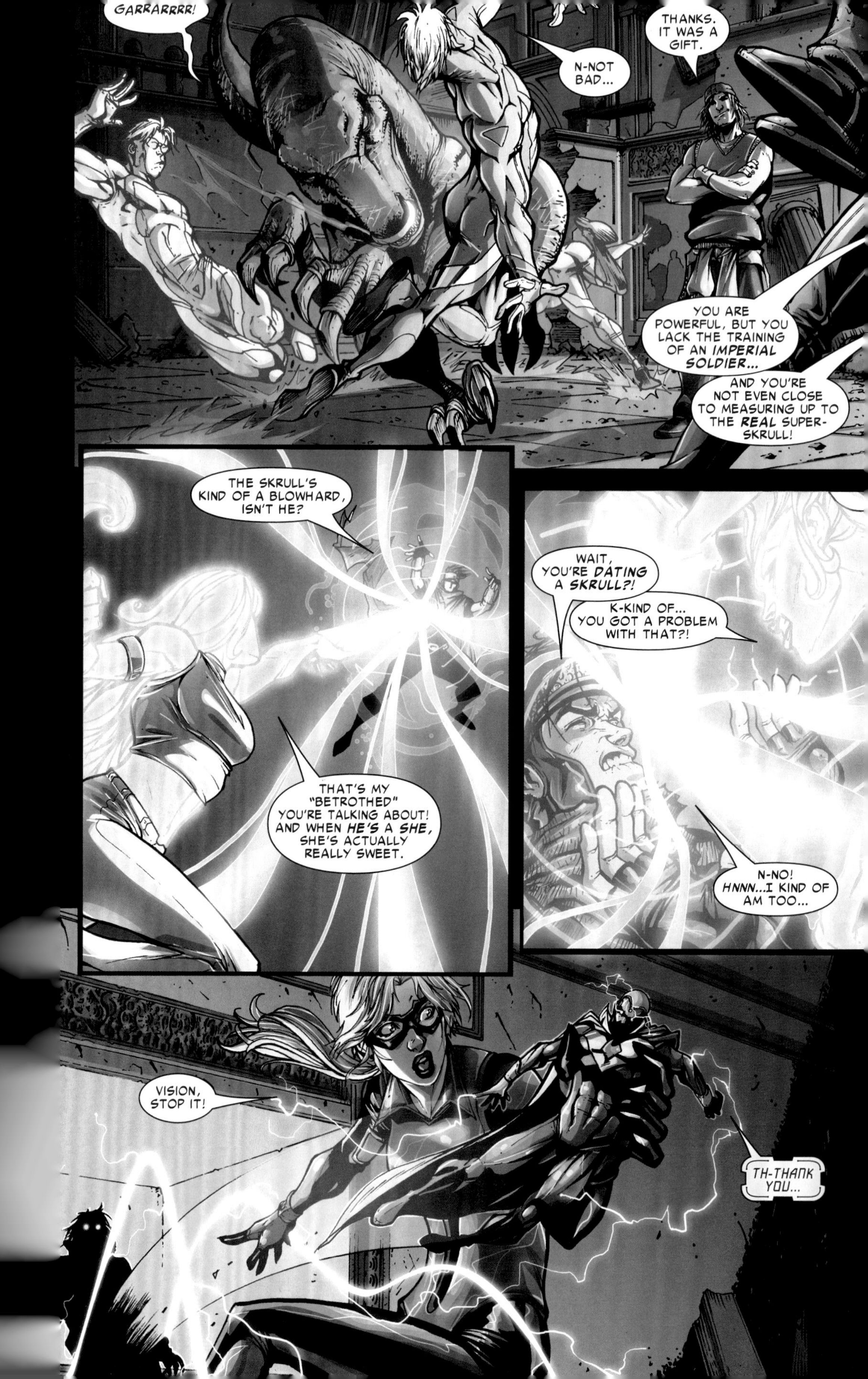
GARRARRRR!
N-NOT BAD...
THANKS. IT WAS A GIFT.
YOU ARE POWERFUL, BUT YOU LACK THE TRAINING OF AN IMPERIAL SOLDIER...
AND YOU'RE NOT EVEN CLOSE TO MEASURING UP TO THE REAL SUPER-SKRULL!
THE SKRULL'S KIND OF A BLOWHARD, ISN'T HE?
THAT'S MY "BETROTHED" YOU'RE TALKING ABOUT! AND WHEN HE'S A SHE, SHE'S ACTUALLY REALLY SWEET.
WAIT, YOU'RE DATING A SKRULL?!
K-KIND OF... YOU GOT A PROBLEM WITH THAT?!
N-NO! HNNN...I KIND OF AM TOO...
VISION, STOP IT!
TH-THANK YOU...

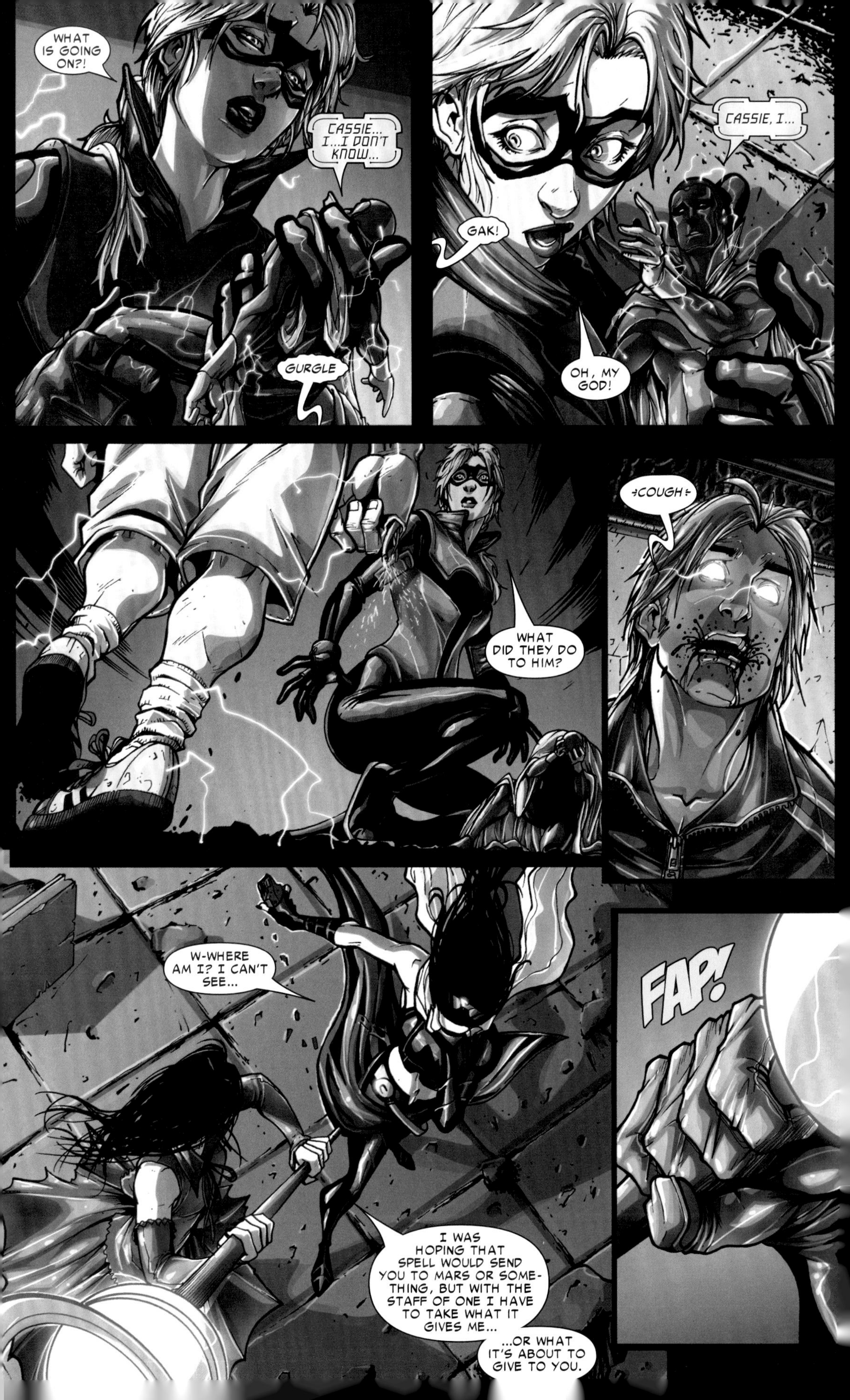
WHAT IS GOING ON?!
CASSIE... I...I DON'T KNOW...
GURGLE
CASSIE, I...
GAK!
OH, MY GOD!
WHAT DID THEY DO TO HIM?
COUGH
W-WHERE AM I? I CAN'T SEE...
I WAS HOPING THAT SPELL WOULD SEND YOU TO MARS OR SOME-THING, BUT WITH THE STAFF OF ONE I HAVE TO TAKE WHAT IT GIVES ME...
...OR WHAT IT'S ABOUT TO GIVE TO YOU.
FAP!

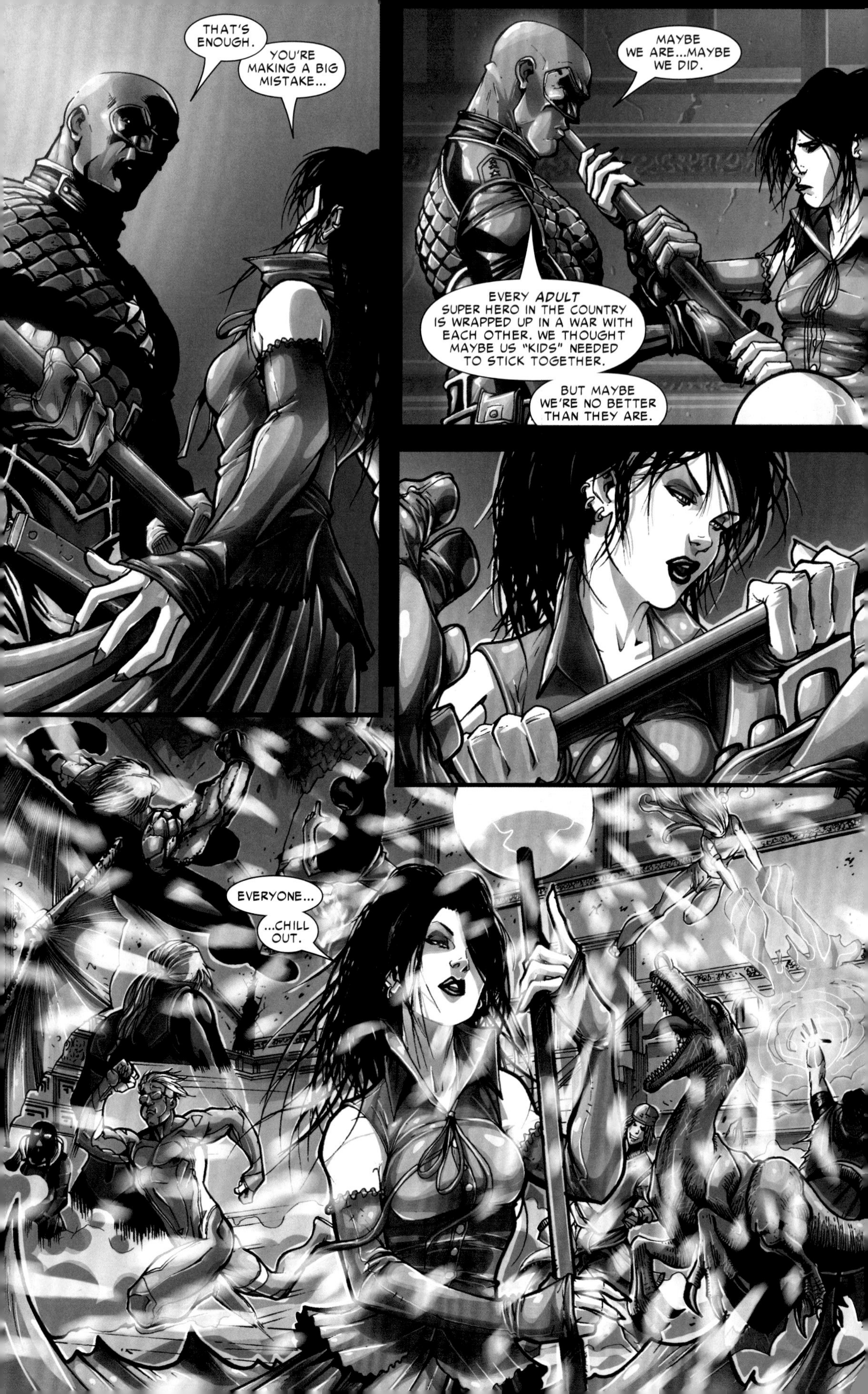
THAT'S ENOUGH.
YOU'RE MAKING A BIG MISTAKE...
MAYBE WE ARE...MAYBE WE DID.
EVERY ADULT SUPER HERO IN THE COUNTRY IS WRAPPED UP IN A WAR WITH EACH OTHER. WE THOUGHT MAYBE US "KIDS" NEEDED TO STICK TOGETHER.
BUT MAYBE WE'RE NO BETTER THAN THEY ARE.
EVERYONE...
...CHILL OUT.

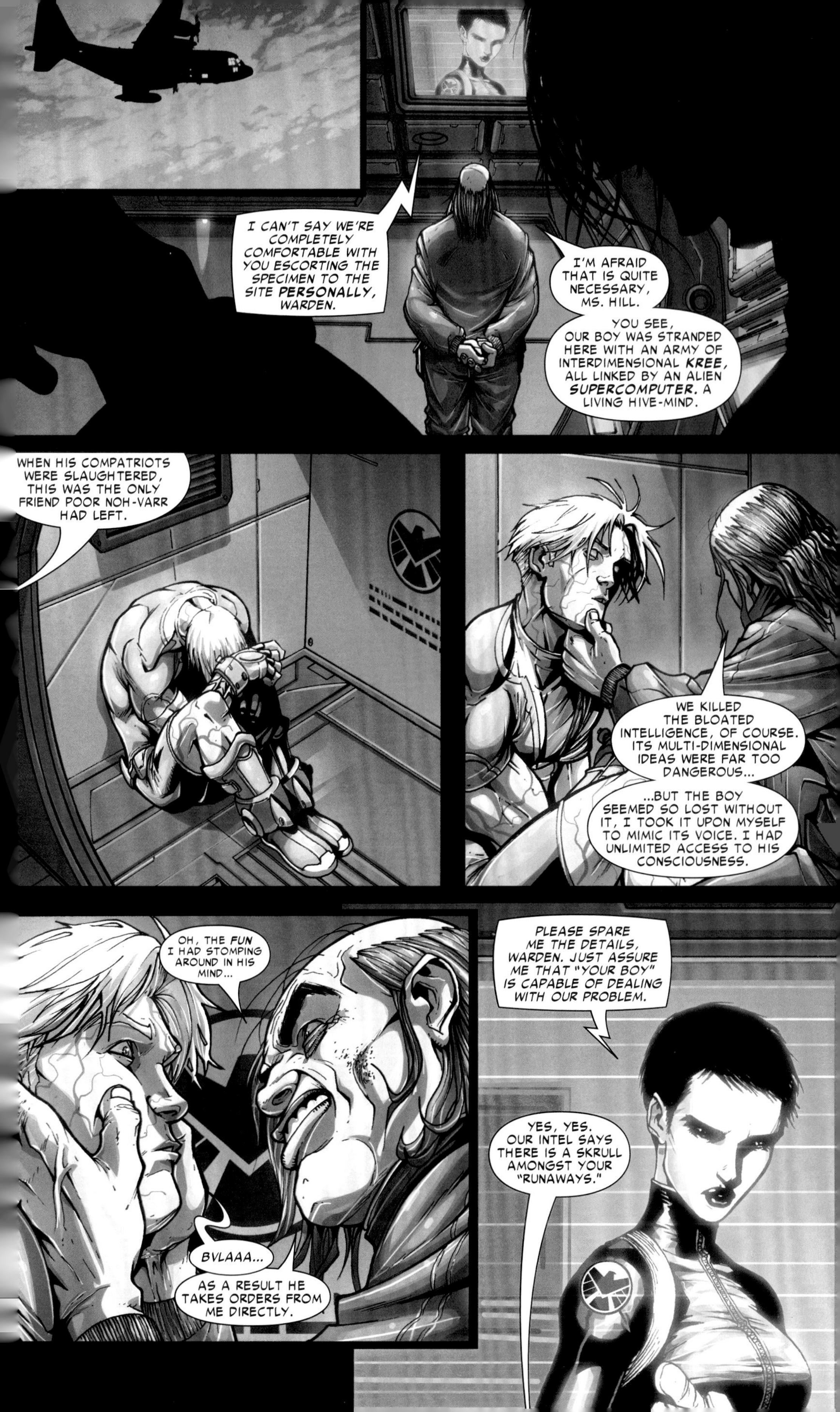
I CAN'T SAY WE'RE COMPLETELY COMFORTABLE WITH YOU ESCORTING THE SPECIMEN TO THE SITE PERSONALLY, WARDEN.
I'M AFRAID THAT IS QUITE NECESSARY, MS. HILL.
YOU SEE, OUR BOY WAS STRANDED HERE WITH AN ARMY OF INTERDIMENSIONAL KREE, ALL LINKED BY AN ALIEN SUPERCOMPUTER. A LIVING HIVE-MIND.
WHEN HIS COMPATRIOTS WERE SLAUGHTERED, THIS WAS THE ONLY FRIEND POOR NOH-VARR HAD LEFT.
WE KILLED THE BLOATED INTELLIGENCE, OF COURSE. ITS MULTI-DIMENSIONAL IDEAS WERE FAR TOO DANGEROUS...
...BUT THE BOY SEEMED SO LOST WITHOUT IT, I TOOK IT UPON MYSELF TO MIMIC ITS VOICE. I HAD UNLIMITED ACCESS TO HIS CONSCIOUSNESS.
OH, THE FUN I HAD STOMPING AROUND IN HIS MIND...
BVLAAA...
AS A RESULT HE TAKES ORDERS FROM ME DIRECTLY.
PLEASE SPARE ME THE DETAILS, WARDEN. JUST ASSURE ME THAT "YOUR BOY" IS CAPABLE OF DEALING WITH OUR PROBLEM.
YES, YES. OUR INTEL SAYS THERE IS A SKRULL AMONGST YOUR "RUNAWAYS."

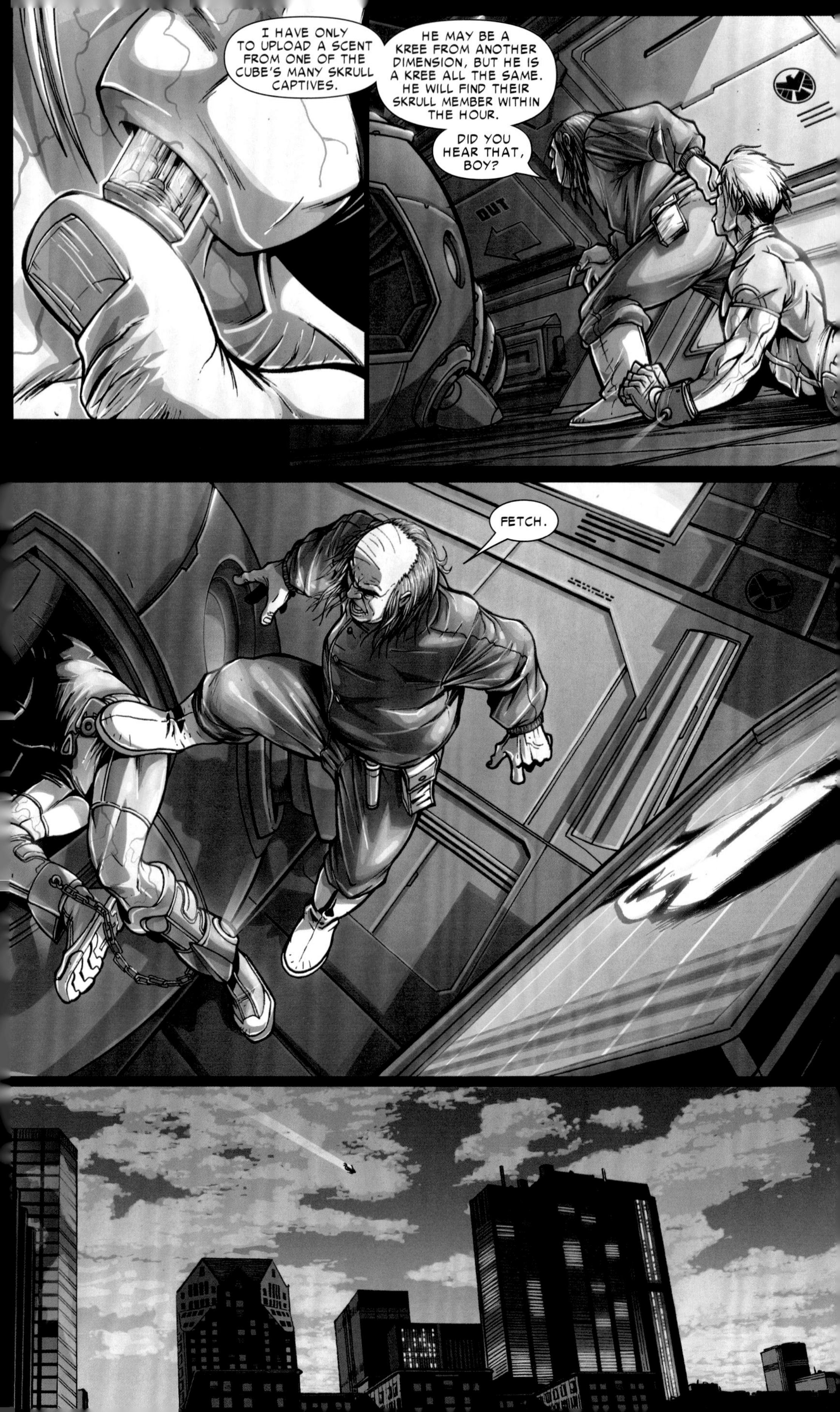
I HAVE ONLY TO UPLOAD A SCENT FROM ONE OF THE CUBE'S MANY SKRULL CAPTIVES.
HE MAY BE A KREE FROM ANOTHER DIMENSION, BUT HE IS A KREE ALL THE SAME. HE WILL FIND THEIR SKRULL MEMBER WITHIN THE HOUR.
DID YOU HEAR THAT, BOY?
OUT
FETCH.

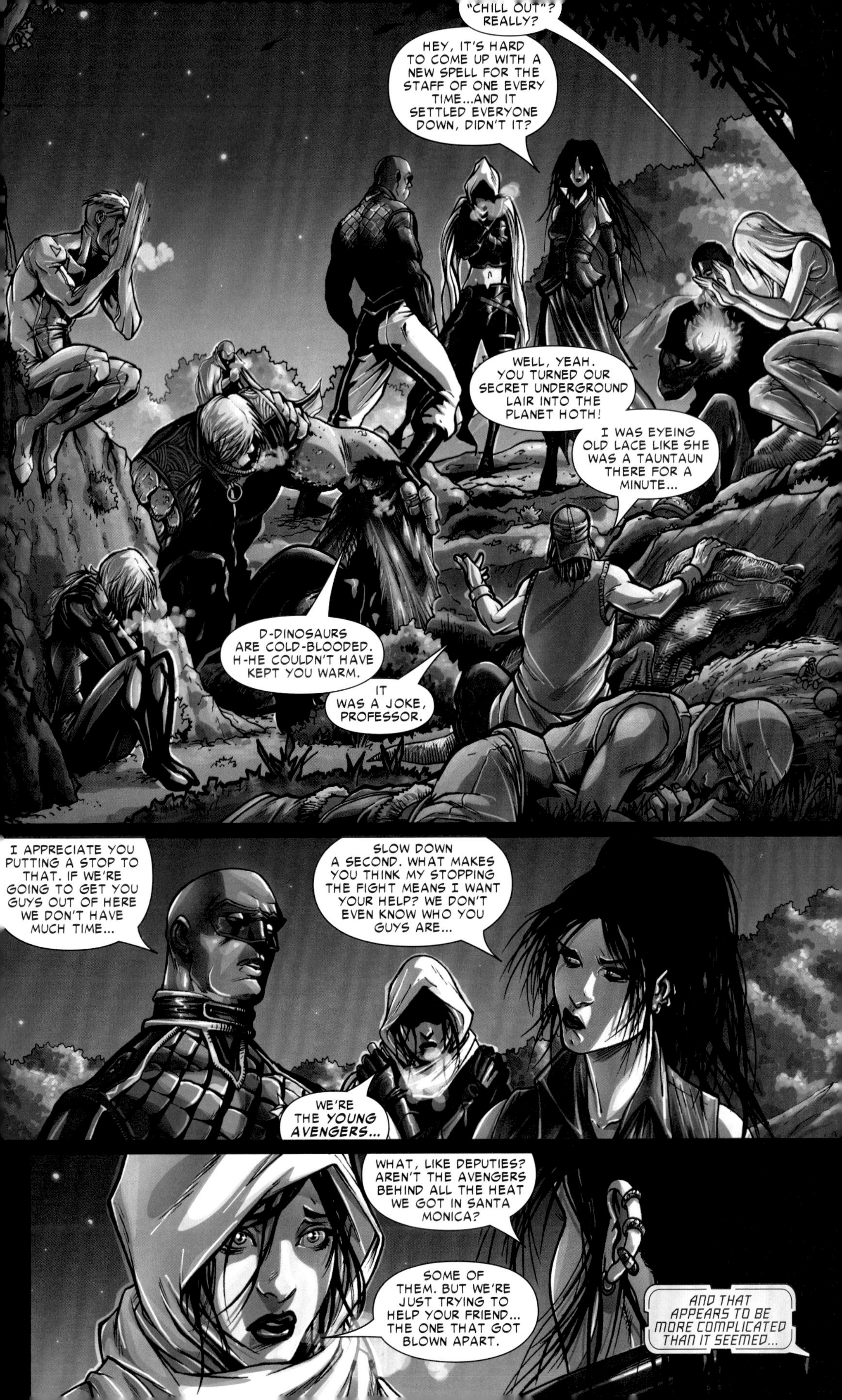
"CHILL OUT"? REALLY?
HEY, IT'S HARD TO COME UP WITH A NEW SPELL FOR THE STAFF OF ONE EVERY TIME...AND IT SETTLED EVERYONE DOWN, DIDN'T IT?
WELL, YEAH. YOU TURNED OUR SECRET UNDERGROUND LAIR INTO THE PLANET HOTH!
I WAS EYEING OLD LACE LIKE SHE WAS A TAUNTAUN THERE FOR A MINUTE...
D-DINOSAURS ARE COLD-BLOODED. H-HE COULDN'T HAVE KEPT YOU WARM.
IT WAS A JOKE, PROFESSOR.
I APPRECIATE YOU PUTTING A STOP TO THAT. IF WE'RE GOING TO GET YOU GUYS OUT OF HERE WE DON'T HAVE MUCH TIME...
SLOW DOWN A SECOND. WHAT MAKES YOU THINK MY STOPPING THE FIGHT MEANS I WANT YOUR HELP? WE DON'T EVEN KNOW WHO YOU GUYS ARE...
WE'RE THE *YOUNG AVENGERS*...
WHAT, LIKE DEPUTIES? AREN'T THE AVENGERS BEHIND ALL THE HEAT WE GOT IN SANTA MONICA?
SOME OF THEM. BUT WE'RE JUST TRYING TO HELP YOUR FRIEND... THE ONE THAT GOT BLOWN APART.
AND THAT APPEARS TO BE MORE COMPLICATED THAN IT SEEMED...

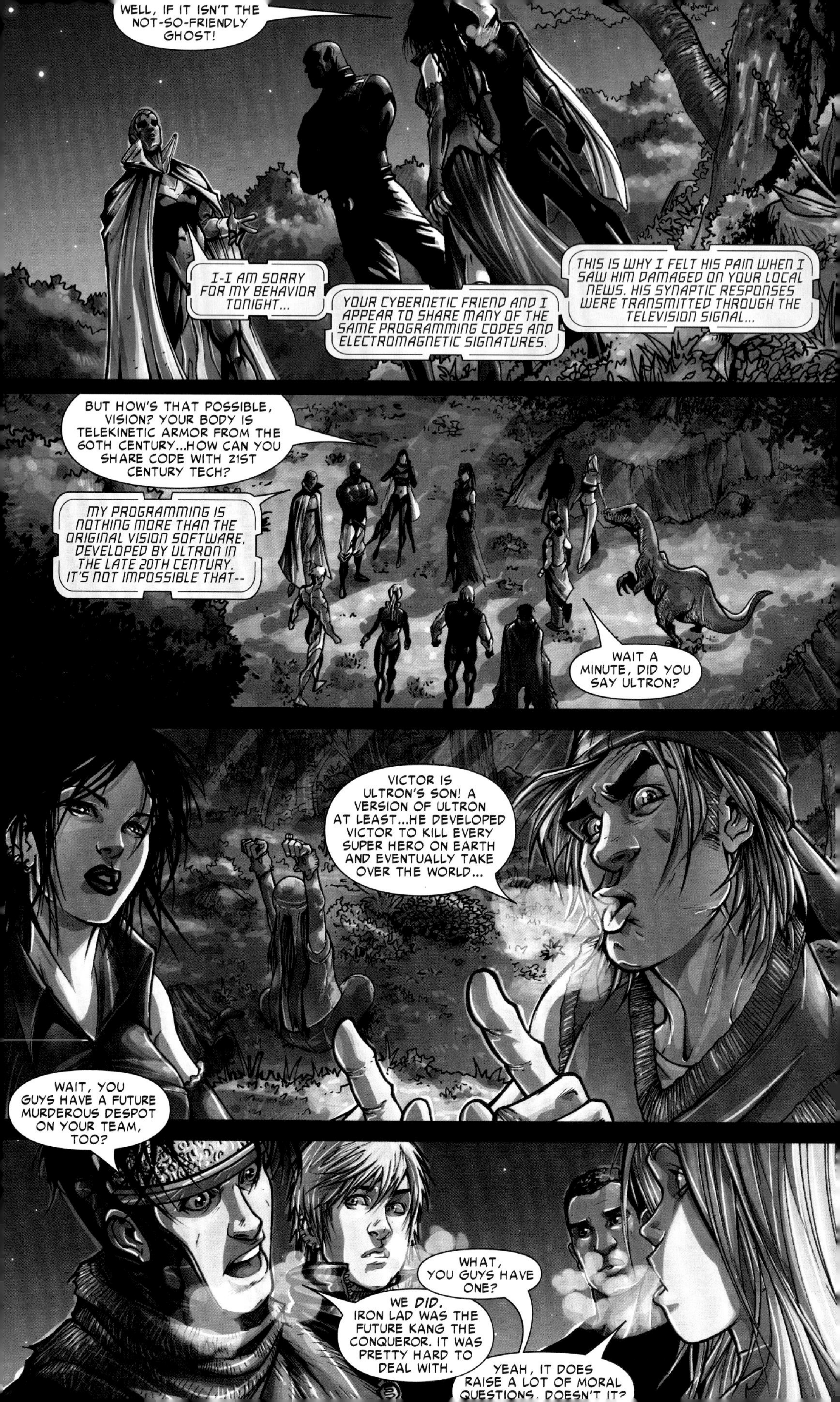
WELL, IF IT ISN'T THE NOT-SO-FRIENDLY GHOST!
I-I AM SORRY FOR MY BEHAVIOR TONIGHT...
YOUR CYBERNETIC FRIEND AND I APPEAR TO SHARE MANY OF THE SAME PROGRAMMING CODES AND ELECTROMAGNETIC SIGNATURES.
THIS IS WHY I FELT HIS PAIN WHEN I SAW HIM DAMAGED ON YOUR LOCAL NEWS. HIS SYNAPTIC RESPONSES WERE TRANSMITTED THROUGH THE TELEVISION SIGNAL...
BUT HOW'S THAT POSSIBLE, VISION? YOUR BODY IS TELEKINETIC ARMOR FROM THE 60TH CENTURY...HOW CAN YOU SHARE CODE WITH 21ST CENTURY TECH?
MY PROGRAMMING IS NOTHING MORE THAN THE ORIGINAL VISION SOFTWARE, DEVELOPED BY ULTRON IN THE LATE 20TH CENTURY. IT'S NOT IMPOSSIBLE THAT--
WAIT A MINUTE, DID YOU SAY ULTRON?
VICTOR IS ULTRON'S SON! A VERSION OF ULTRON AT LEAST...HE DEVELOPED VICTOR TO KILL EVERY SUPER HERO ON EARTH AND EVENTUALLY TAKE OVER THE WORLD...
WAIT, YOU GUYS HAVE A FUTURE MURDEROUS DESPOT ON YOUR TEAM, TOO?
WHAT, YOU GUYS HAVE ONE?
WE *DID*. IRON LAD WAS THE FUTURE KANG THE CONQUEROR. IT WAS PRETTY HARD TO DEAL WITH.
YEAH, IT DOES RAISE A LOT OF MORAL QUESTIONS, DOESN'T IT?

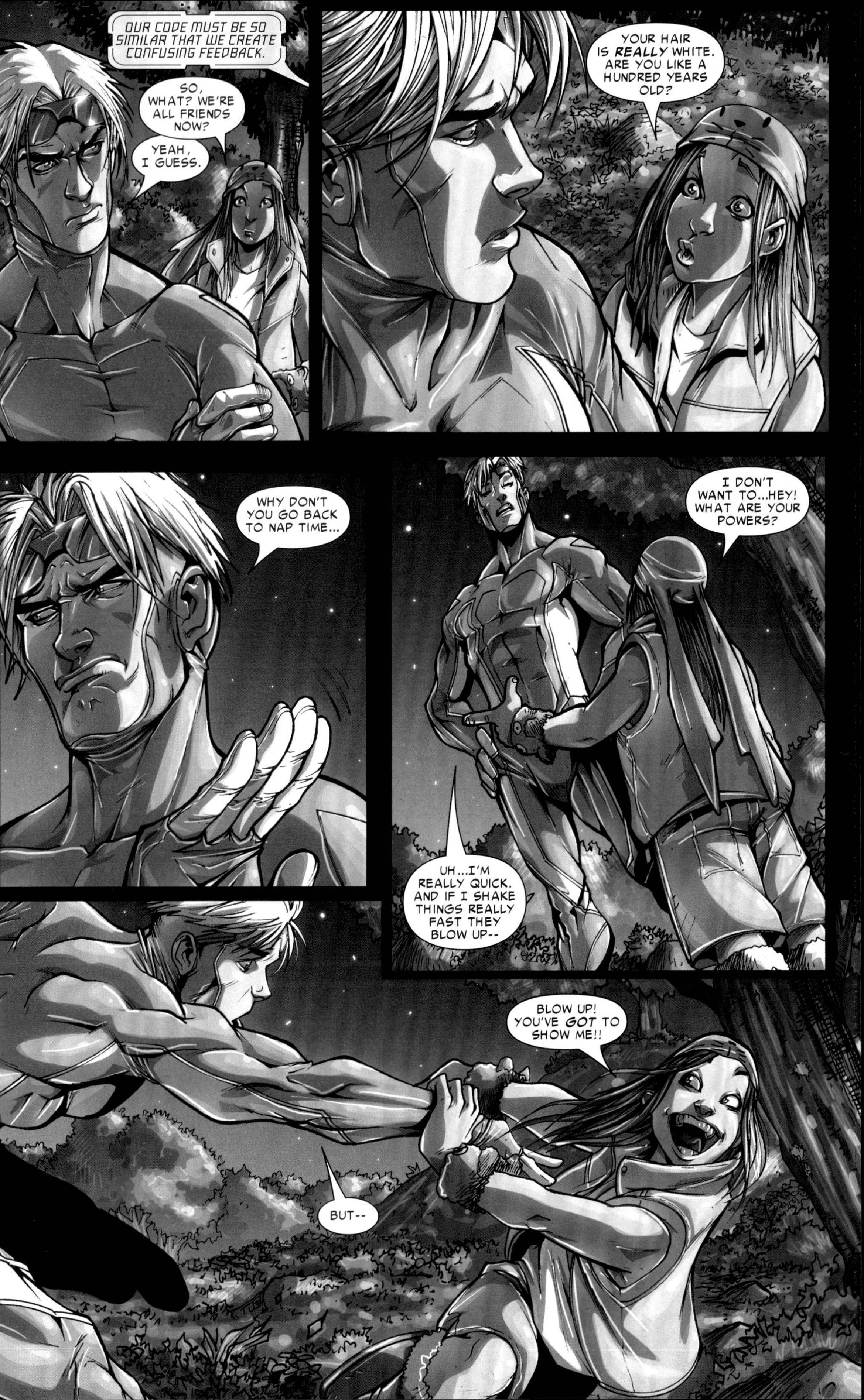
OUR CODE MUST BE SO SIMILAR THAT WE CREATE CONFUSING FEEDBACK.
SO, WHAT? WE'RE ALL FRIENDS NOW?
YEAH, I GUESS.
YOUR HAIR IS REALLY WHITE. ARE YOU LIKE A HUNDRED YEARS OLD?
WHY DON'T YOU GO BACK TO NAP TIME...
I DON'T WANT TO...HEY! WHAT ARE YOUR POWERS?
UH...I'M REALLY QUICK. AND IF I SHAKE THINGS REALLY FAST THEY BLOW UP--
BLOW UP! YOU'VE GOT TO SHOW ME!!
BUT--

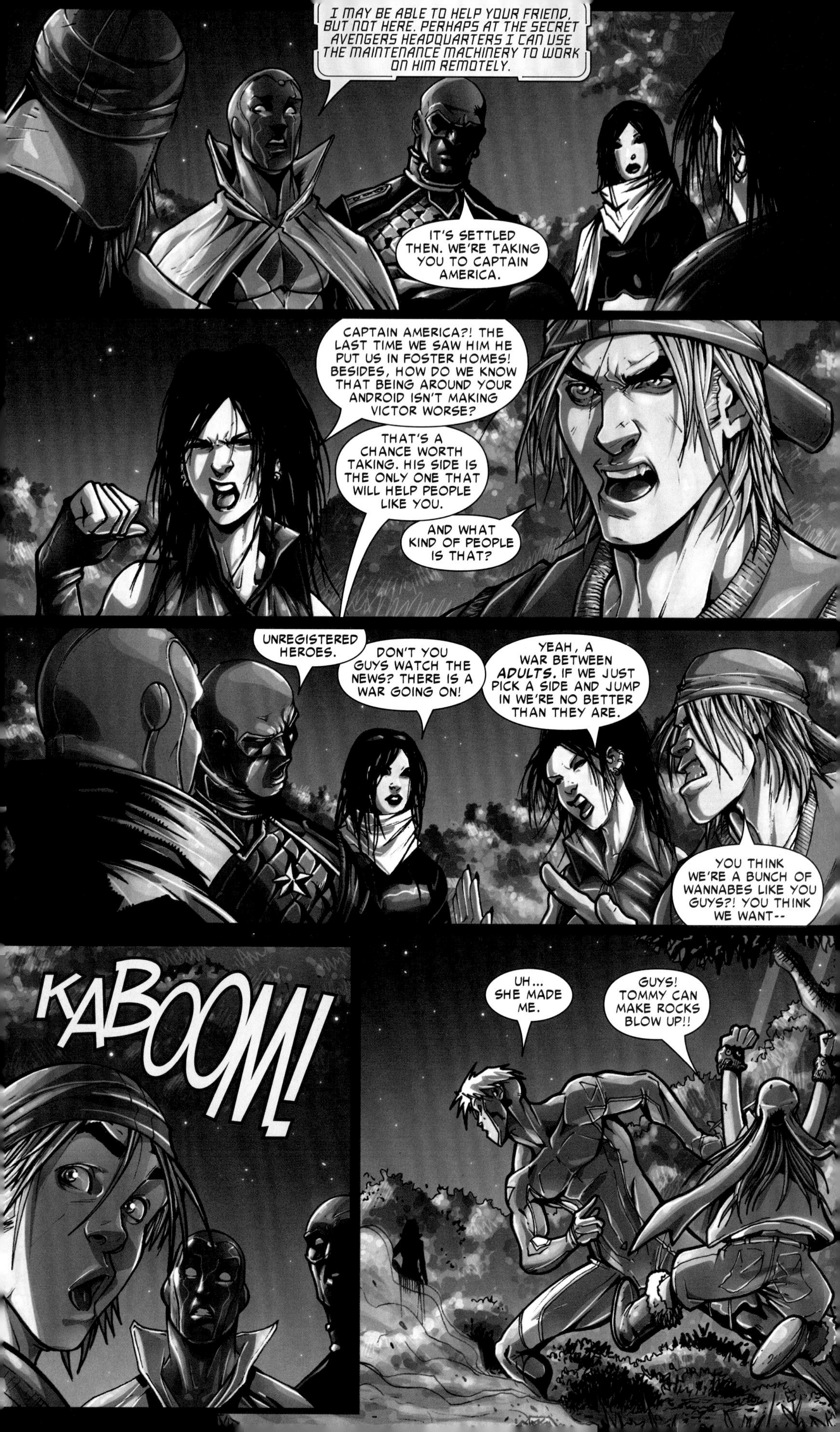
I MAY BE ABLE TO HELP YOUR FRIEND, BUT NOT HERE. PERHAPS AT THE SECRET AVENGERS HEADQUARTERS I CAN USE THE MAINTENANCE MACHINERY TO WORK ON HIM REMOTELY.
IT'S SETTLED THEN. WE'RE TAKING YOU TO CAPTAIN AMERICA.
CAPTAIN AMERICA?! THE LAST TIME WE SAW HIM HE PUT US IN FOSTER HOMES! BESIDES, HOW DO WE KNOW THAT BEING AROUND YOUR ANDROID ISN'T MAKING VICTOR WORSE?
THAT'S A CHANCE WORTH TAKING. HIS SIDE IS THE ONLY ONE THAT WILL HELP PEOPLE LIKE YOU.
AND WHAT KIND OF PEOPLE IS THAT?
UNREGISTERED HEROES.
DON'T YOU GUYS WATCH THE NEWS? THERE IS A WAR GOING ON!
YEAH, A WAR BETWEEN ADULTS. IF WE JUST PICK A SIDE AND JUMP IN WE'RE NO BETTER THAN THEY ARE.
YOU THINK WE'RE A BUNCH OF WANNABES LIKE YOU GUYS?! YOU THINK WE WANT--
KABOOM!
UH... SHE MADE ME.
GUYS! TOMMY CAN MAKE ROCKS BLOW UP!!

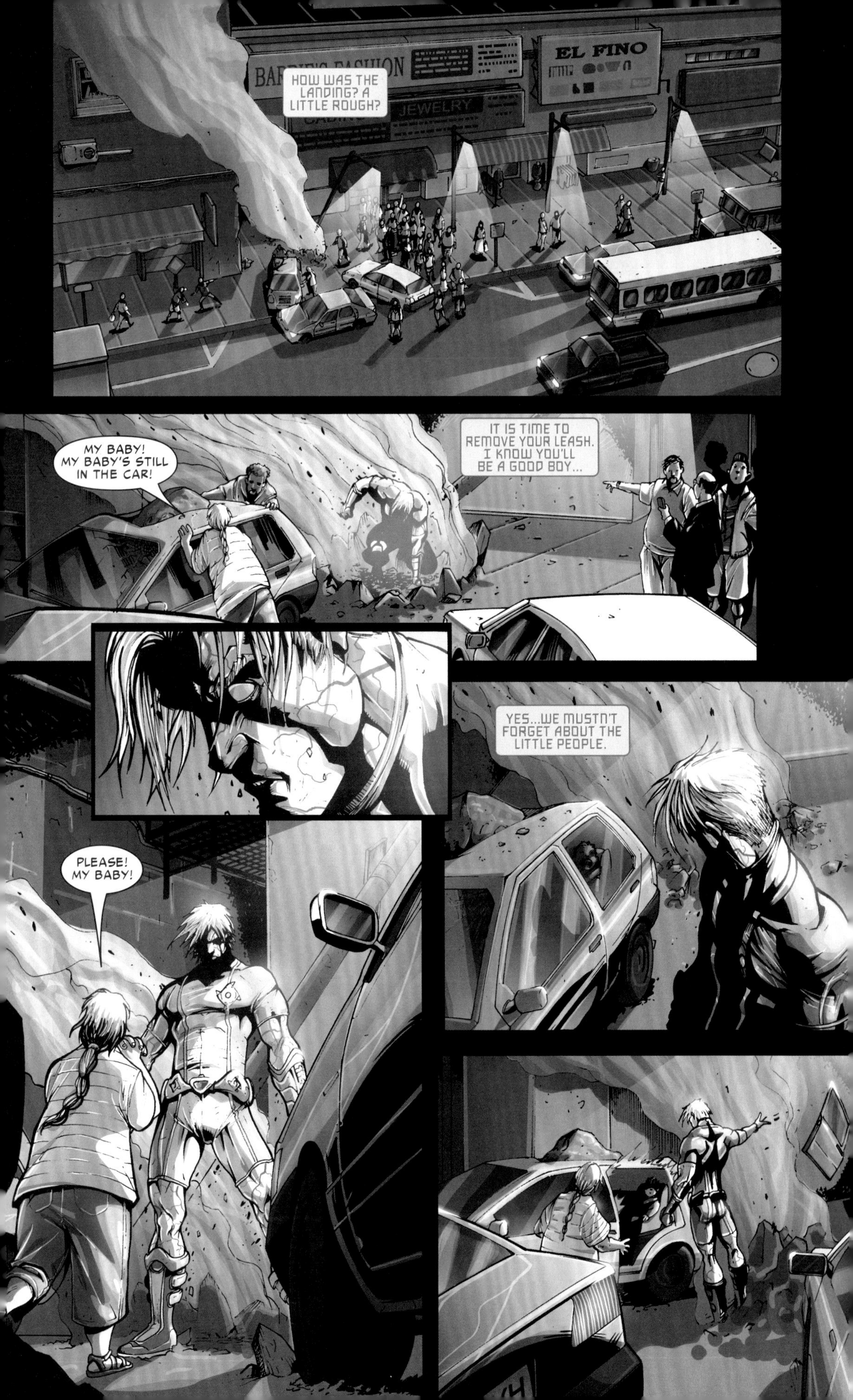
EL FINO
JEWELRY
HOW WAS THE LANDING? A LITTLE ROUGH?
MY BABY! MY BABY'S STILL IN THE CAR!
IT IS TIME TO REMOVE YOUR LEASH. I KNOW YOU'LL BE A GOOD BOY...
PLEASE! MY BABY!
YES...WE MUSTN'T FORGET ABOUT THE LITTLE PEOPLE.

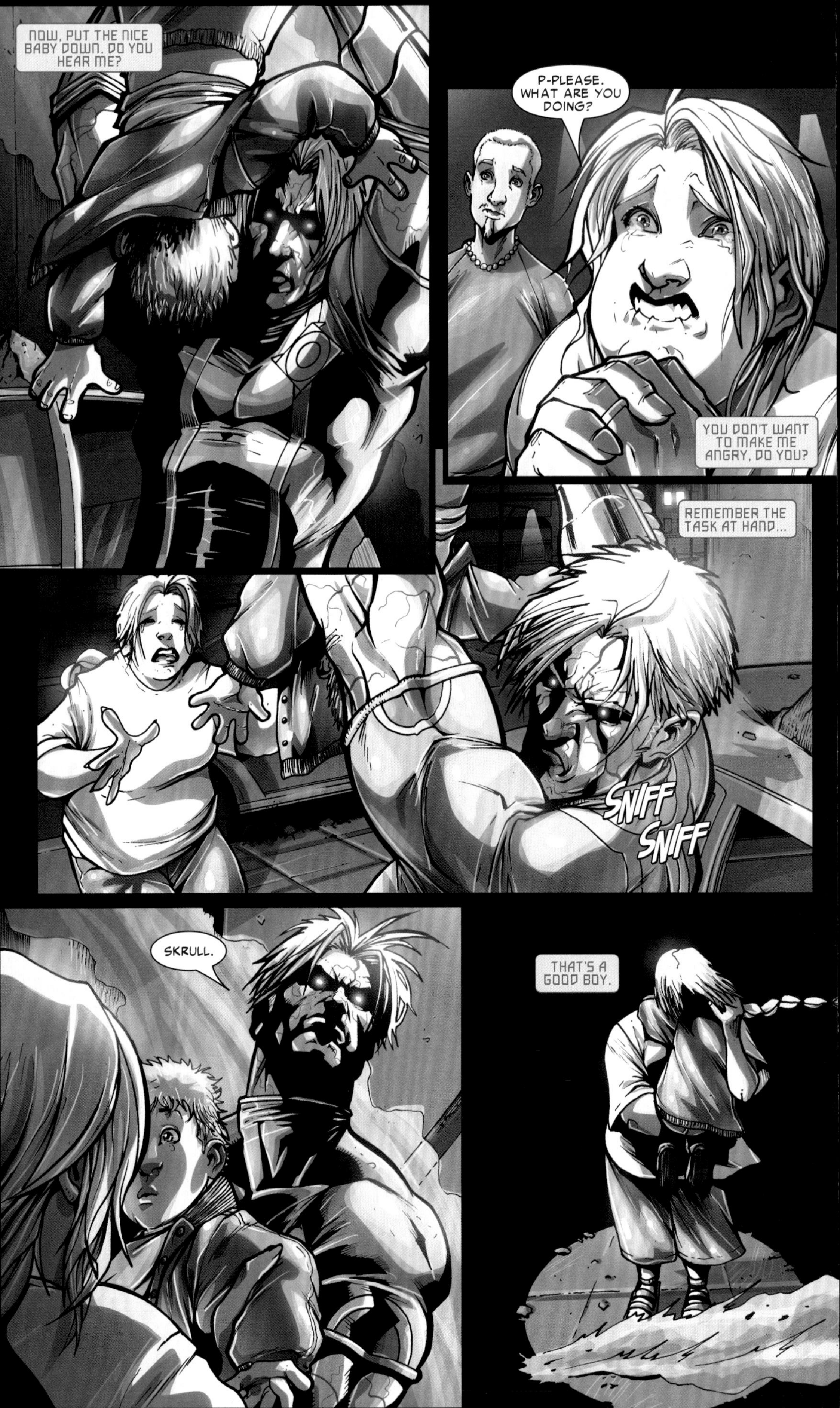
NOW, PUT THE NICE BABY DOWN. DO YOU HEAR ME?
P-PLEASE. WHAT ARE YOU DOING?
YOU DON'T WANT TO MAKE ME ANGRY, DO YOU?
REMEMBER THE TASK AT HAND...
SNIFF
SNIFF
SKRULL.
THAT'S A GOOD BOY.

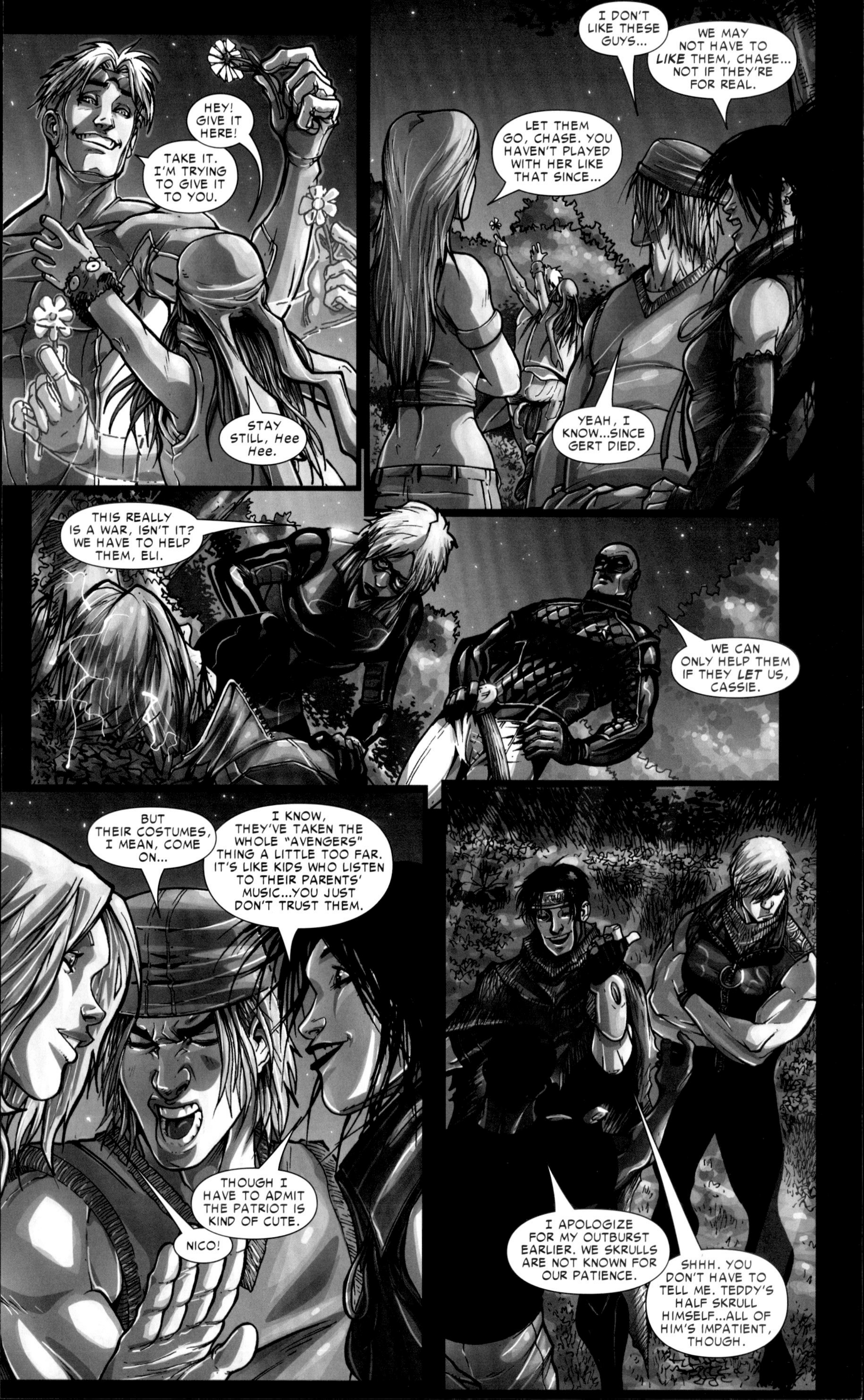
HEY! GIVE IT HERE!
TAKE IT. I'M TRYING TO GIVE IT TO YOU.
STAY STILL, *Hee Hee.*
I DON'T LIKE THESE GUYS...
WE MAY NOT HAVE TO *LIKE* THEM, CHASE... NOT IF THEY'RE FOR REAL.
LET THEM GO, CHASE. YOU HAVEN'T PLAYED WITH HER LIKE THAT SINCE...
YEAH, I KNOW...SINCE GERT DIED.
THIS REALLY IS A WAR, ISN'T IT? WE HAVE TO HELP THEM, ELI.
WE CAN ONLY HELP THEM IF THEY *LET* US, CASSIE.
BUT THEIR COSTUMES, I MEAN, COME ON...
I KNOW, THEY'VE TAKEN THE WHOLE "AVENGERS" THING A LITTLE TOO FAR. IT'S LIKE KIDS WHO LISTEN TO THEIR PARENTS' MUSIC...YOU JUST DON'T TRUST THEM.
THOUGH I HAVE TO ADMIT THE PATRIOT IS KIND OF CUTE.
NICO!
I APOLOGIZE FOR MY OUTBURST EARLIER. WE SKRULLS ARE NOT KNOWN FOR OUR PATIENCE.
SHHH. YOU DON'T HAVE TO TELL ME. TEDDY'S HALF SKRULL HIMSELF...ALL OF HIM'S IMPATIENT, THOUGH.

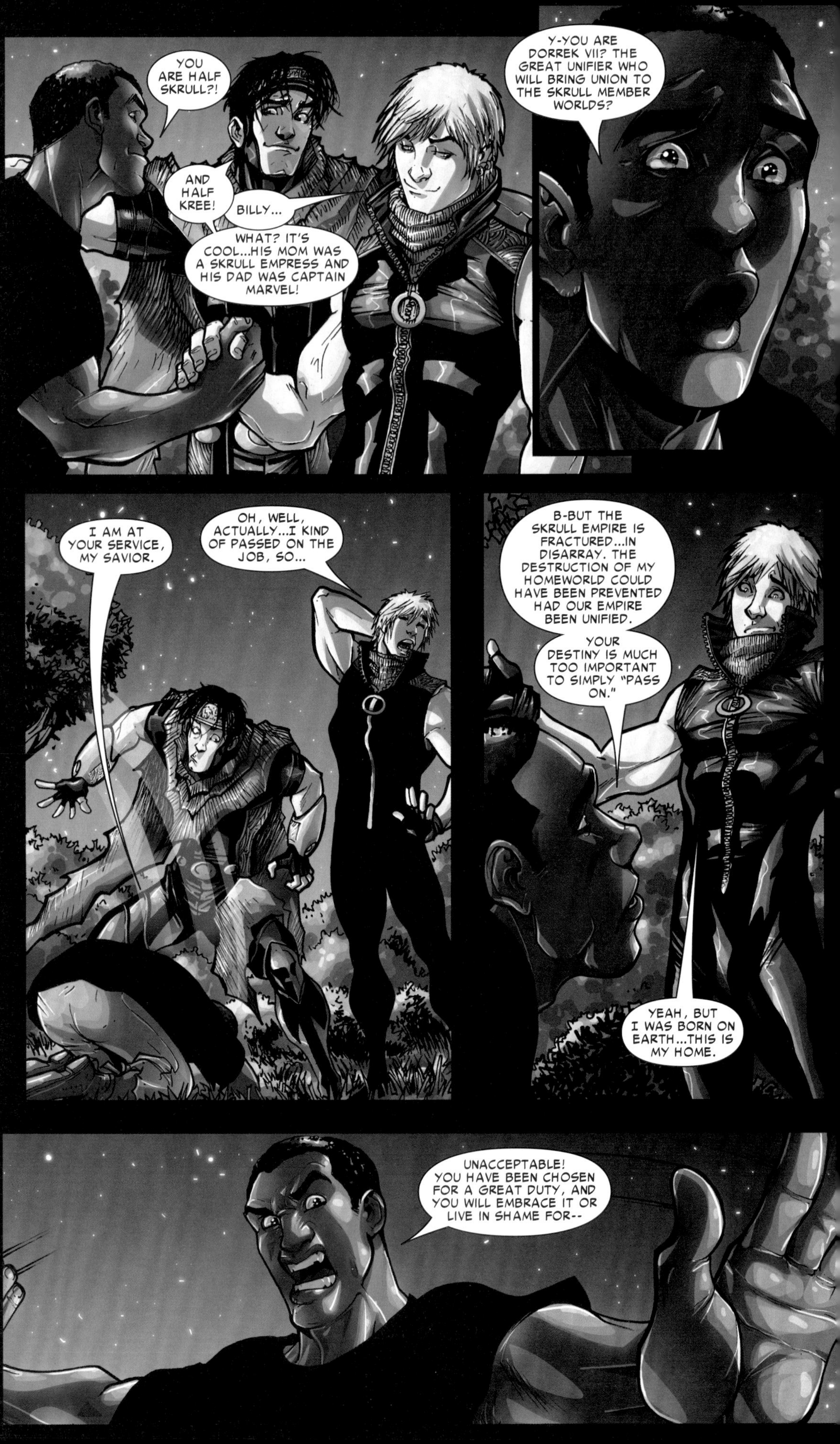
YOU ARE HALF SKRULL?!
AND HALF KREE!
BILLY...
WHAT? IT'S COOL...HIS MOM WAS A SKRULL EMPRESS AND HIS DAD WAS CAPTAIN MARVEL!
Y-YOU ARE DORREK VII? THE GREAT UNIFIER WHO WILL BRING UNION TO THE SKRULL MEMBER WORLDS?
I AM AT YOUR SERVICE, MY SAVIOR.
OH, WELL, ACTUALLY...I KIND OF PASSED ON THE JOB, SO...
B-BUT THE SKRULL EMPIRE IS FRACTURED...IN DISARRAY. THE DESTRUCTION OF MY HOMEWORLD COULD HAVE BEEN PREVENTED HAD OUR EMPIRE BEEN UNIFIED.
YOUR DESTINY IS MUCH TOO IMPORTANT TO SIMPLY "PASS ON."
YEAH, BUT I WAS BORN ON EARTH...THIS IS MY HOME.
UNACCEPTABLE! YOU HAVE BEEN CHOSEN FOR A GREAT DUTY, AND YOU WILL EMBRACE IT OR LIVE IN SHAME FOR--

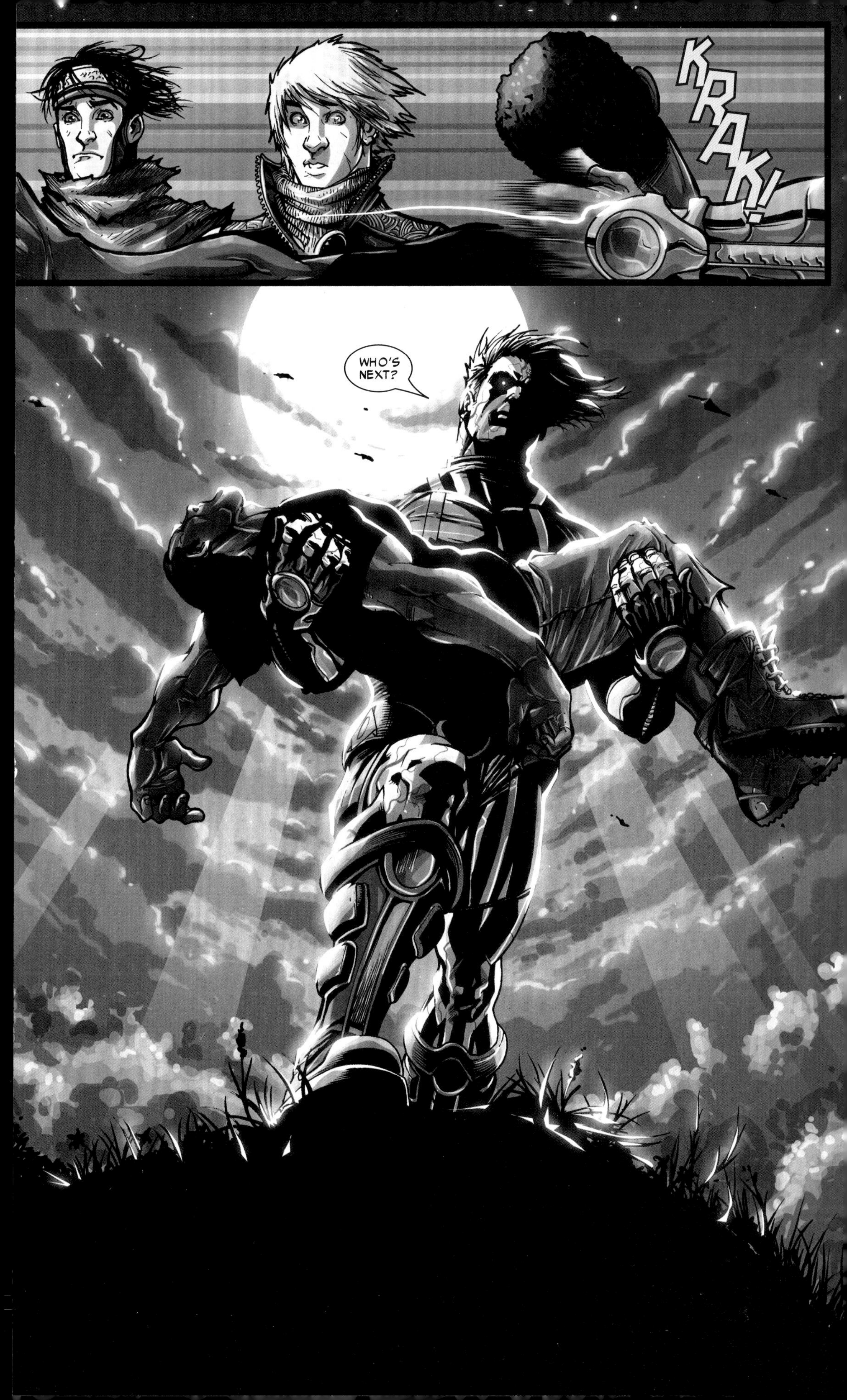
KRAK!
WHO'S NEXT?

YOUNG AVENGERS
& RUNAWAYS
A MARVEL COMICS EVENT

CIVIL
WAR

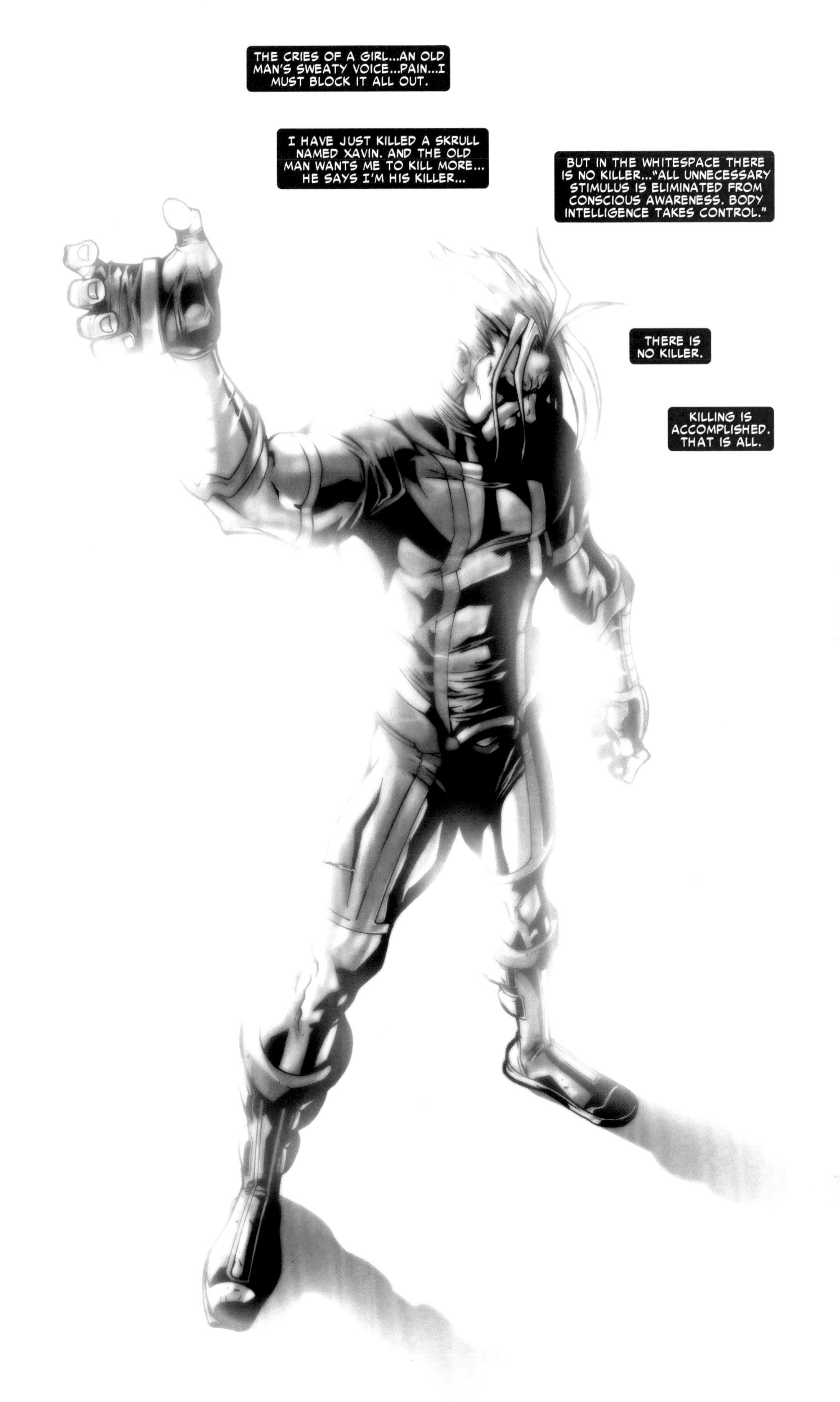
THE CRIES OF A GIRL...AN OLD MAN'S SWEATY VOICE...PAIN...I MUST BLOCK IT ALL OUT.
I HAVE JUST KILLED A SKRULL NAMED XAVIN. AND THE OLD MAN WANTS ME TO KILL MORE... HE SAYS I'M HIS KILLER...
BUT IN THE WHITESPACE THERE IS NO KILLER..."ALL UNNECESSARY STIMULUS IS ELIMINATED FROM CONSCIOUS AWARENESS. BODY INTELLIGENCE TAKES CONTROL."
THERE IS NO KILLER.
KILLING IS ACCOMPLISHED. THAT IS ALL.

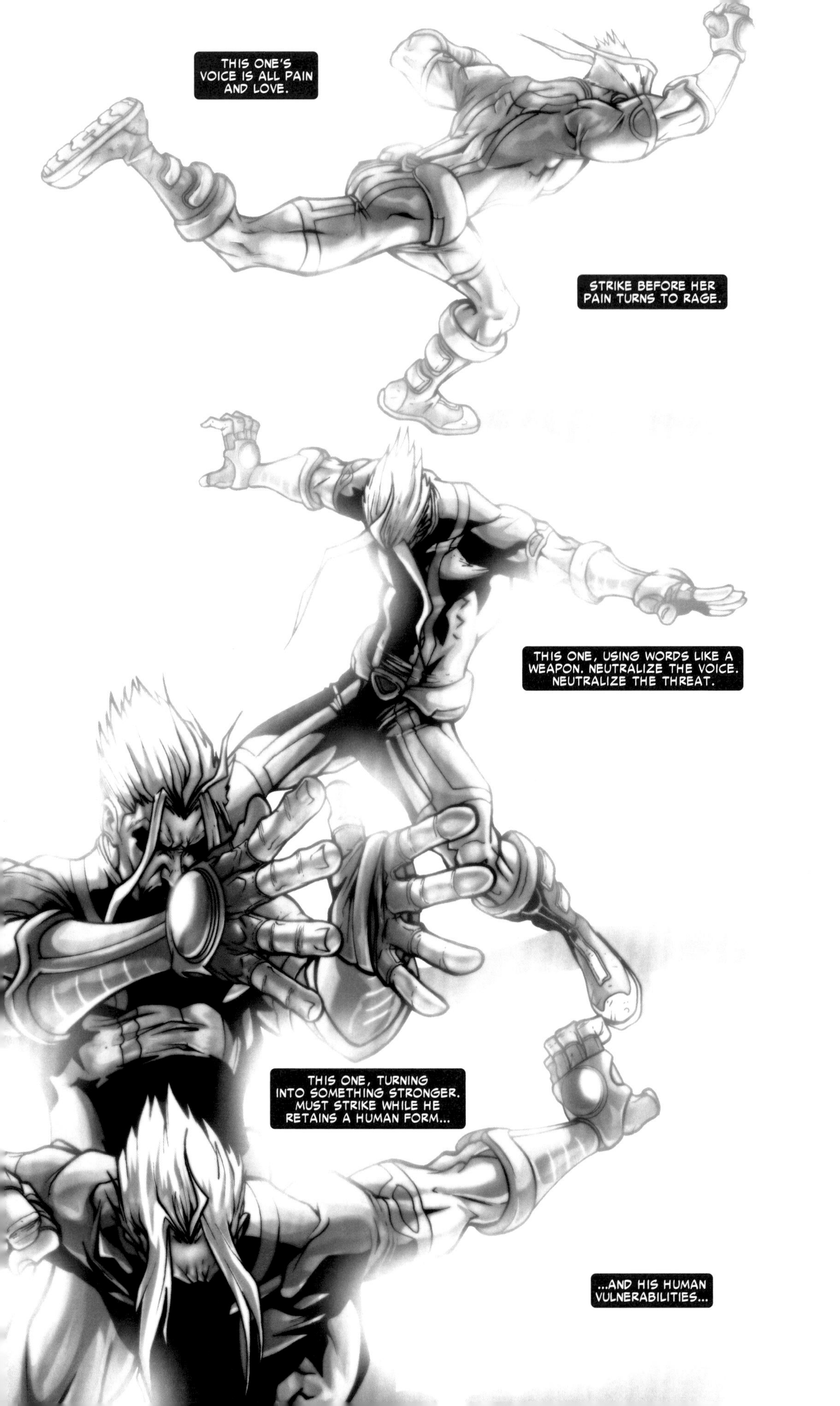
THIS ONE'S VOICE IS ALL PAIN AND LOVE.
STRIKE BEFORE HER PAIN TURNS TO RAGE.
THIS ONE, USING WORDS LIKE A WEAPON. NEUTRALIZE THE VOICE. NEUTRALIZE THE THREAT.
THIS ONE, TURNING INTO SOMETHING STRONGER. MUST STRIKE WHILE HE RETAINS A HUMAN FORM...
...AND HIS HUMAN VULNERABILITIES...

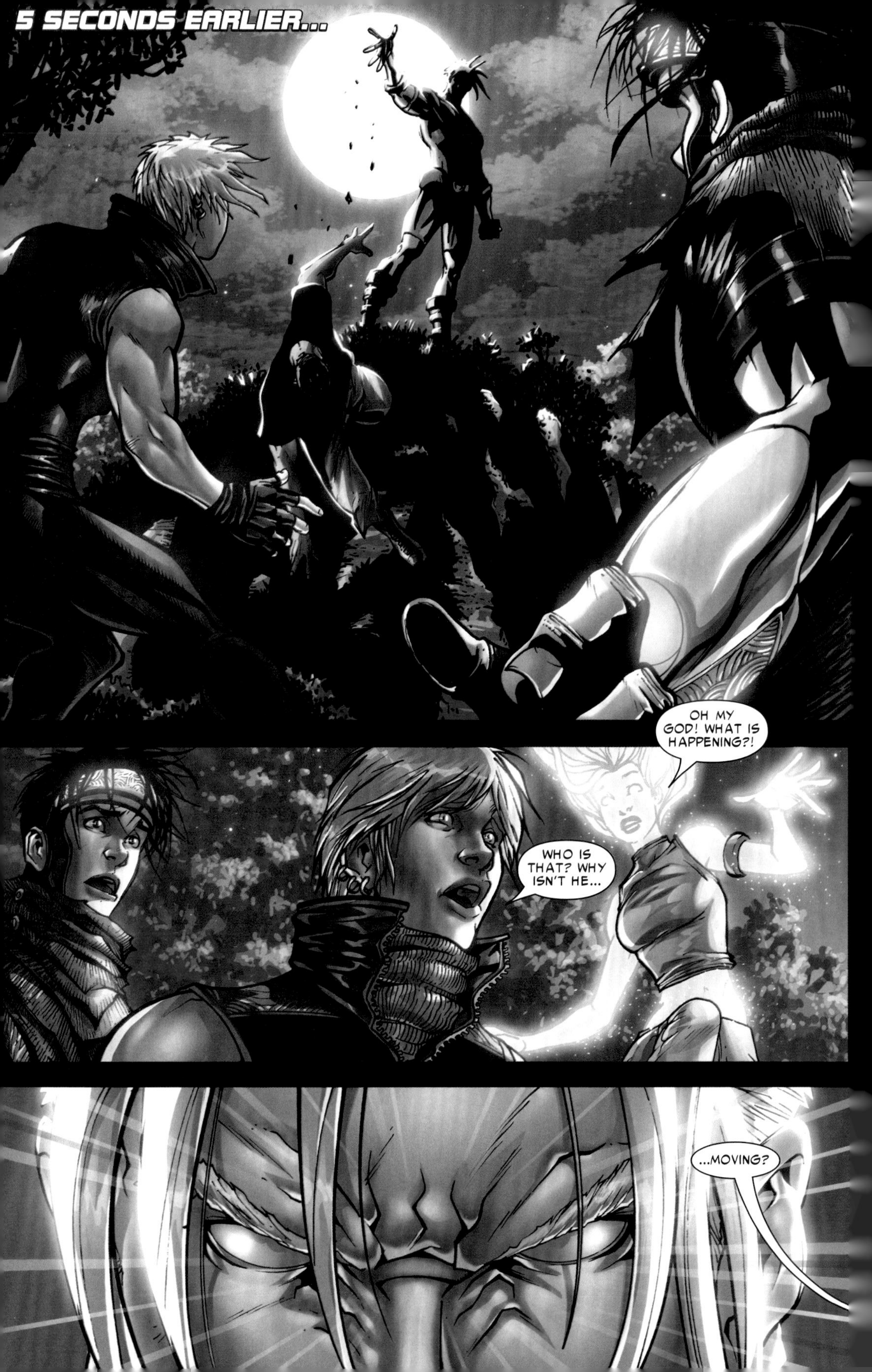
5 SECONDS EARLIER...
OH MY GOD! WHAT IS HAPPENING?!
WHO IS THAT? WHY ISN'T HE...
...MOVING?

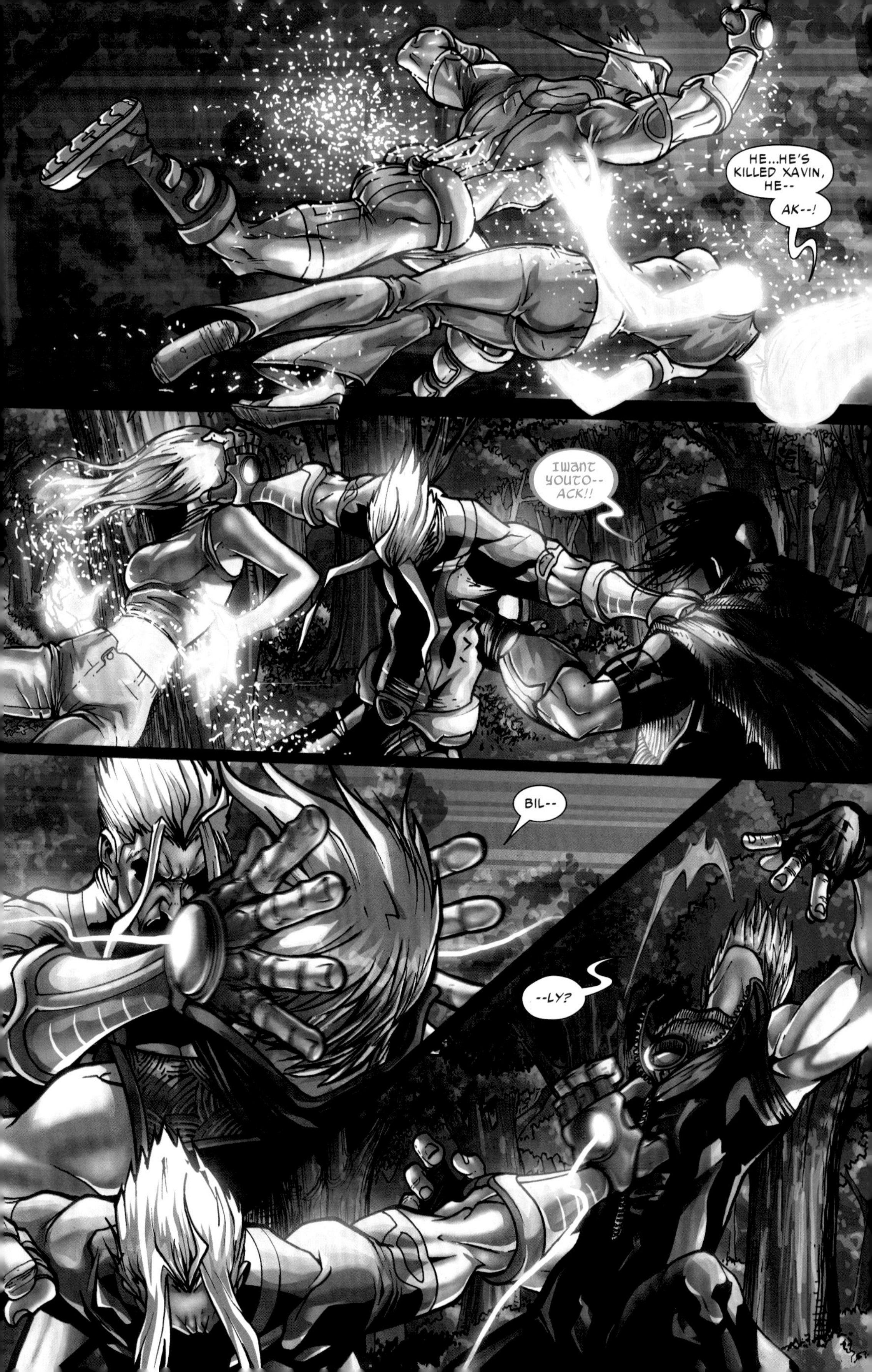
HE...HE'S KILLED XAVIN, HE--
AK--!
IWANT YOUTO--ACK!!
BIL--
--LY?

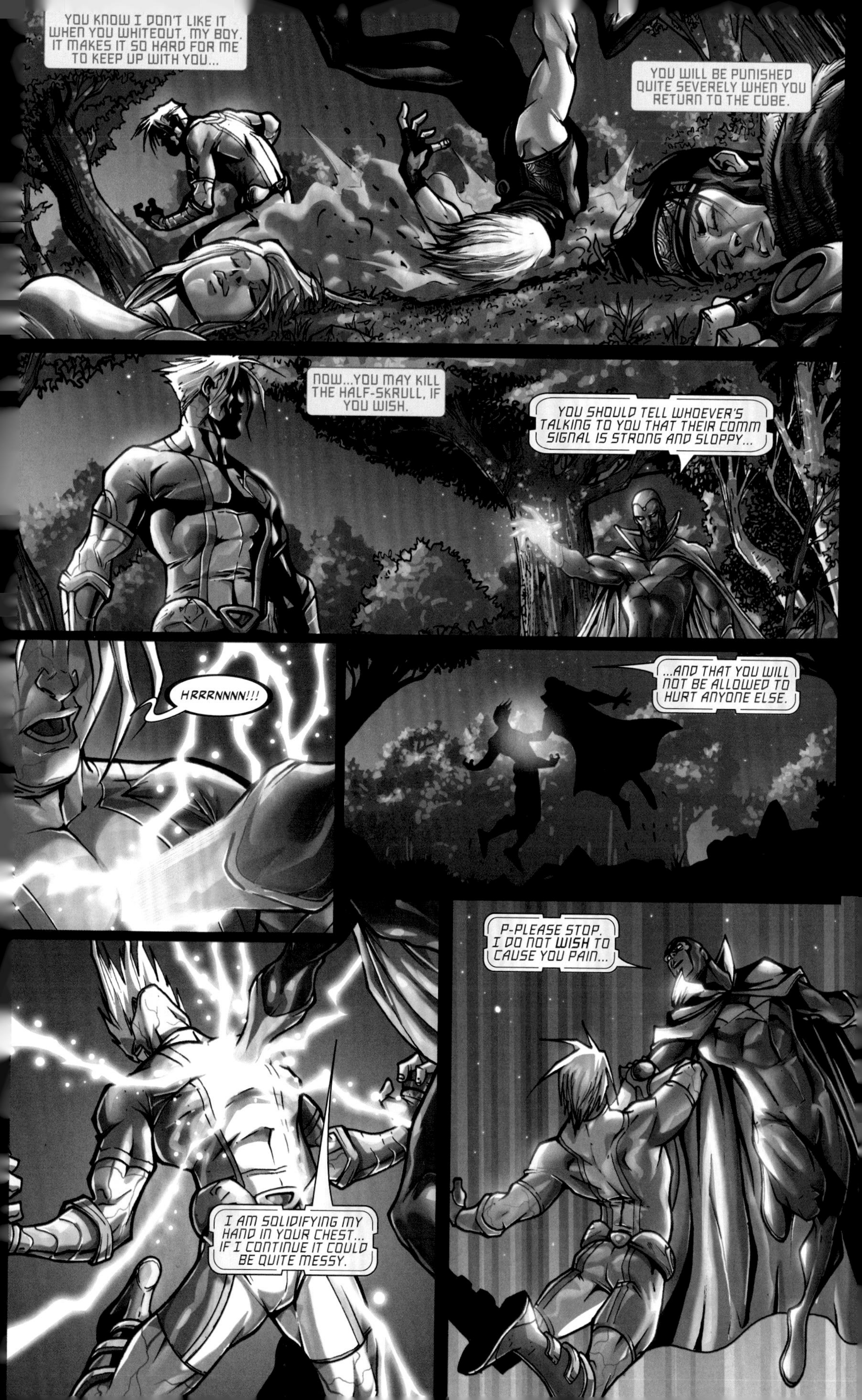
YOU KNOW I DON'T LIKE IT WHEN YOU WHITEOUT, MY BOY. IT MAKES IT SO HARD FOR ME TO KEEP UP WITH YOU...
YOU WILL BE PUNISHED QUITE SEVERELY WHEN YOU RETURN TO THE CUBE.
NOW...YOU MAY KILL THE HALF-SKRULL, IF YOU WISH.
YOU SHOULD TELL WHOEVER'S TALKING TO YOU THAT THEIR COMM SIGNAL IS STRONG AND SLOPPY...
HRRRNNNN!!!
...AND THAT YOU WILL NOT BE ALLOWED TO HURT ANYONE ELSE.
I AM SOLIDIFYING MY HAND IN YOUR CHEST... IF I CONTINUE IT COULD BE QUITE MESSY.
P-PLEASE STOP. I DO NOT WISH TO CAUSE YOU PAIN...

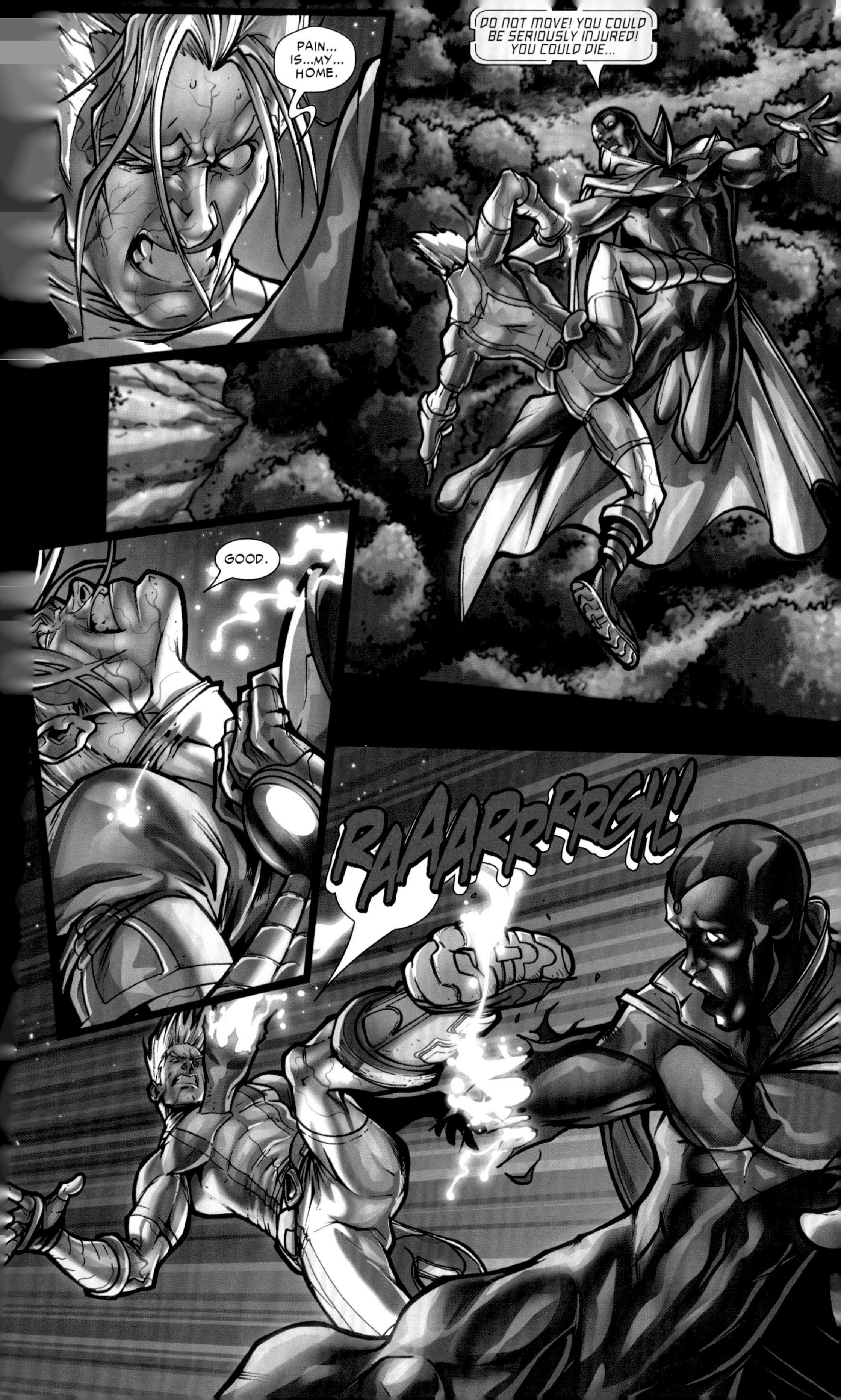
PAIN... IS...MY... HOME.
DO NOT MOVE! YOU COULD BE SERIOUSLY INJURED! YOU COULD DIE...
GOOD.
RAAARRRRGH!

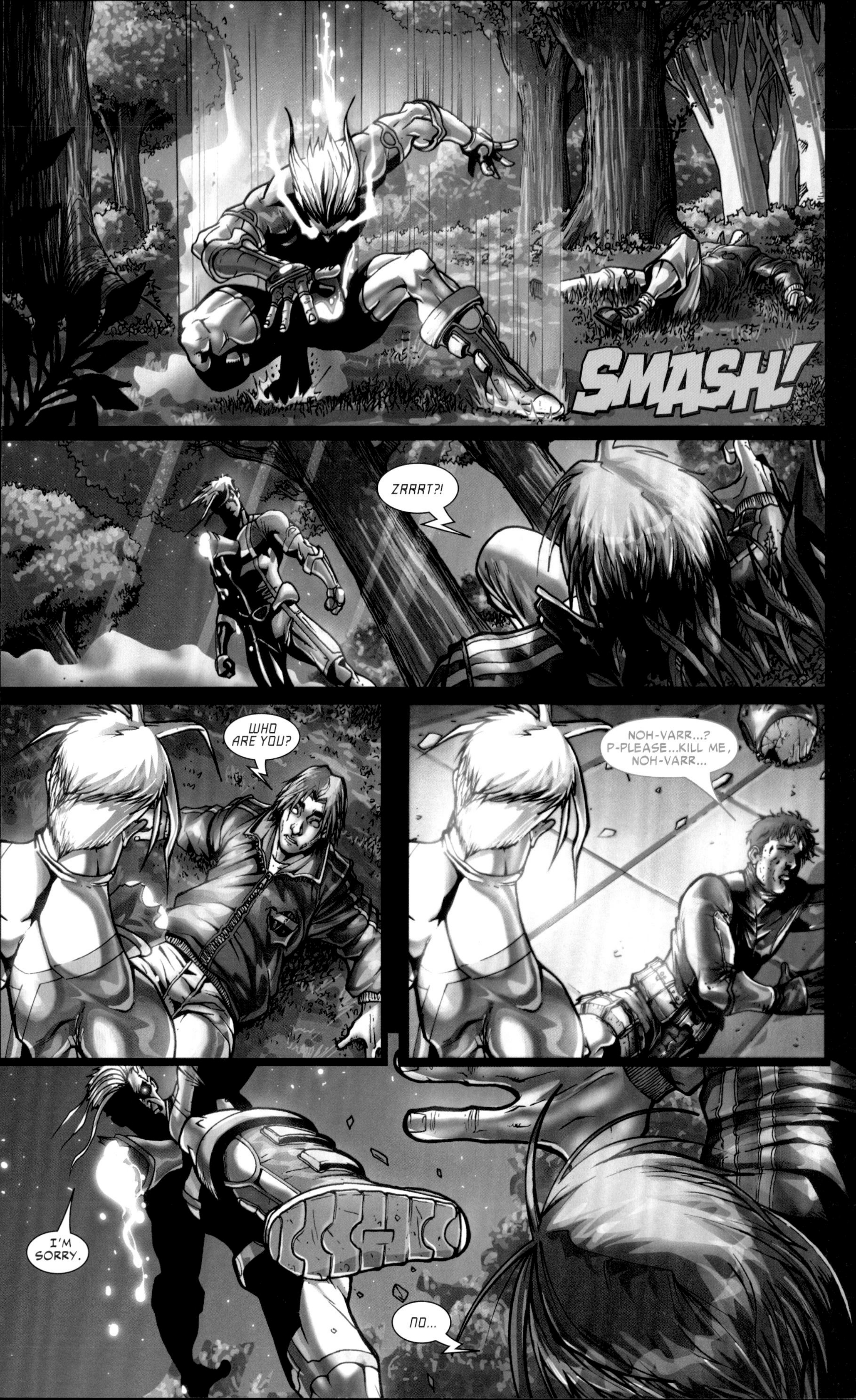
SMASH!
ZRRRT?!
WHO ARE YOU?
NOH-VARR...? P-PLEASE...KILL ME, NOH-VARR...
I'M SORRY.
NO...

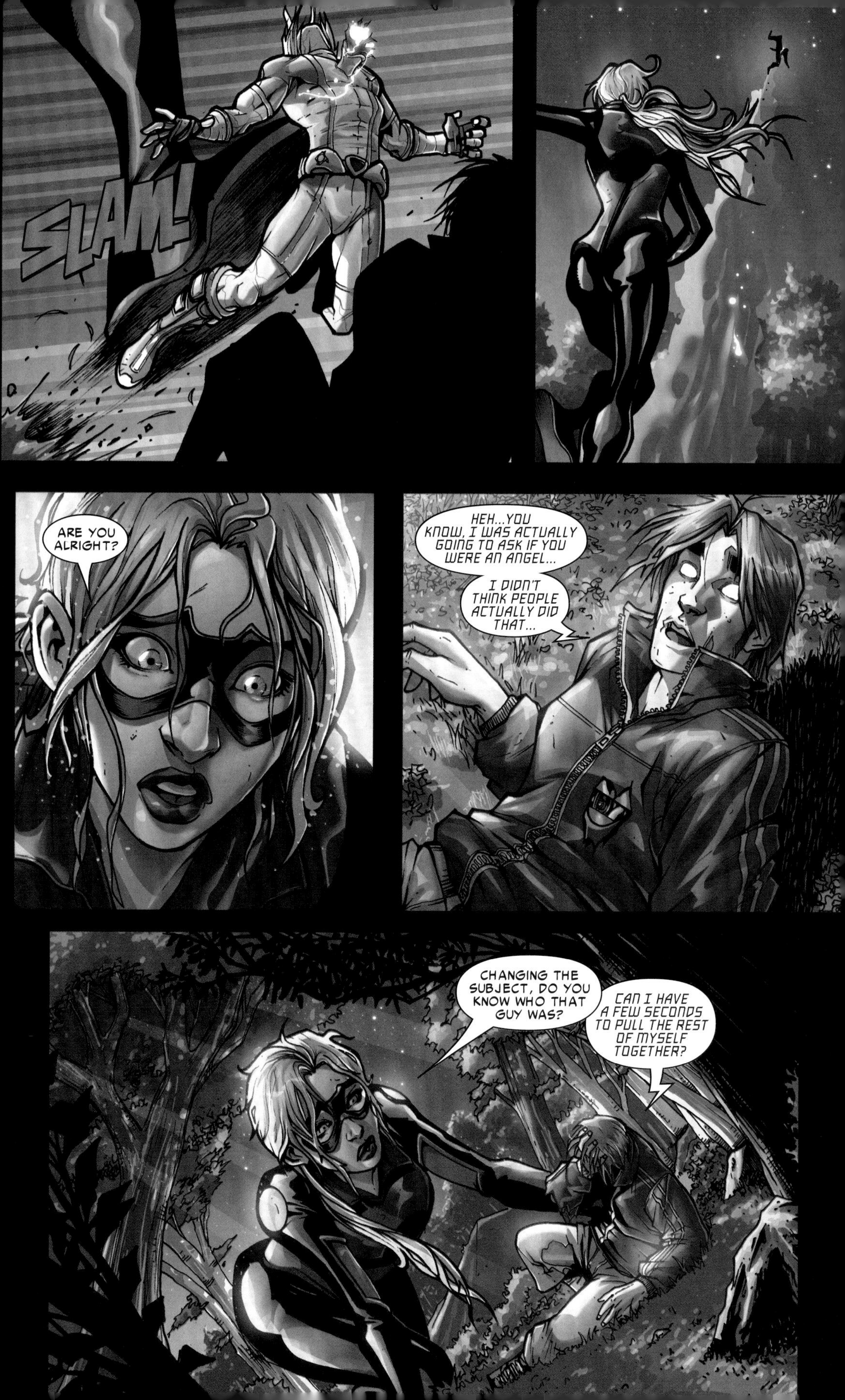
SLAM!
ARE YOU ALRIGHT?
HEH...YOU KNOW, I WAS ACTUALLY GOING TO ASK IF YOU WERE AN ANGEL...
I DIDN'T THINK PEOPLE ACTUALLY DID THAT...
CHANGING THE SUBJECT, DO YOU KNOW WHO THAT GUY WAS?
CAN I HAVE A FEW SECONDS TO PULL THE REST OF MYSELF TOGETHER?

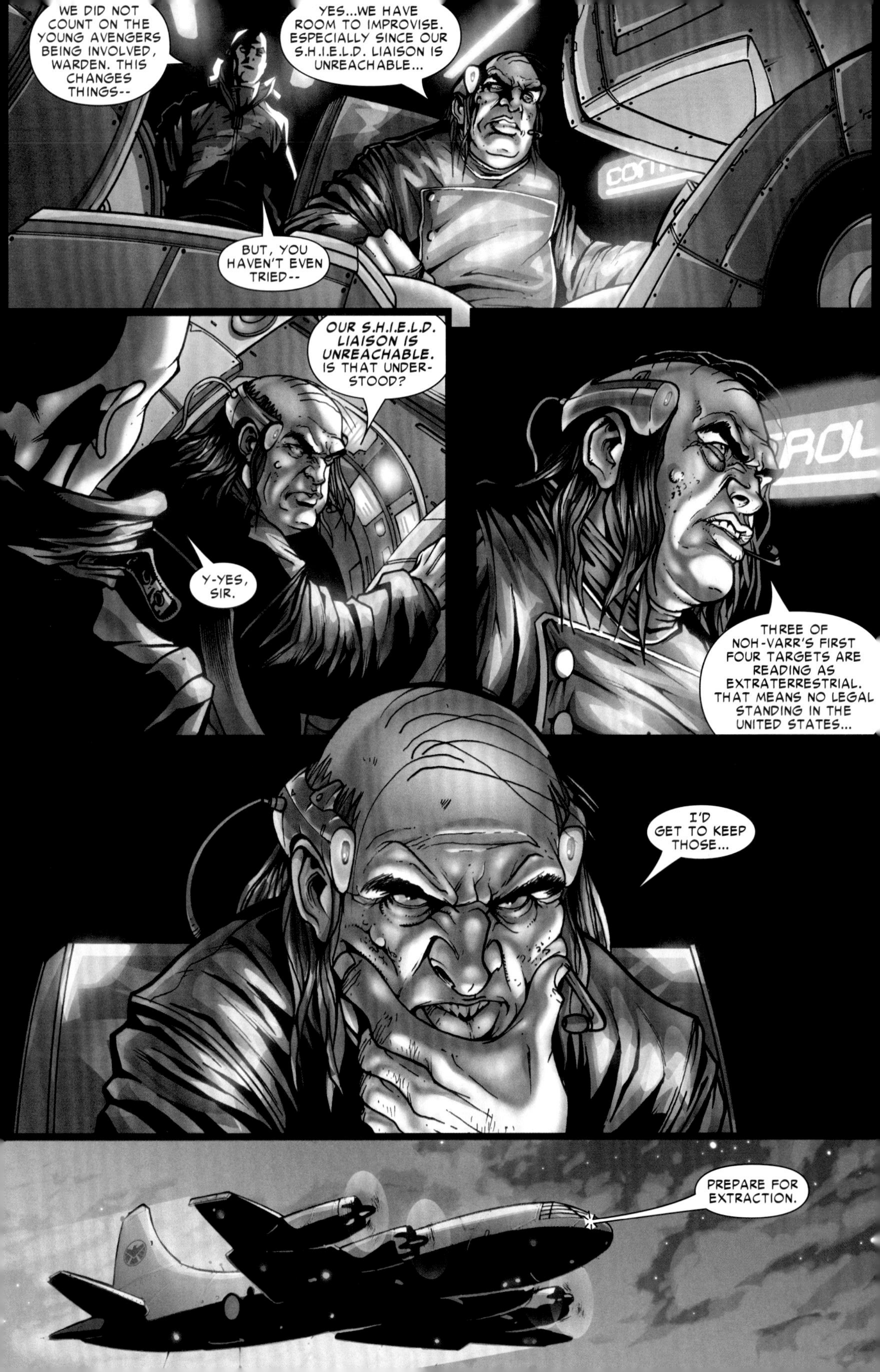
WE DID NOT COUNT ON THE YOUNG AVENGERS BEING INVOLVED, WARDEN. THIS CHANGES THINGS--
YES...WE HAVE ROOM TO IMPROVISE. ESPECIALLY SINCE OUR S.H.I.E.L.D. LIAISON IS UNREACHABLE...
BUT, YOU HAVEN'T EVEN TRIED--
OUR S.H.I.E.L.D. LIAISON IS UNREACHABLE. IS THAT UNDER-STOOD?
Y-YES, SIR.
THREE OF NOH-VARR'S FIRST FOUR TARGETS ARE READING AS EXTRATERRESTRIAL. THAT MEANS NO LEGAL STANDING IN THE UNITED STATES...
I'D GET TO KEEP THOSE...
PREPARE FOR EXTRACTION.

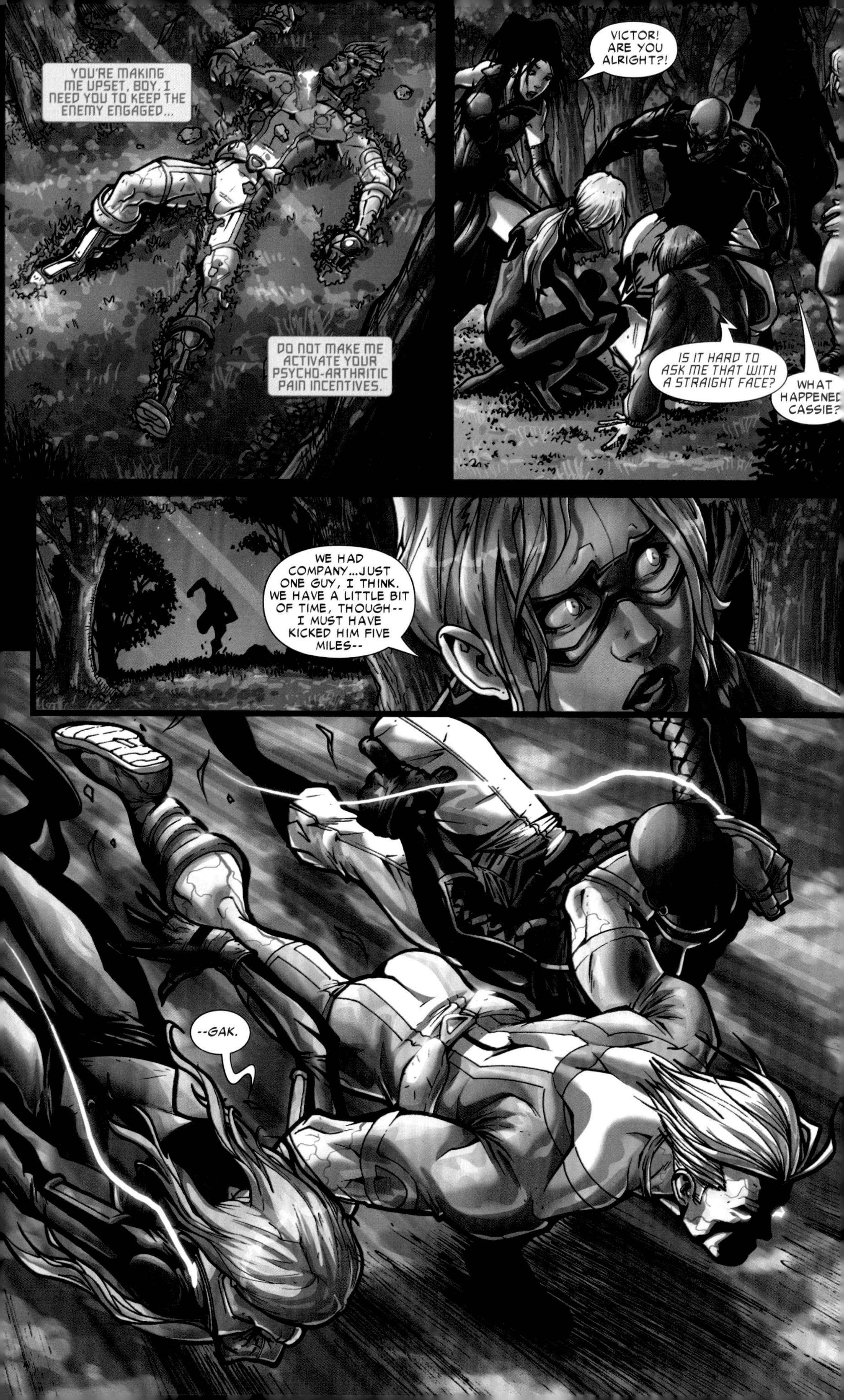
YOU'RE MAKING ME UPSET, BOY. I NEED YOU TO KEEP THE ENEMY ENGAGED...
DO NOT MAKE ME ACTIVATE YOUR PSYCHO-ARTHRITIC PAIN INCENTIVES.
VICTOR! ARE YOU ALRIGHT?!
IS IT HARD TO ASK ME THAT WITH A STRAIGHT FACE?
WHAT HAPPENED CASSIE?
WE HAD COMPANY...JUST ONE GUY, I THINK. WE HAVE A LITTLE BIT OF TIME, THOUGH-- I MUST HAVE KICKED HIM FIVE MILES--
--GAK.

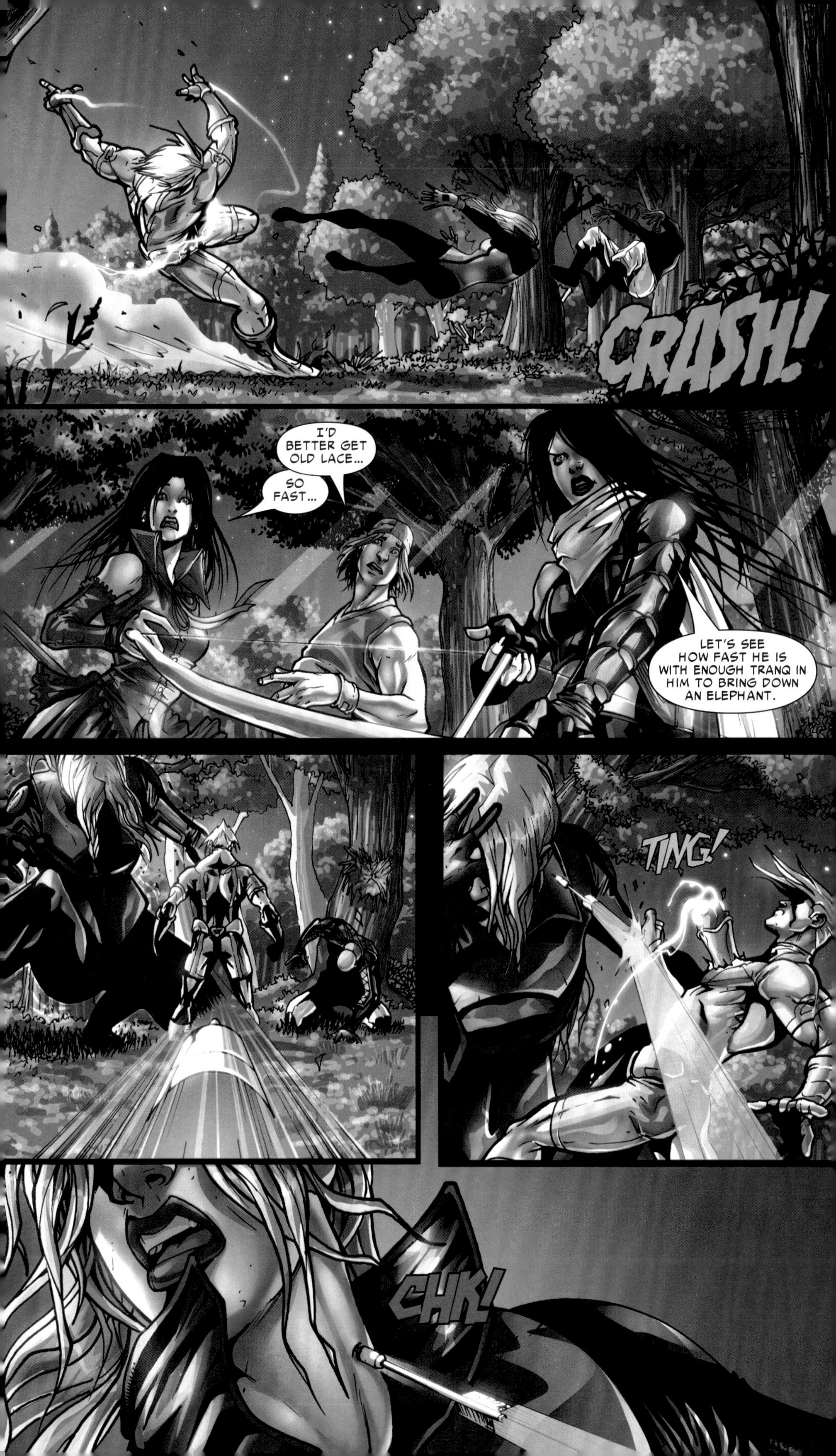
CRASH!
I'D BETTER GET OLD LACE...
SO FAST...
LET'S SEE HOW FAST HE IS WITH ENOUGH TRANQ IN HIM TO BRING DOWN AN ELEPHANT.
TING!
CHK!

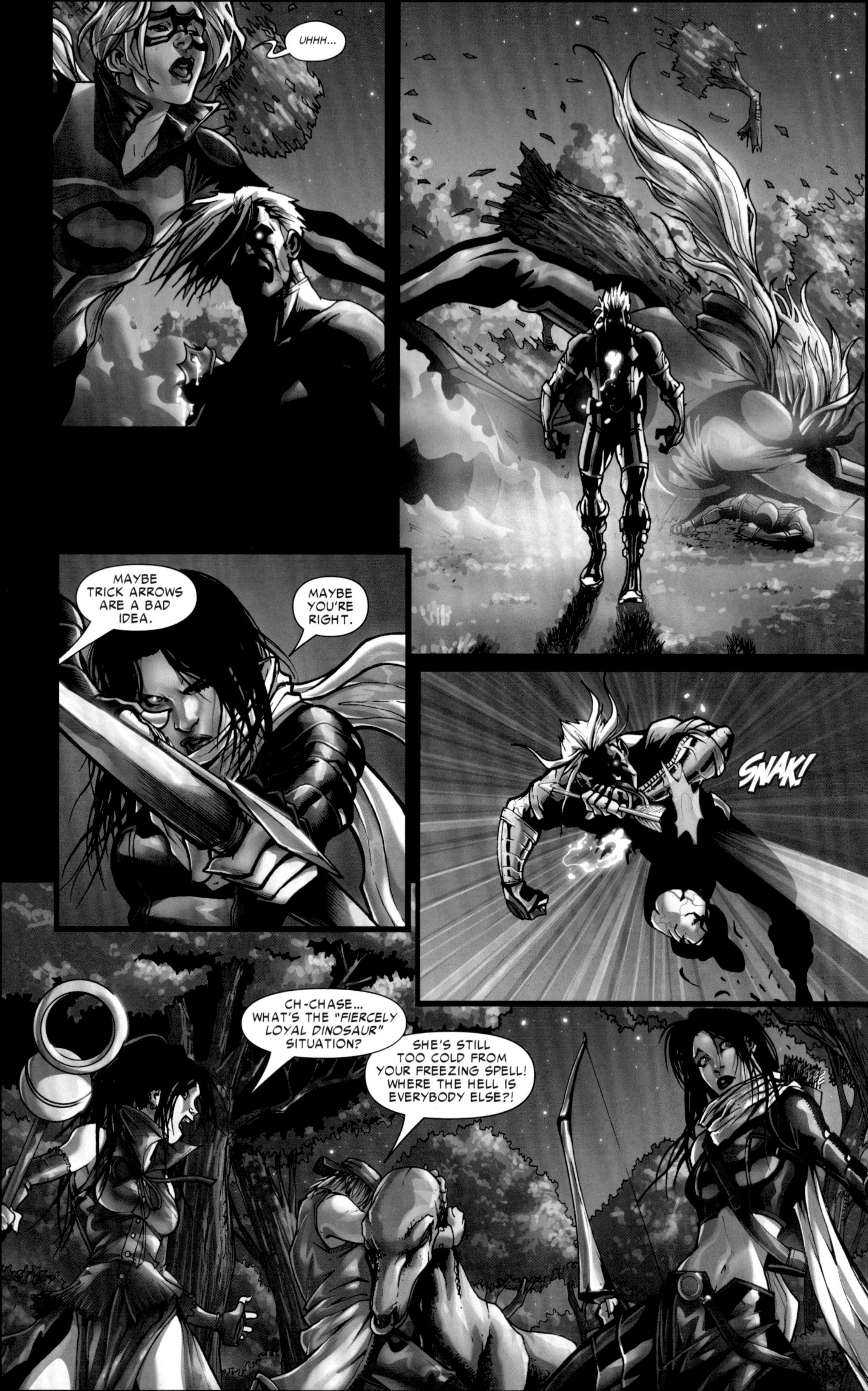
UHHH...
MAYBE TRICK ARROWS ARE A BAD IDEA.
MAYBE YOU'RE RIGHT.
SNAK!
CH-CHASE... WHAT'S THE "FIERCELY LOYAL DINOSAUR" SITUATION?
SHE'S STILL TOO COLD FROM YOUR FREEZING SPELL! WHERE THE HELL IS EVERYBODY ELSE?!

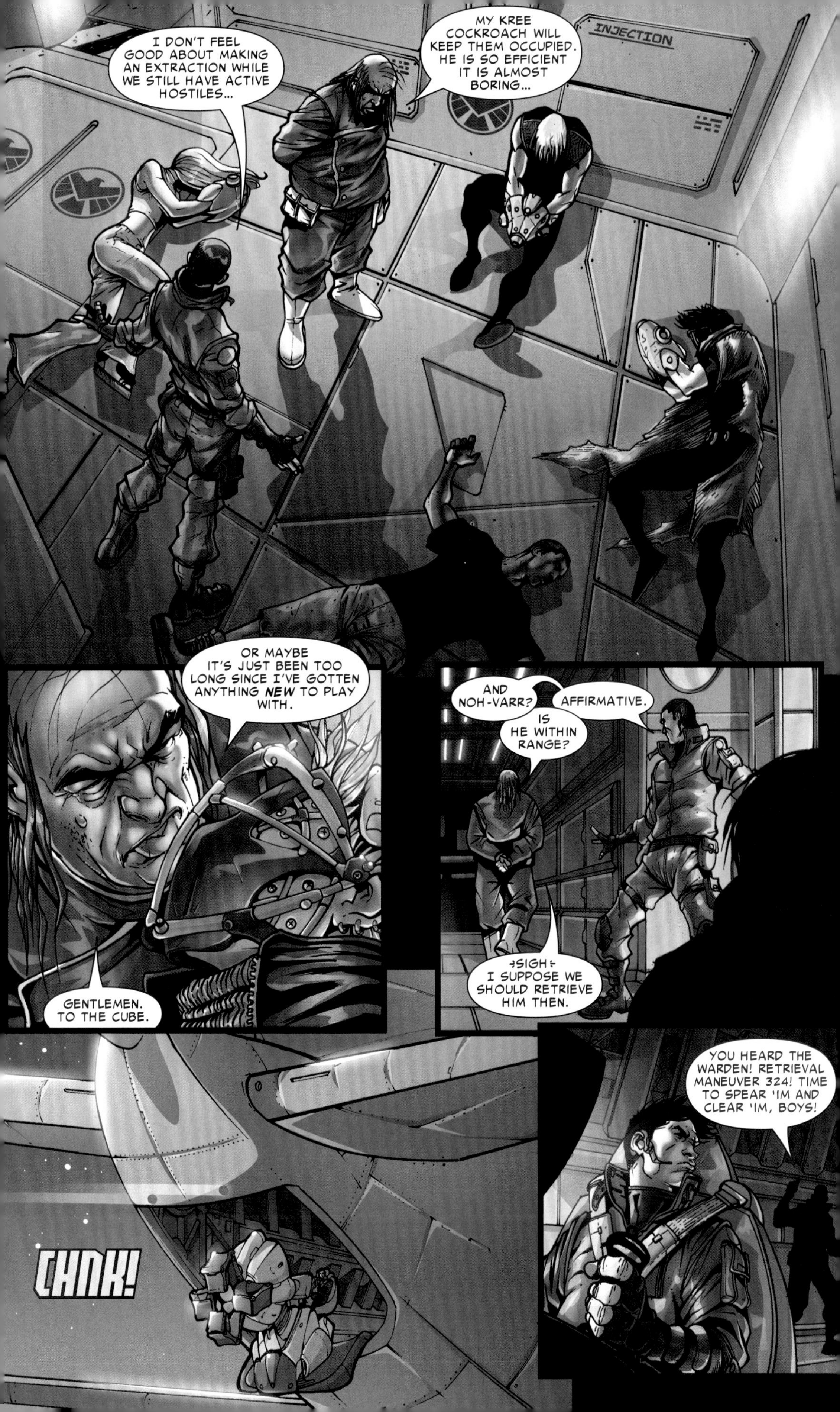
I DON'T FEEL GOOD ABOUT MAKING AN EXTRACTION WHILE WE STILL HAVE ACTIVE HOSTILES...
MY KREE COCKROACH WILL KEEP THEM OCCUPIED. HE IS SO EFFICIENT IT IS ALMOST BORING...
INJECTION
OR MAYBE IT'S JUST BEEN TOO LONG SINCE I'VE GOTTEN ANYTHING NEW TO PLAY WITH.
GENTLEMEN. TO THE CUBE.
AND NOH-VARR?
IS HE WITHIN RANGE?
AFFIRMATIVE.
SIGH
I SUPPOSE WE SHOULD RETRIEVE HIM THEN.
CHNK!
YOU HEARD THE WARDEN! RETRIEVAL MANEUVER 324! TIME TO SPEAR 'IM AND CLEAR 'IM, BOYS!

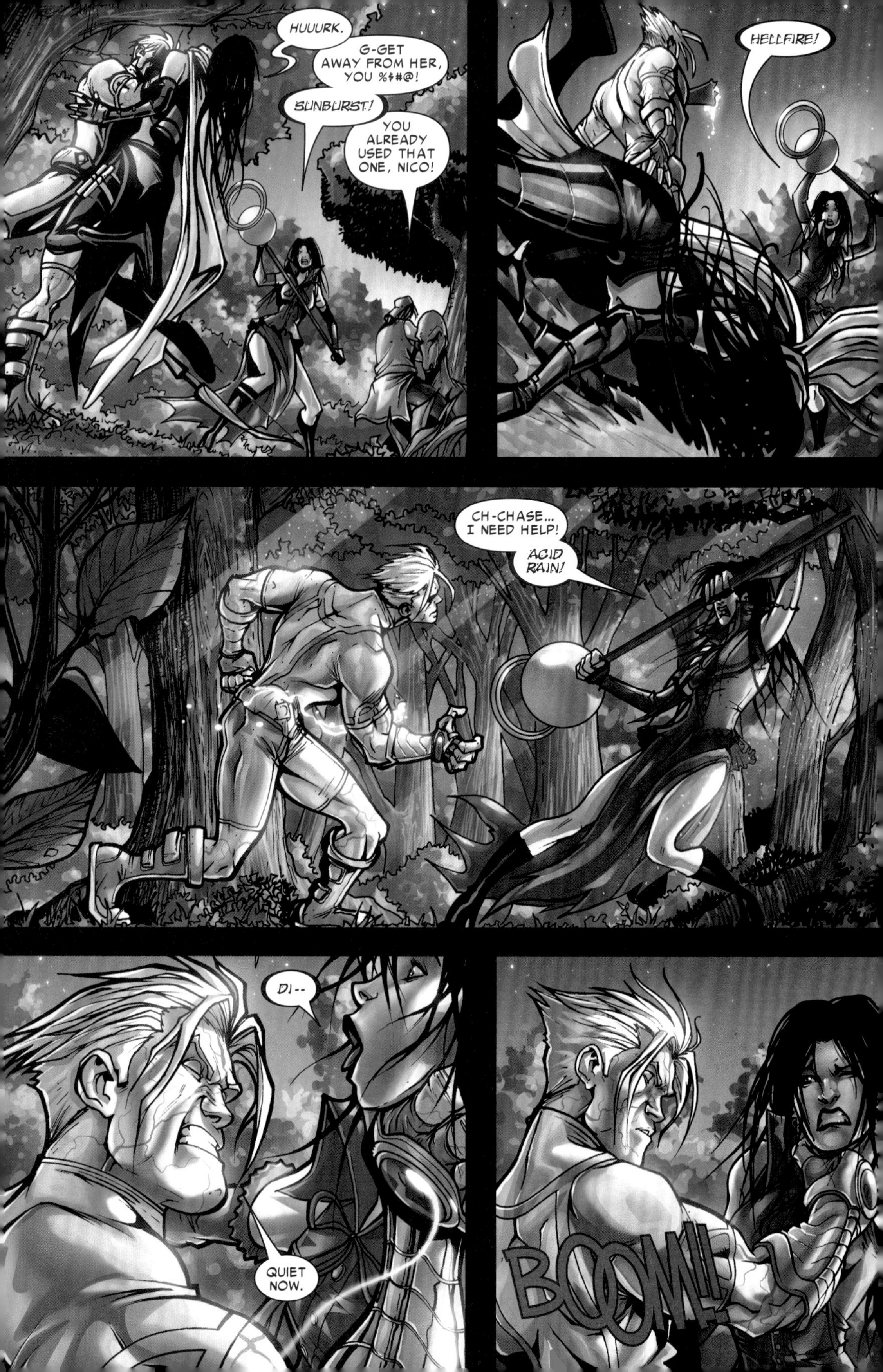
HUUURK.
G-GET AWAY FROM HER, YOU %$#@!
SUNBURST!
YOU ALREADY USED THAT ONE, NICO!
HELLFIRE!
CH-CHASE... I NEED HELP!
ACID RAIN!
DI--
QUIET NOW.
BOOM!!

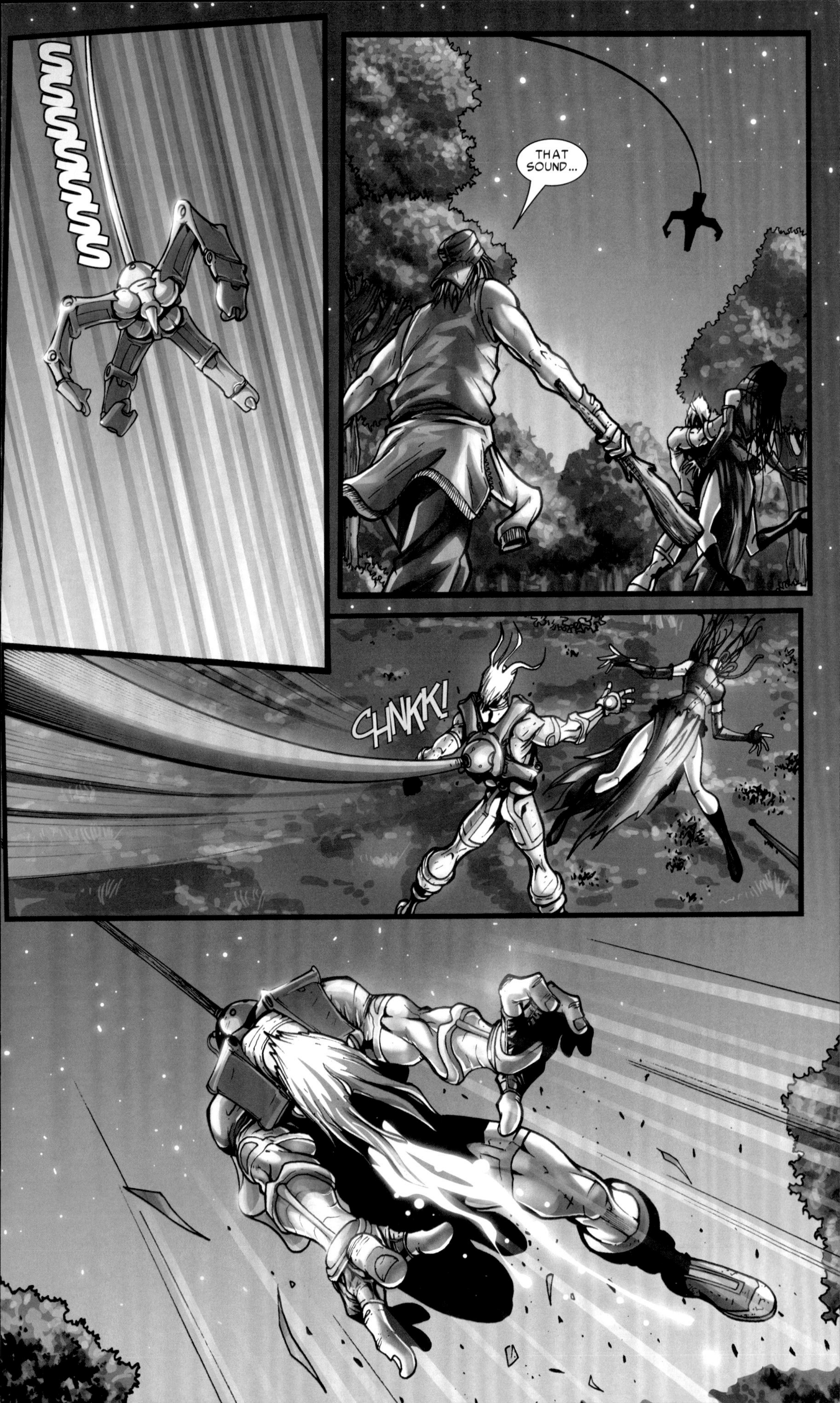

SSSSSSSSS
THAT SOUND...
CHNKK!

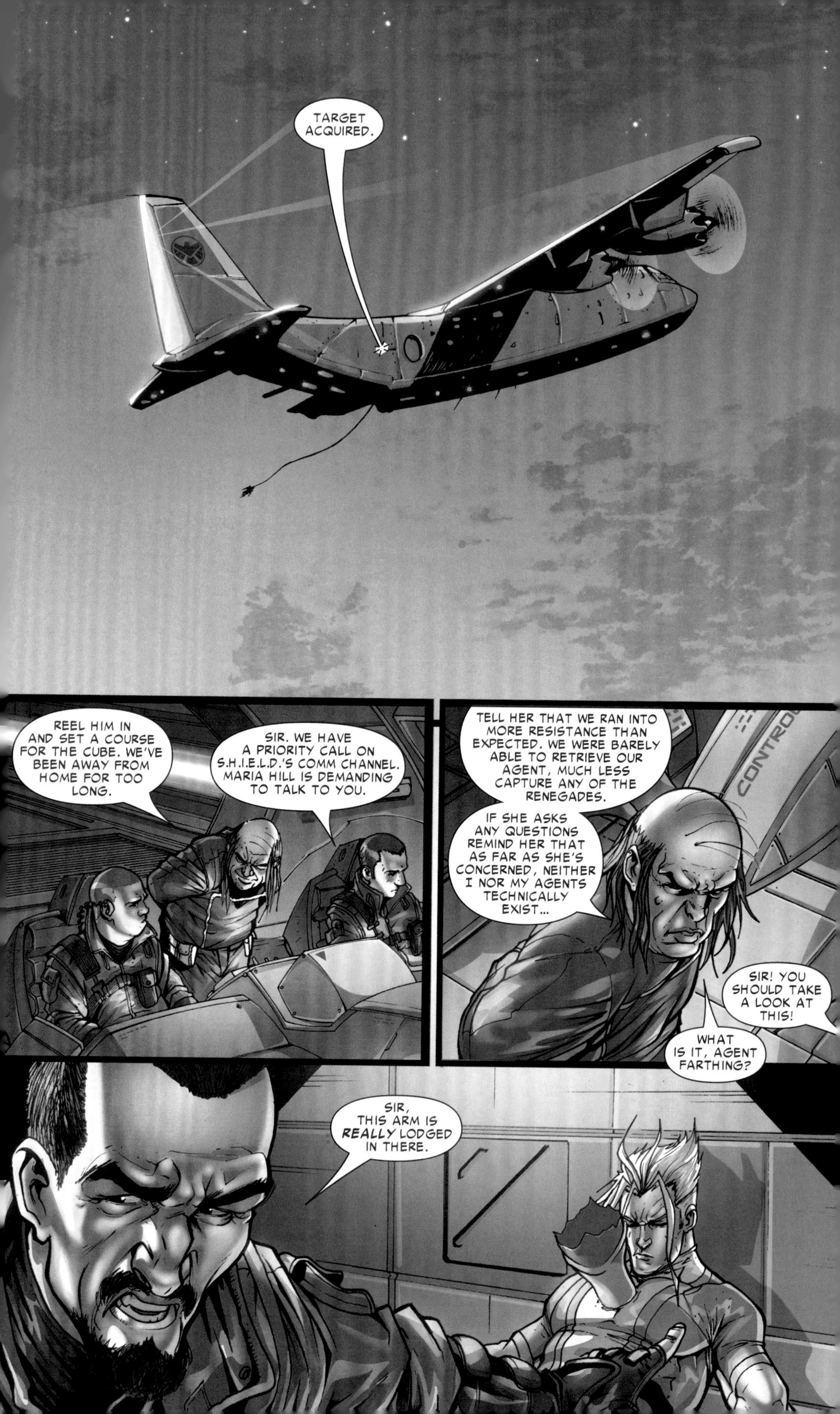
TARGET ACQUIRED.
REEL HIM IN AND SET A COURSE FOR THE CUBE. WE'VE BEEN AWAY FROM HOME FOR TOO LONG.
SIR. WE HAVE A PRIORITY CALL ON S.H.I.E.L.D.'S COMM CHANNEL. MARIA HILL IS DEMANDING TO TALK TO YOU.
TELL HER THAT WE RAN INTO MORE RESISTANCE THAN EXPECTED. WE WERE BARELY ABLE TO RETRIEVE OUR AGENT, MUCH LESS CAPTURE ANY OF THE RENEGADES.
IF SHE ASKS ANY QUESTIONS REMIND HER THAT AS FAR AS SHE'S CONCERNED, NEITHER I NOR MY AGENTS TECHNICALLY EXIST...
SIR! YOU SHOULD TAKE A LOOK AT THIS!
WHAT IS IT, AGENT FARTHING?
SIR, THIS ARM IS *REALLY* LODGED IN THERE.

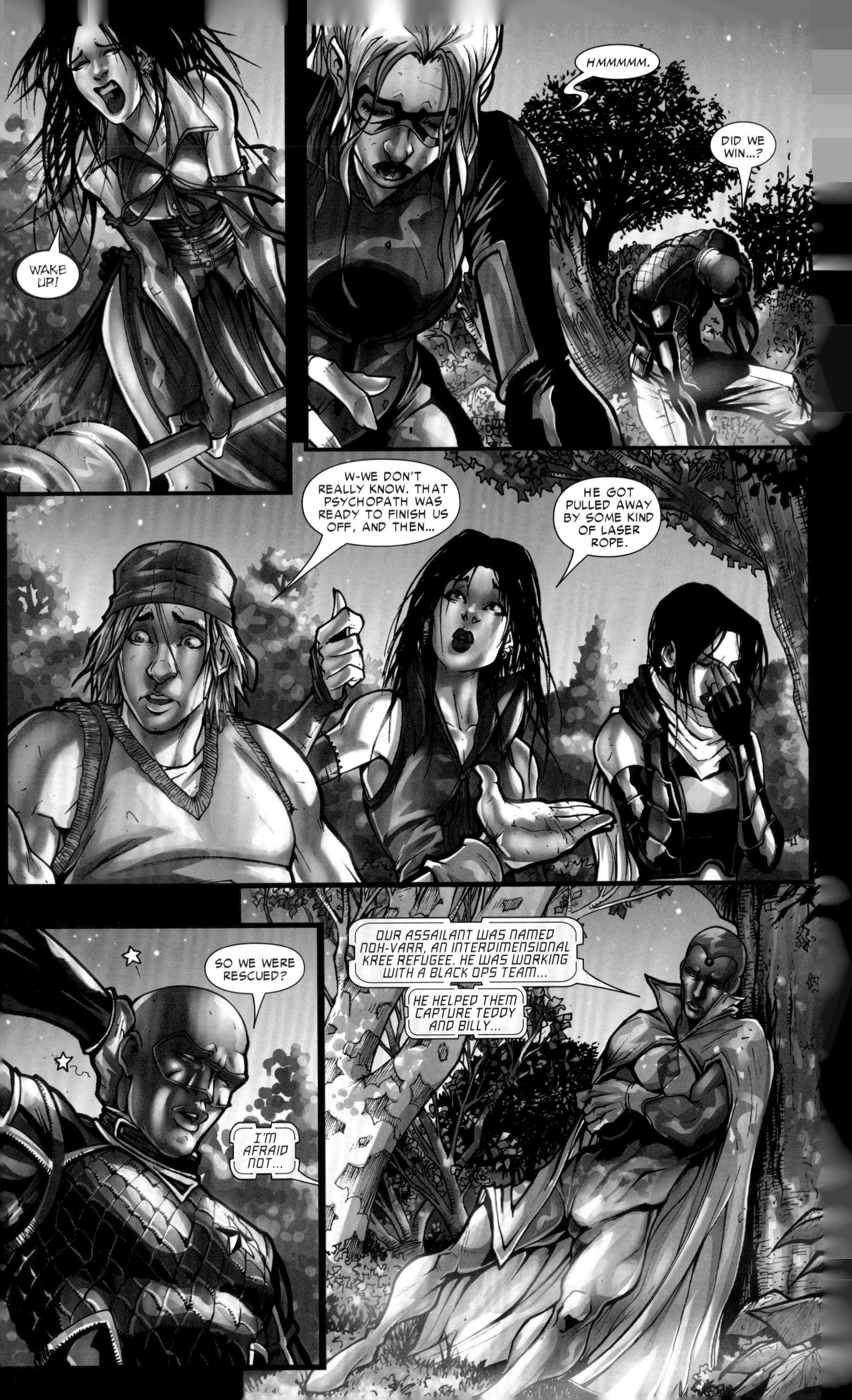
WAKE UP!
HMMMMM.
DID WE WIN...?
W-WE DON'T REALLY KNOW. THAT PSYCHOPATH WAS READY TO FINISH US OFF, AND THEN...
HE GOT PULLED AWAY BY SOME KIND OF LASER ROPE.
SO WE WERE RESCUED?
I'M AFRAID NOT...
OUR ASSAILANT WAS NAMED NOH-VARR, AN INTERDIMENSIONAL KREE REFUGEE. HE WAS WORKING WITH A BLACK OPS TEAM...
HE HELPED THEM CAPTURE TEDDY AND BILLY...

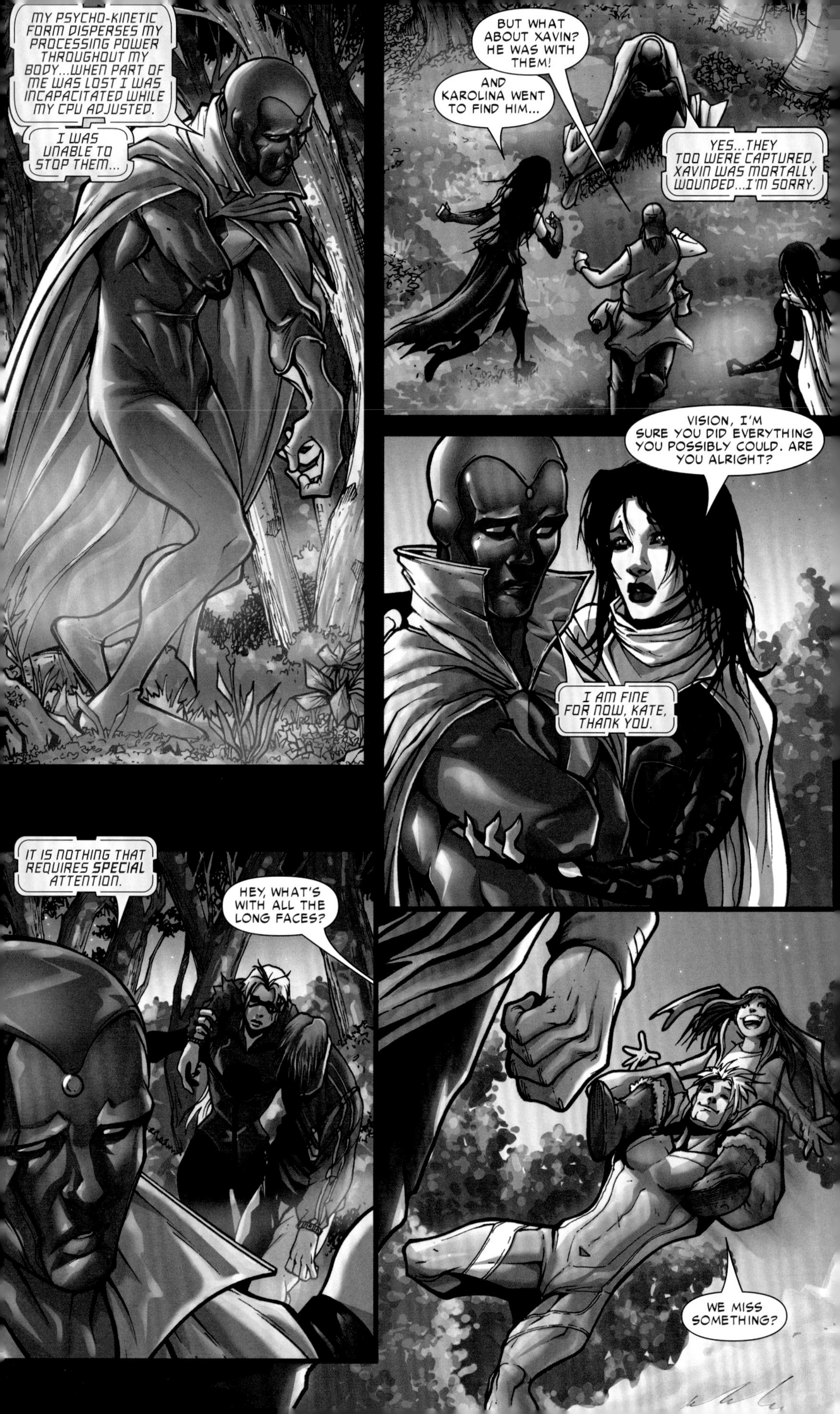
MY PSYCHO-KINETIC FORM DISPERSES MY PROCESSING POWER THROUGHOUT MY BODY...WHEN PART OF ME WAS LOST I WAS INCAPACITATED WHILE MY CPU ADJUSTED.
I WAS UNABLE TO STOP THEM...
AND KAROLINA WENT TO FIND HIM...
BUT WHAT ABOUT XAVIN? HE WAS WITH THEM!
YES...THEY TOO WERE CAPTURED. XAVIN WAS MORTALLY WOUNDED...I'M SORRY.
VISION, I'M SURE YOU DID EVERYTHING YOU POSSIBLY COULD. ARE YOU ALRIGHT?
I AM FINE FOR NOW, KATE, THANK YOU.
IT IS NOTHING THAT REQUIRES SPECIAL ATTENTION.
HEY, WHAT'S WITH ALL THE LONG FACES?
WE MISS SOMETHING?

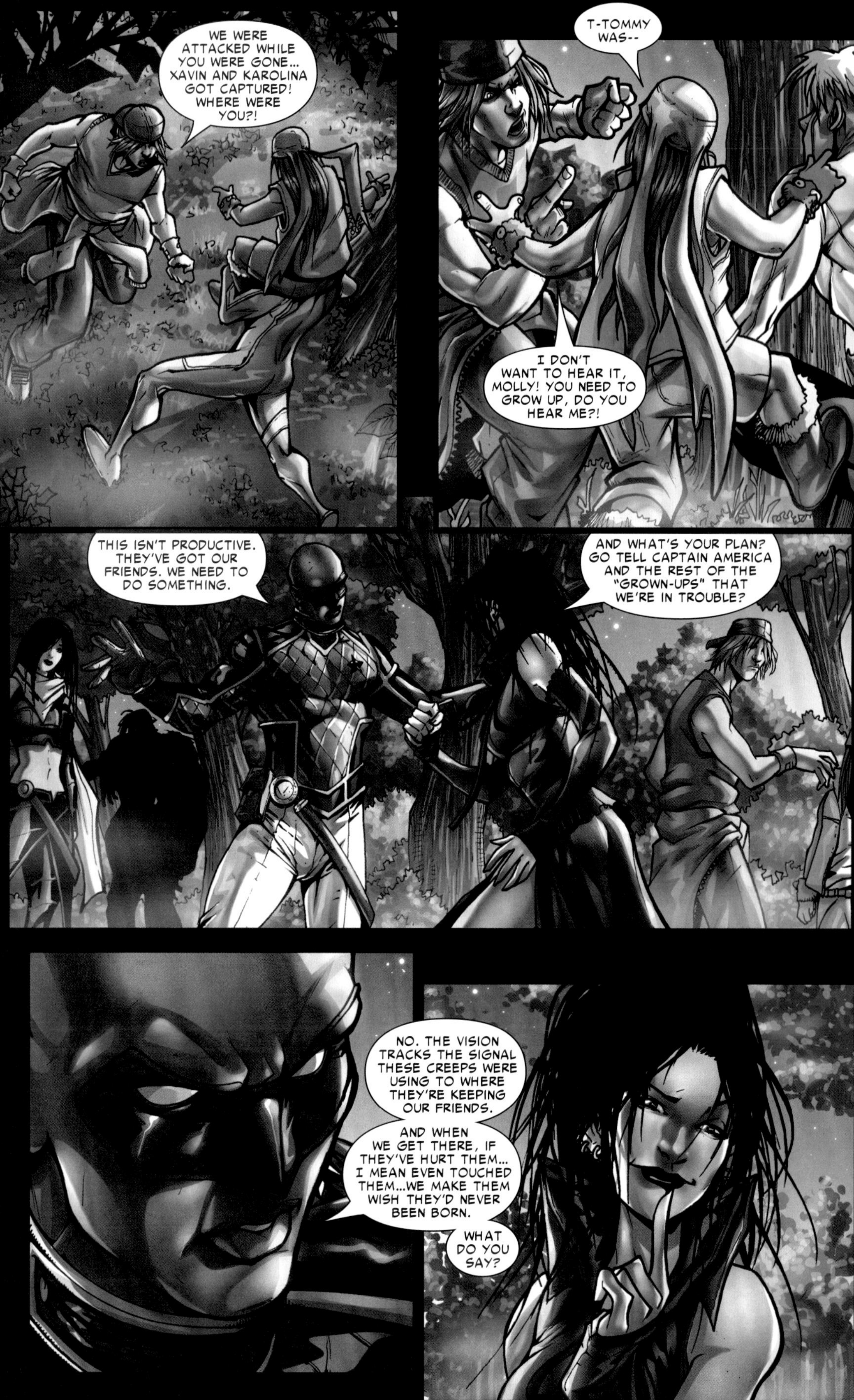
WE WERE ATTACKED WHILE YOU WERE GONE... XAVIN AND KAROLINA GOT CAPTURED! WHERE WERE YOU?!
T-TOMMY WAS--
I DON'T WANT TO HEAR IT, MOLLY! YOU NEED TO GROW UP, DO YOU HEAR ME?!
THIS ISN'T PRODUCTIVE. THEY'VE GOT OUR FRIENDS. WE NEED TO DO SOMETHING.
AND WHAT'S YOUR PLAN? GO TELL CAPTAIN AMERICA AND THE REST OF THE "GROWN-UPS" THAT WE'RE IN TROUBLE?
NO. THE VISION TRACKS THE SIGNAL THESE CREEPS WERE USING TO WHERE THEY'RE KEEPING OUR FRIENDS.
AND WHEN WE GET THERE, IF THEY'VE HURT THEM... I MEAN EVEN TOUCHED THEM...WE MAKE THEM WISH THEY'D NEVER BEEN BORN.
WHAT DO YOU SAY?

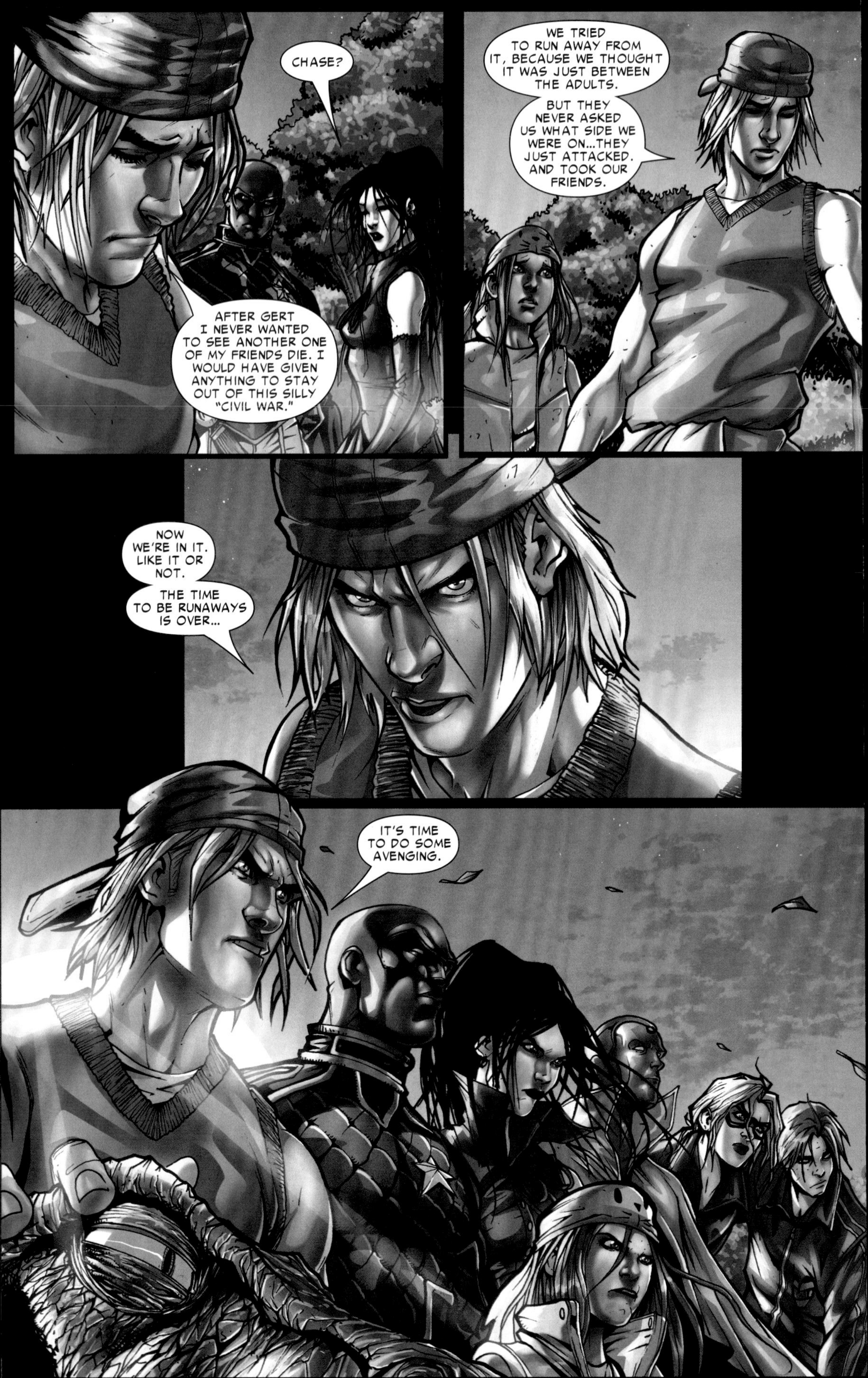
CHASE?
AFTER GERT I NEVER WANTED TO SEE ANOTHER ONE OF MY FRIENDS DIE. I WOULD HAVE GIVEN ANYTHING TO STAY OUT OF THIS SILLY "CIVIL WAR."
WE TRIED TO RUN AWAY FROM IT, BECAUSE WE THOUGHT IT WAS JUST BETWEEN THE ADULTS.
BUT THEY NEVER ASKED US WHAT SIDE WE WERE ON...THEY JUST ATTACKED. AND TOOK OUR FRIENDS.
NOW WE'RE IN IT. LIKE IT OR NOT.
THE TIME TO BE RUNAWAYS IS OVER...
IT'S TIME TO DO SOME AVENGING.

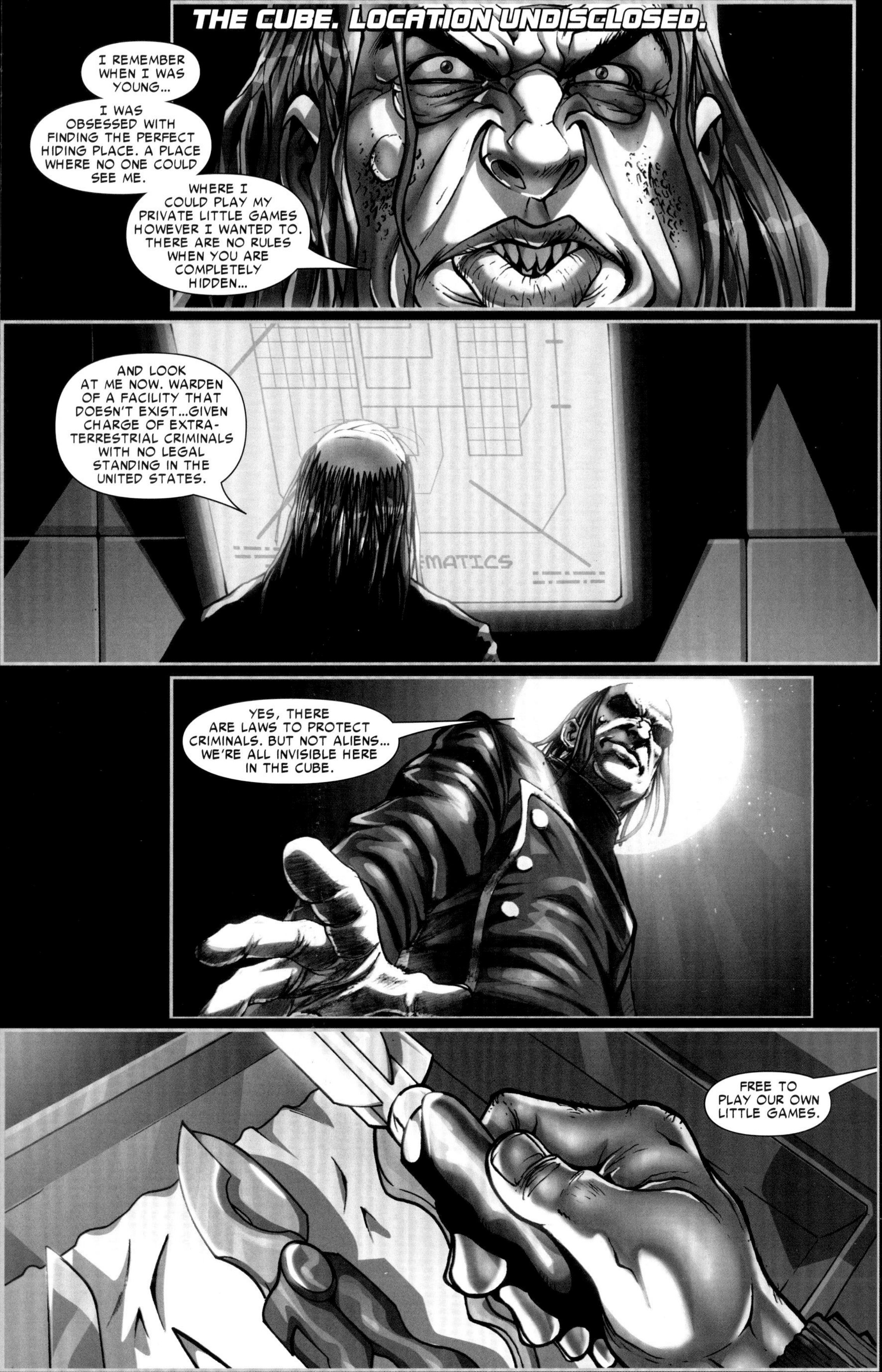
THE CUBE. LOCATION UNDISCLOSED.
I REMEMBER WHEN I WAS YOUNG...
I WAS OBSESSED WITH FINDING THE PERFECT HIDING PLACE. A PLACE WHERE NO ONE COULD SEE ME.
WHERE I COULD PLAY MY PRIVATE LITTLE GAMES HOWEVER I WANTED TO. THERE ARE NO RULES WHEN YOU ARE COMPLETELY HIDDEN...
AND LOOK AT ME NOW. WARDEN OF A FACILITY THAT DOESN'T EXIST...GIVEN CHARGE OF EXTRA-TERRESTRIAL CRIMINALS WITH NO LEGAL STANDING IN THE UNITED STATES.
MATICS
YES, THERE ARE LAWS TO PROTECT CRIMINALS. BUT NOT ALIENS... WE'RE ALL INVISIBLE HERE IN THE CUBE.
FREE TO PLAY OUR OWN LITTLE GAMES.

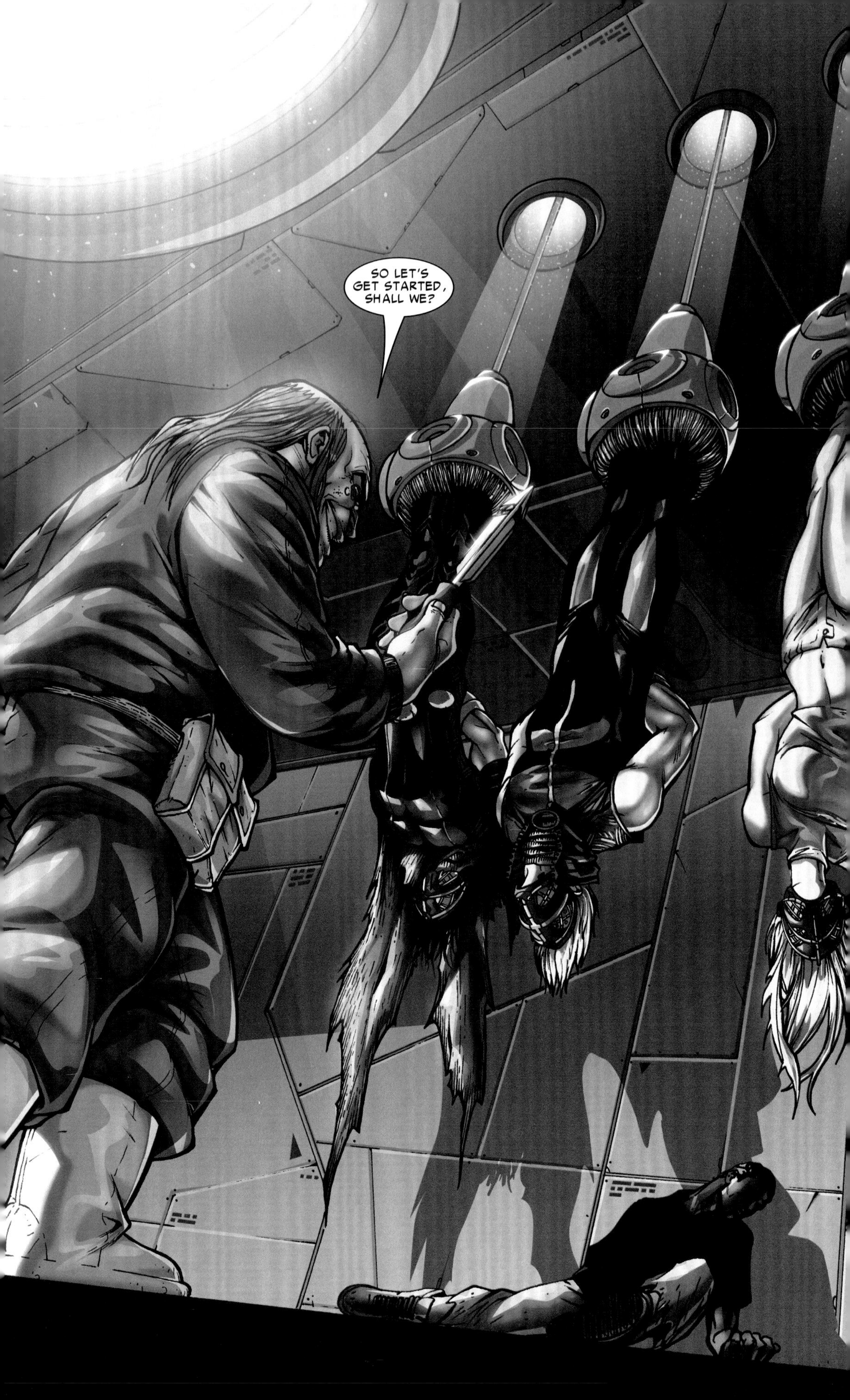
SO LET'S GET STARTED, SHALL WE?

YOUNG AVENGERS
& RUNAWAYS
A MARVEL COMICS EVENT

CIVIL
WAR

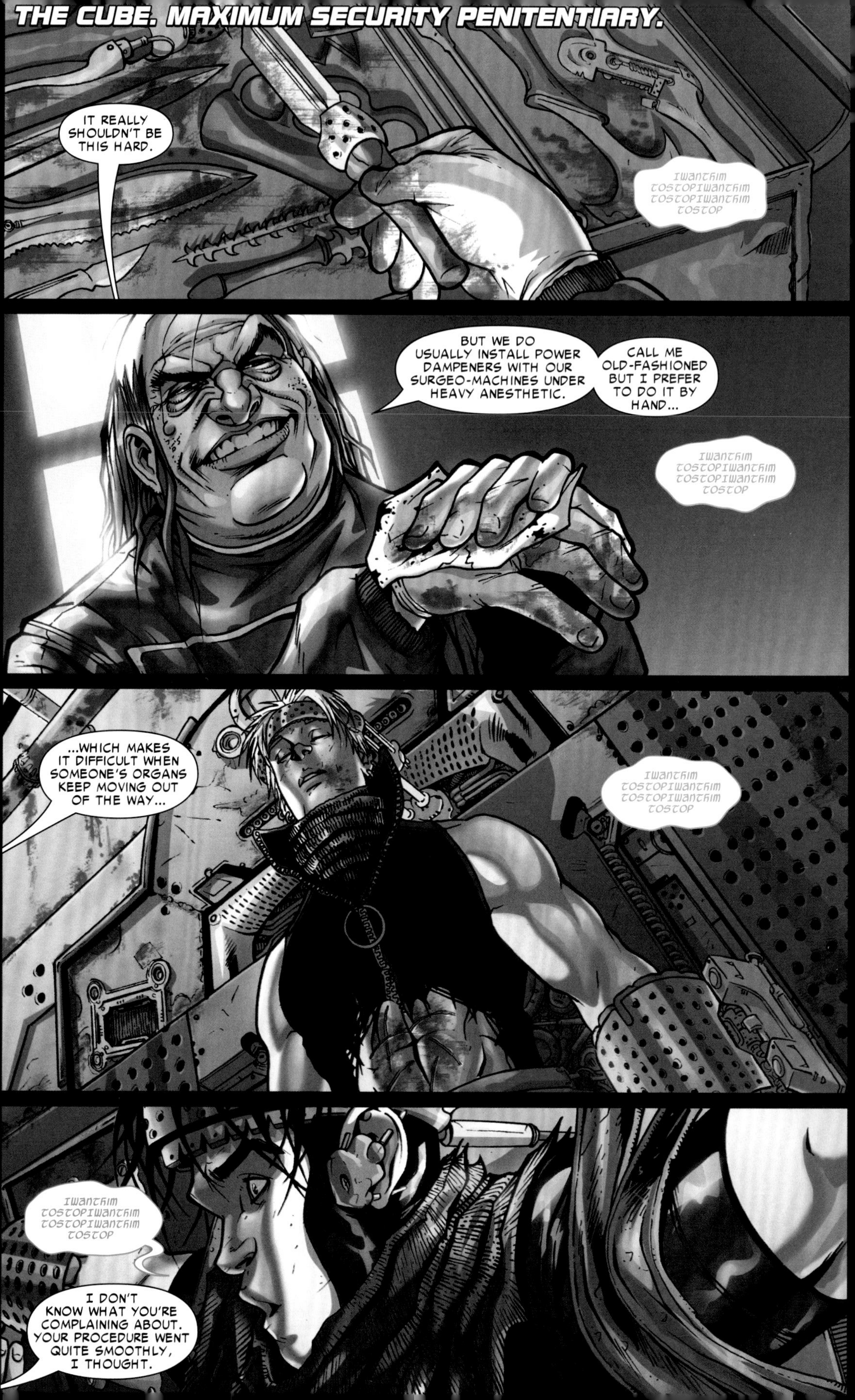

THE CUBE. MAXIMUM SECURITY PENITENTIARY.
IT REALLY SHOULDN'T BE THIS HARD.
IWANTHIM TOSTOPIWANTHIM TOSTOPIWANTHIM TOSTOP
BUT WE DO USUALLY INSTALL POWER DAMPENERS WITH OUR SURGEO-MACHINES UNDER HEAVY ANESTHETIC.
CALL ME OLD-FASHIONED BUT I PREFER TO DO IT BY HAND...
IWANTHIM TOSTOPIWANTHIM TOSTOPIWANTHIM TOSTOP
...WHICH MAKES IT DIFFICULT WHEN SOMEONE'S ORGANS KEEP MOVING OUT OF THE WAY...
IWANTHIM TOSTOPIWANTHIM TOSTOPIWANTHIM TOSTOP
IWANTHIM TOSTOPIWANTHIM TOSTOPIWANTHIM TOSTOP
I DON'T KNOW WHAT YOU'RE COMPLAINING ABOUT. YOUR PROCEDURE WENT QUITE SMOOTHLY, I THOUGHT.

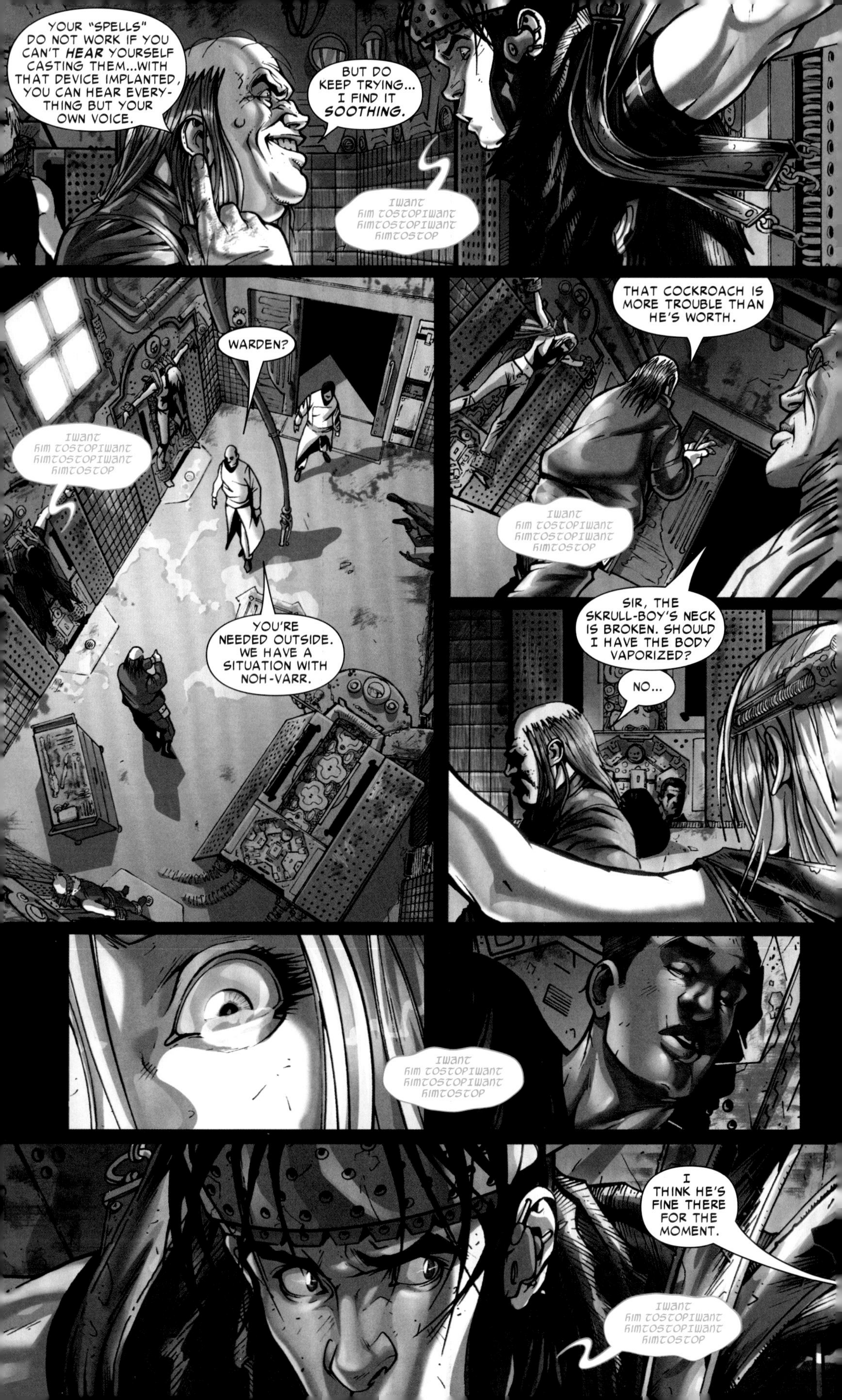

YOUR "SPELLS" DO NOT WORK IF YOU CAN'T HEAR YOURSELF CASTING THEM...WITH THAT DEVICE IMPLANTED, YOU CAN HEAR EVERYTHING BUT YOUR OWN VOICE.
BUT DO KEEP TRYING... I FIND IT SOOTHING.
IWANT HIM TOSTOPIWANT HIMTOSTOPIWANT HIMTOSTOP
WARDEN?
IWANT HIM TOSTOPIWANT HIMTOSTOPIWANT HIMTOSTOP
YOU'RE NEEDED OUTSIDE. WE HAVE A SITUATION WITH NOH-VARR.
THAT COCKROACH IS MORE TROUBLE THAN HE'S WORTH.
IWANT HIM TOSTOPIWANT HIMTOSTOPIWANT HIMTOSTOP
SIR, THE SKRULL-BOY'S NECK IS BROKEN. SHOULD I HAVE THE BODY VAPORIZED?
NO...
IWANT HIM TOSTOPIWANT HIMTOSTOPIWANT HIMTOSTOP
I THINK HE'S FINE THERE FOR THE MOMENT.
IWANT HIM TOSTOPIWANT HIMTOSTOPIWANT HIMTOSTOP

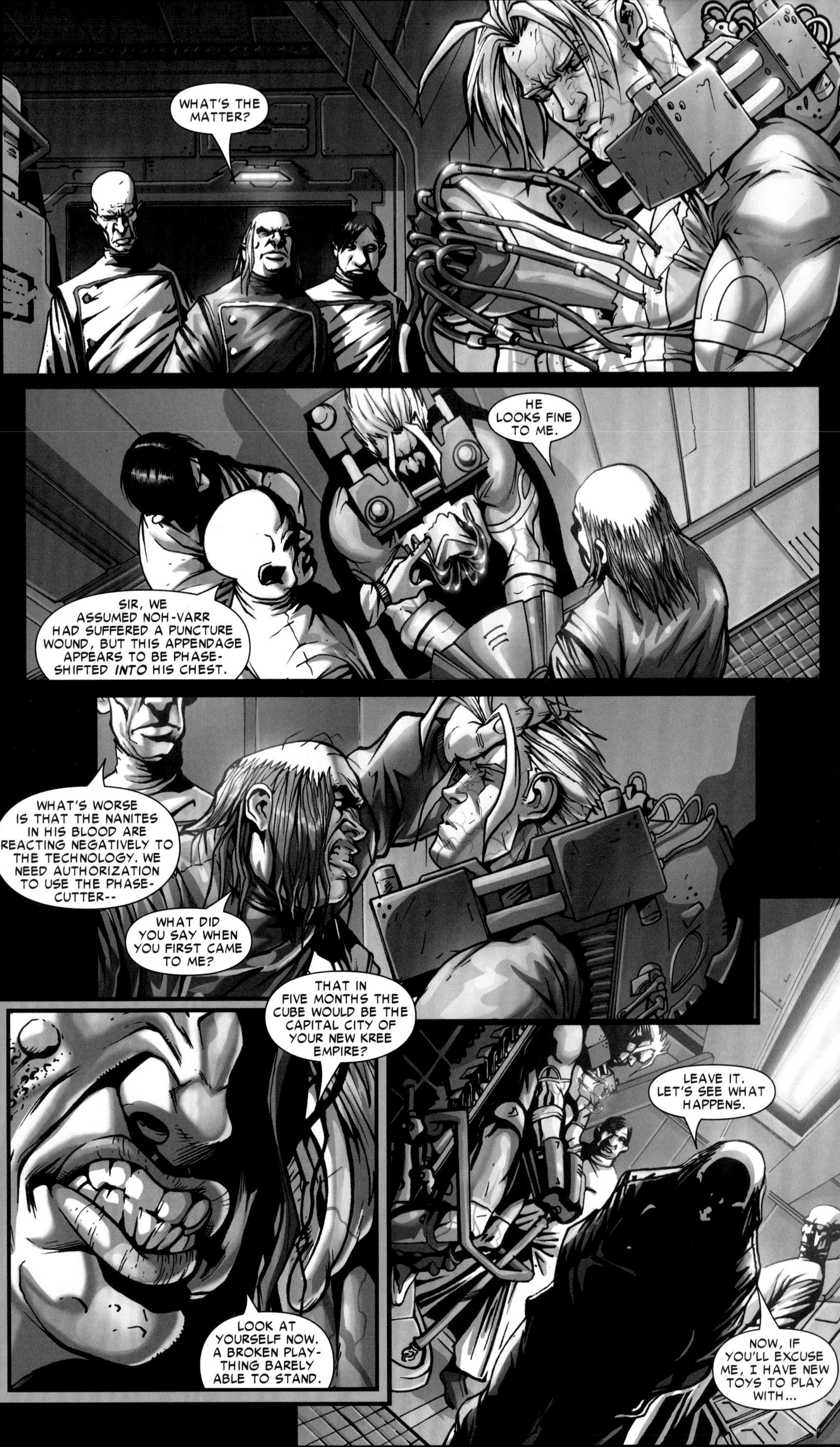
WHAT'S THE MATTER?
HE LOOKS FINE TO ME.
SIR, WE ASSUMED NOH-VARR HAD SUFFERED A PUNCTURE WOUND, BUT THIS APPENDAGE APPEARS TO BE PHASE-SHIFTED *INTO* HIS CHEST.
WHAT'S WORSE IS THAT THE NANITES IN HIS BLOOD ARE REACTING NEGATIVELY TO THE TECHNOLOGY. WE NEED AUTHORIZATION TO USE THE PHASE-CUTTER--
WHAT DID YOU SAY WHEN YOU FIRST CAME TO ME?
THAT IN FIVE MONTHS THE CUBE WOULD BE THE CAPITAL CITY OF YOUR NEW KREE EMPIRE?
LOOK AT YOURSELF NOW. A BROKEN PLAY-THING BARELY ABLE TO STAND.
LEAVE IT. LET'S SEE WHAT HAPPENS.
NOW, IF YOU'LL EXCUSE ME, I HAVE NEW TOYS TO PLAY WITH...

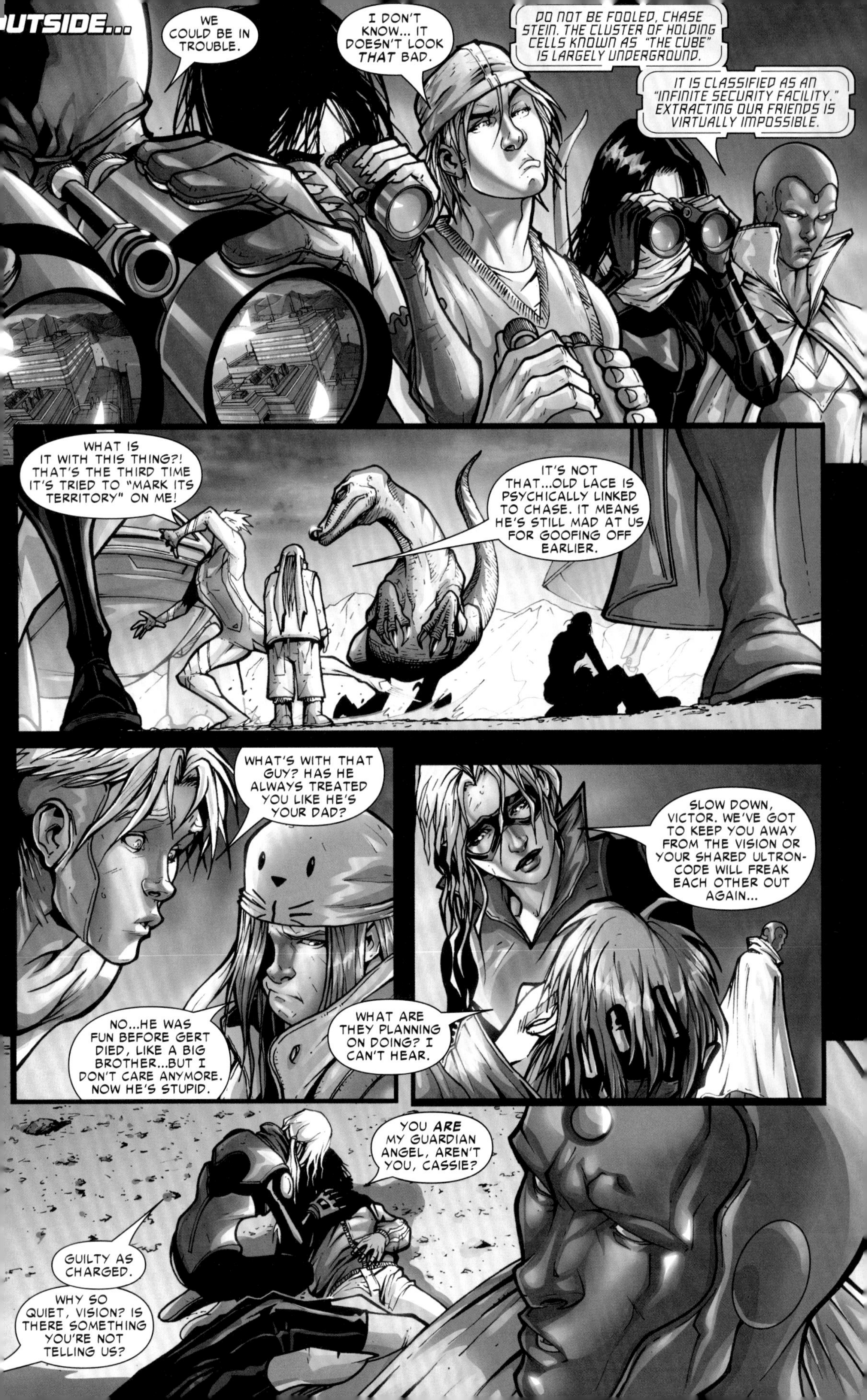
UTSIDE...
WE COULD BE IN TROUBLE.
I DON'T KNOW... IT DOESN'T LOOK THAT BAD.
DO NOT BE FOOLED, CHASE STEIN. THE CLUSTER OF HOLDING CELLS KNOWN AS "THE CUBE" IS LARGELY UNDERGROUND.
IT IS CLASSIFIED AS AN "INFINITE SECURITY FACILITY." EXTRACTING OUR FRIENDS IS VIRTUALLY IMPOSSIBLE.
WHAT IS IT WITH THIS THING?! THAT'S THE THIRD TIME IT'S TRIED TO "MARK ITS TERRITORY" ON ME!
IT'S NOT THAT...OLD LACE IS PSYCHICALLY LINKED TO CHASE. IT MEANS HE'S STILL MAD AT US FOR GOOFING OFF EARLIER.
WHAT'S WITH THAT GUY? HAS HE ALWAYS TREATED YOU LIKE HE'S YOUR DAD?
NO...HE WAS FUN BEFORE GERT DIED, LIKE A BIG BROTHER...BUT I DON'T CARE ANYMORE. NOW HE'S STUPID.
SLOW DOWN, VICTOR. WE'VE GOT TO KEEP YOU AWAY FROM THE VISION OR YOUR SHARED ULTRON-CODE WILL FREAK EACH OTHER OUT AGAIN...
WHAT ARE THEY PLANNING ON DOING? I CAN'T HEAR.
YOU ARE MY GUARDIAN ANGEL, AREN'T YOU, CASSIE?
GUILTY AS CHARGED.
WHY SO QUIET, VISION? IS THERE SOMETHING YOU'RE NOT TELLING US?

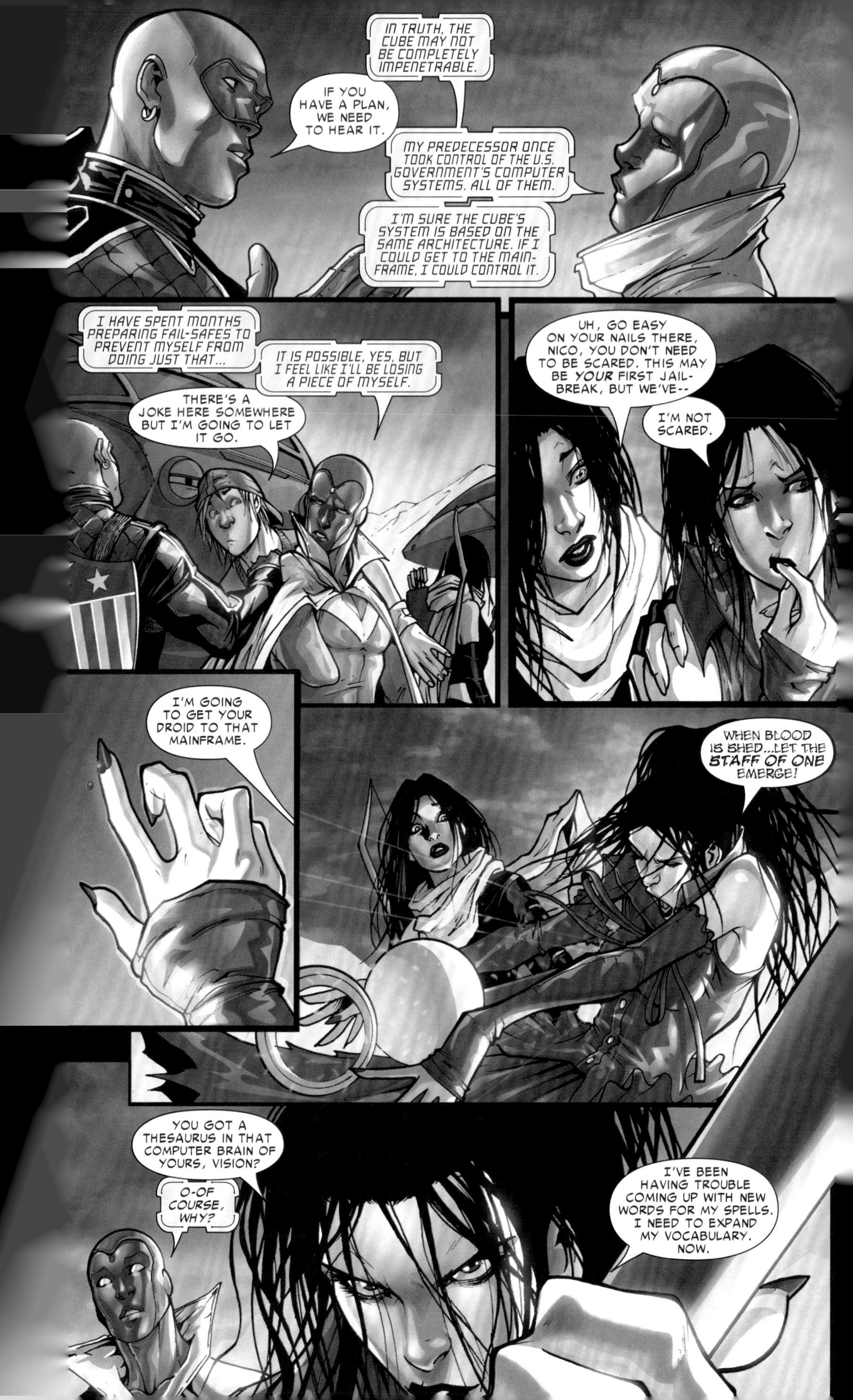
IF YOU HAVE A PLAN, WE NEED TO HEAR IT.
IN TRUTH, THE CUBE MAY NOT BE COMPLETELY IMPENETRABLE.
MY PREDECESSOR ONCE TOOK CONTROL OF THE U.S. GOVERNMENT'S COMPUTER SYSTEMS. ALL OF THEM.
I'M SURE THE CUBE'S SYSTEM IS BASED ON THE SAME ARCHITECTURE. IF I COULD GET TO THE MAIN-FRAME, I COULD CONTROL IT.
I HAVE SPENT MONTHS PREPARING FAIL-SAFES TO PREVENT MYSELF FROM DOING JUST THAT...
IT IS POSSIBLE, YES, BUT I FEEL LIKE I'LL BE LOSING A PIECE OF MYSELF.
THERE'S A JOKE HERE SOMEWHERE BUT I'M GOING TO LET IT GO.
UH, GO EASY ON YOUR NAILS THERE, NICO, YOU DON'T NEED TO BE SCARED. THIS MAY BE YOUR FIRST JAIL-BREAK, BUT WE'VE--
I'M NOT SCARED.
I'M GOING TO GET YOUR DROID TO THAT MAINFRAME.
WHEN BLOOD IS SHED...LET THE STAFF OF ONE EMERGE!
YOU GOT A THESAURUS IN THAT COMPUTER BRAIN OF YOURS, VISION?
O-OF COURSE, WHY?
I'VE BEEN HAVING TROUBLE COMING UP WITH NEW WORDS FOR MY SPELLS. I NEED TO EXPAND MY VOCABULARY. NOW.

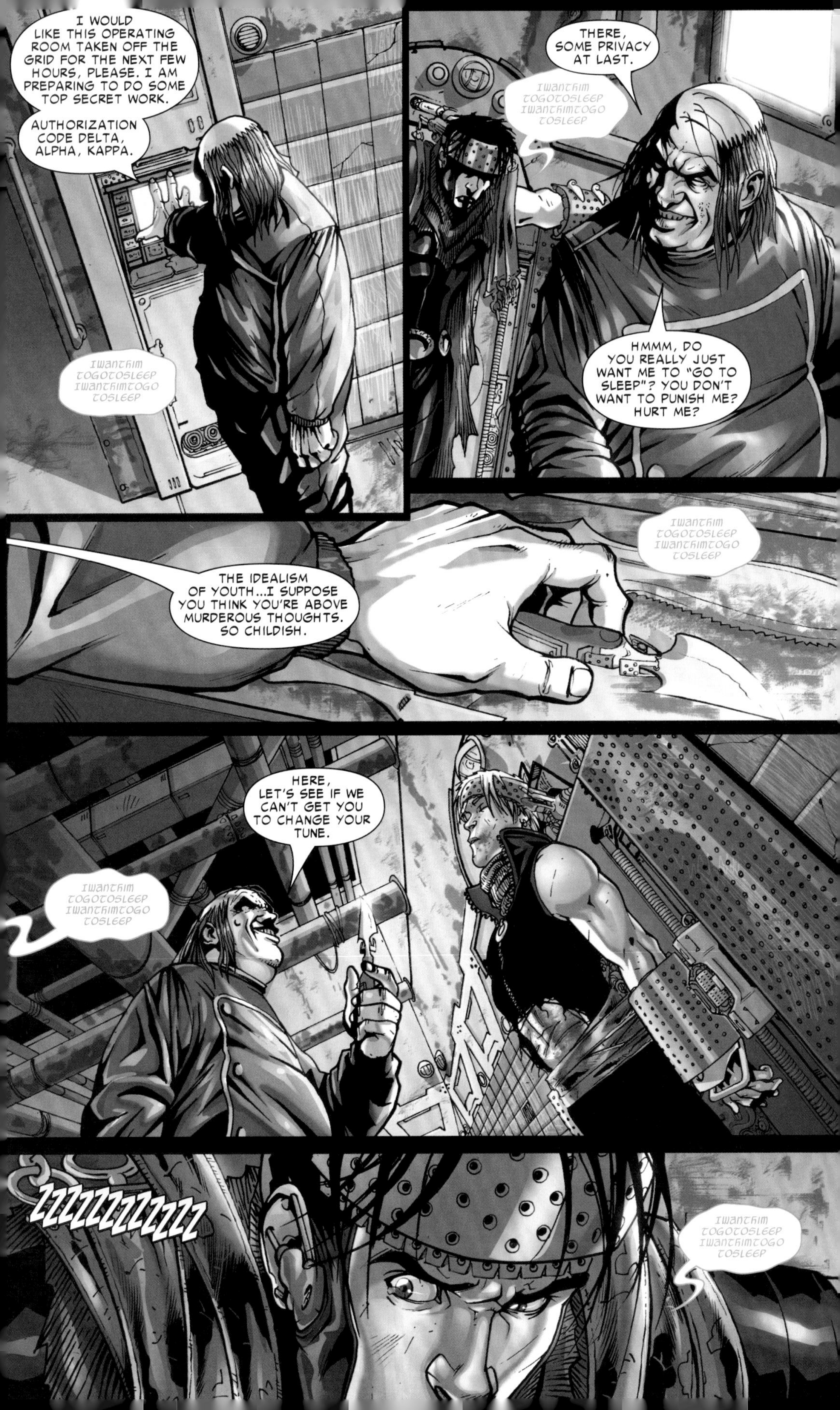
I WOULD LIKE THIS OPERATING ROOM TAKEN OFF THE GRID FOR THE NEXT FEW HOURS, PLEASE. I AM PREPARING TO DO SOME TOP SECRET WORK.
AUTHORIZATION CODE DELTA, ALPHA, KAPPA.
IWANTHIM TOGOTOSLEEP IWANTHIMTOGO TOSLEEP
THERE, SOME PRIVACY AT LAST.
IWANTHIM TOGOTOSLEEP IWANTHIMTOGO TOSLEEP
HMMM, DO YOU REALLY JUST WANT ME TO "GO TO SLEEP"? YOU DON'T WANT TO PUNISH ME? HURT ME?
IWANTHIM TOGOTOSLEEP IWANTHIMTOGO TOSLEEP
THE IDEALISM OF YOUTH...I SUPPOSE YOU THINK YOU'RE ABOVE MURDEROUS THOUGHTS. SO CHILDISH.
HERE, LET'S SEE IF WE CAN'T GET YOU TO CHANGE YOUR TUNE.
IWANTHIM TOGOTOSLEEP IWANTHIMTOGO TOSLEEP
ZZZZZZZZZZZZ
IWANTHIM TOGOTOSLEEP IWANTHIMTOGO TOSLEEP

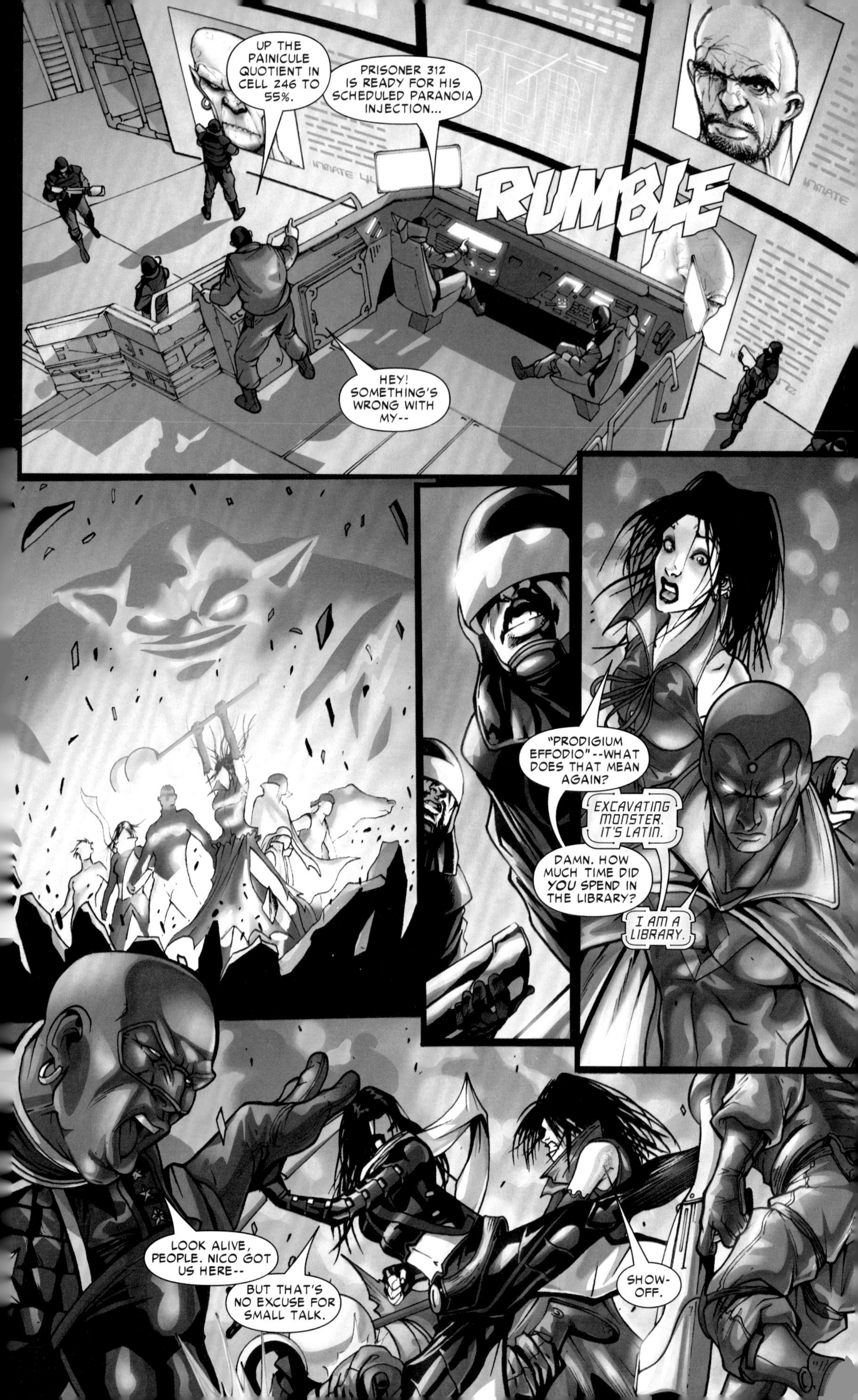
UP THE PAINICULE QUOTIENT IN CELL 246 TO 55%.
PRISONER 312 IS READY FOR HIS SCHEDULED PARANOIA INJECTION...
RUMBLE
HEY! SOMETHING'S WRONG WITH MY--
"PRODIGIUM EFFODIO"--WHAT DOES THAT MEAN AGAIN?
EXCAVATING MONSTER. IT'S LATIN.
DAMN. HOW MUCH TIME DID YOU SPEND IN THE LIBRARY?
I AM A LIBRARY.
LOOK ALIVE, PEOPLE. NICO GOT US HERE--
BUT THAT'S NO EXCUSE FOR SMALL TALK.
SHOW-OFF.

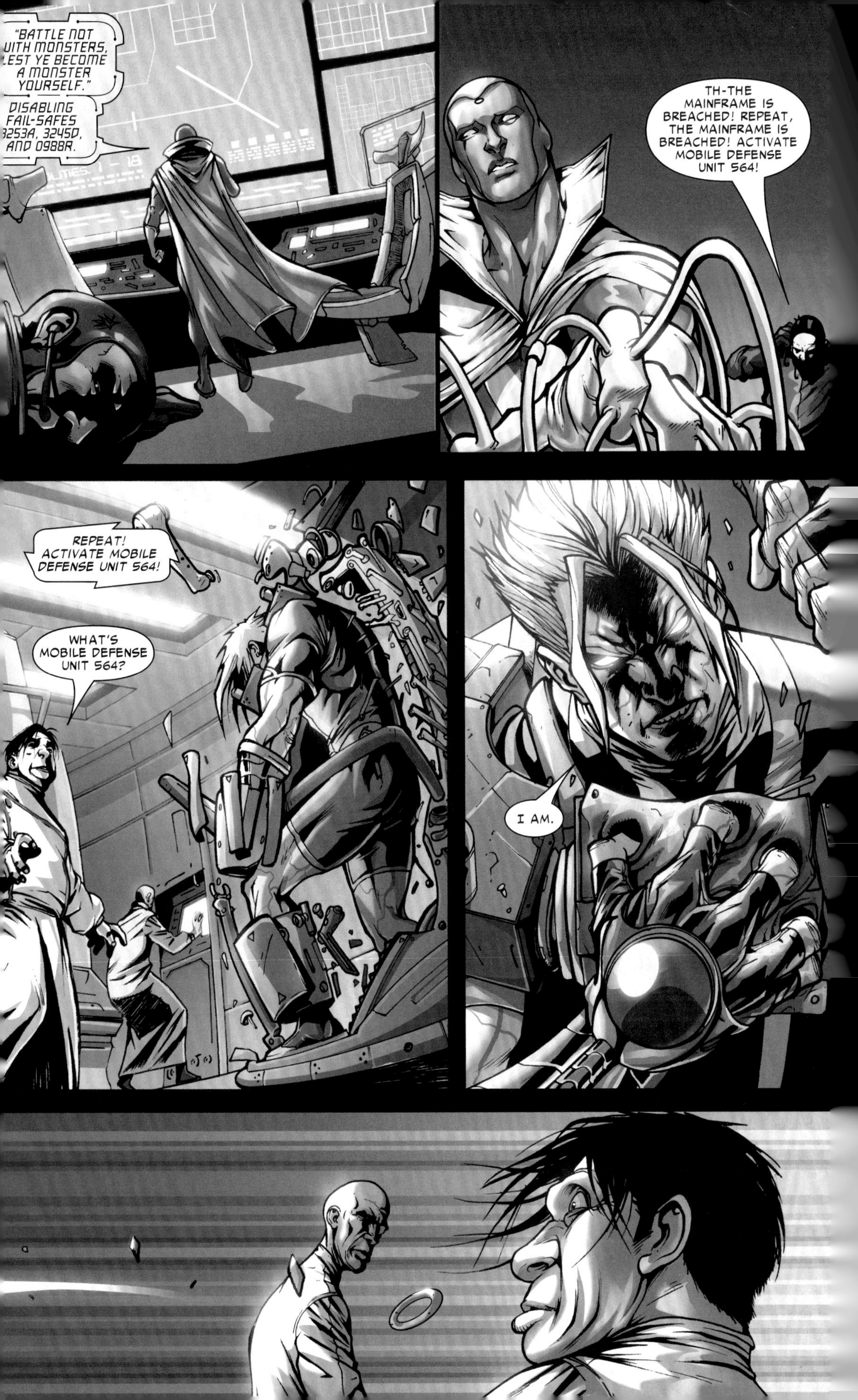
"BATTLE NOT WITH MONSTERS, LEST YE BECOME A MONSTER YOURSELF."
DISABLING FAIL-SAFES 3253A, 3245D, AND 0988R.
TH-THE MAINFRAME IS BREACHED! REPEAT, THE MAINFRAME IS BREACHED! ACTIVATE MOBILE DEFENSE UNIT 564!
REPEAT! ACTIVATE MOBILE DEFENSE UNIT 564!
WHAT'S MOBILE DEFENSE UNIT 564?
I AM.

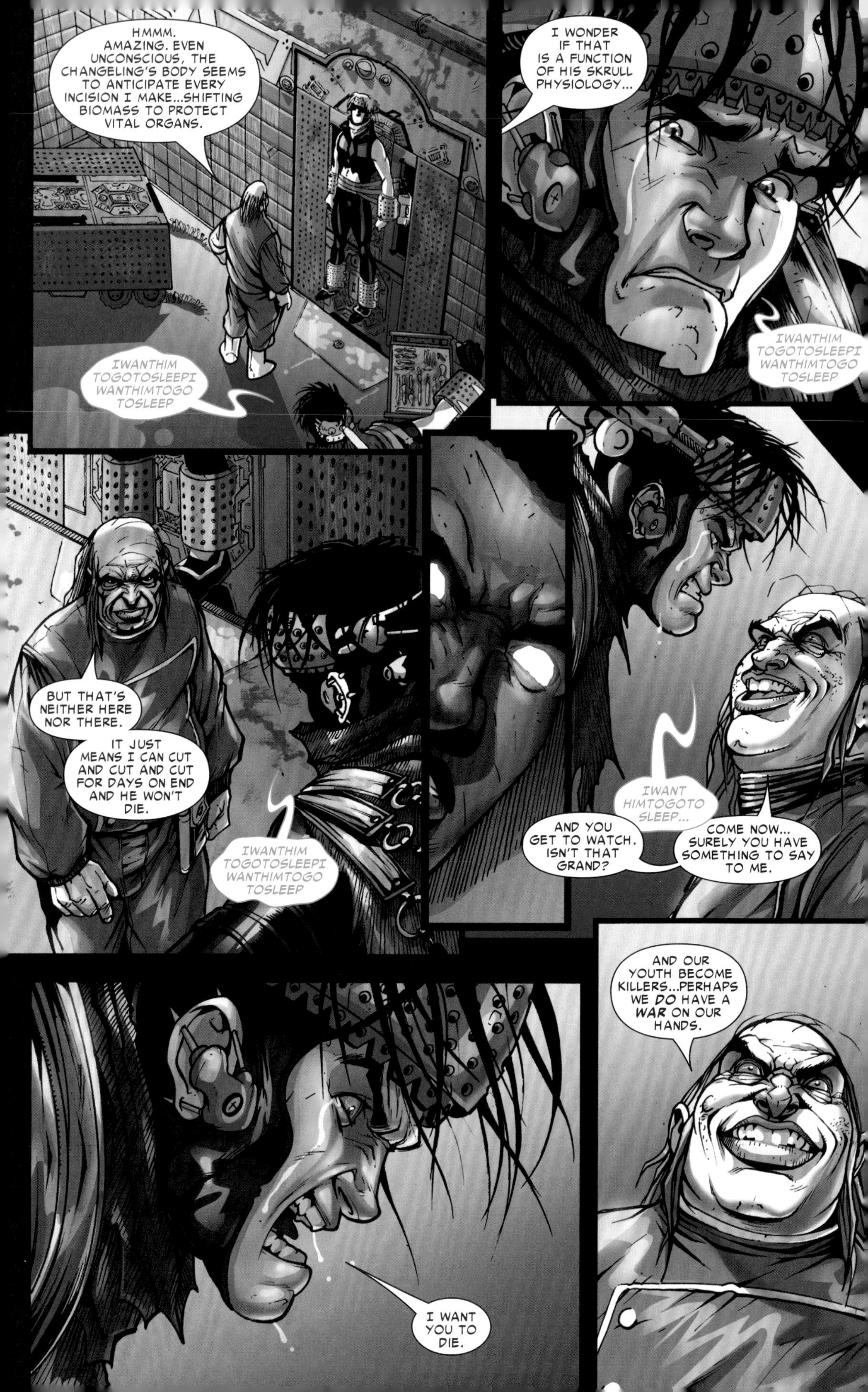
HMMM. AMAZING. EVEN UNCONSCIOUS, THE CHANGELING'S BODY SEEMS TO ANTICIPATE EVERY INCISION I MAKE...SHIFTING BIOMASS TO PROTECT VITAL ORGANS.
IWANTHIM TOGOTOSLEEPI WANTHIMTOGO TOSLEEP
I WONDER IF THAT IS A FUNCTION OF HIS SKRULL PHYSIOLOGY...
IWANTHIM TOGOTOSLEEPI WANTHIMTOGO TOSLEEP
BUT THAT'S NEITHER HERE NOR THERE.
IT JUST MEANS I CAN CUT AND CUT AND CUT FOR DAYS ON END AND HE WON'T DIE.
IWANTHIM TOGOTOSLEEPI WANTHIMTOGO TOSLEEP
IWANT HIMTOGOTO SLEEP...
AND YOU GET TO WATCH. ISN'T THAT GRAND?
COME NOW... SURELY YOU HAVE SOMETHING TO SAY TO ME.
I WANT YOU TO DIE.
AND OUR YOUTH BECOME KILLERS...PERHAPS WE DO HAVE A WAR ON OUR HANDS.

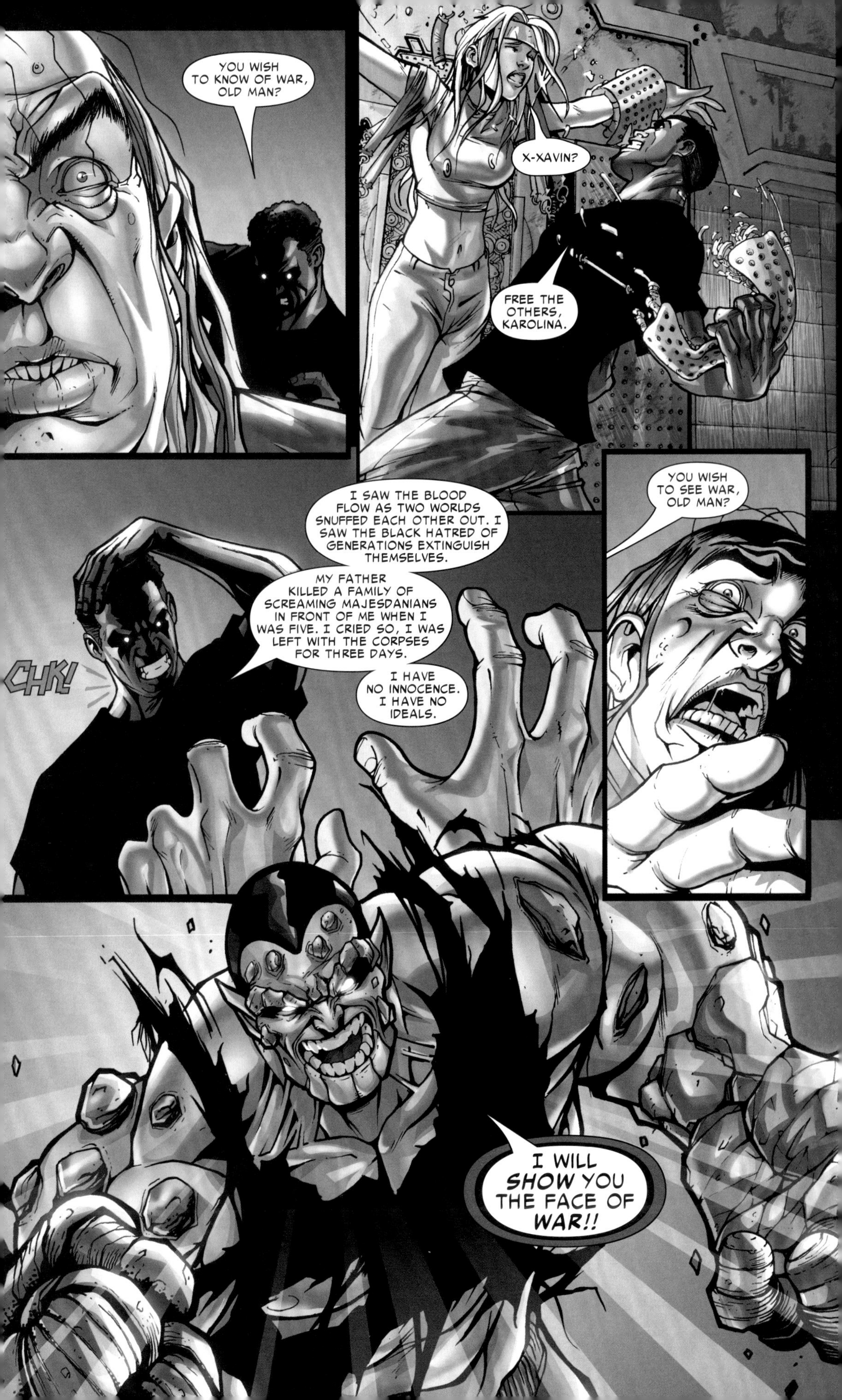
YOU WISH TO KNOW OF WAR, OLD MAN?
X-XAVIN?
FREE THE OTHERS, KAROLINA.
YOU WISH TO SEE WAR, OLD MAN?
I SAW THE BLOOD FLOW AS TWO WORLDS SNUFFED EACH OTHER OUT. I SAW THE BLACK HATRED OF GENERATIONS EXTINGUISH THEMSELVES.
MY FATHER KILLED A FAMILY OF SCREAMING MAJESDANIANS IN FRONT OF ME WHEN I WAS FIVE. I CRIED SO, I WAS LEFT WITH THE CORPSES FOR THREE DAYS.
I HAVE NO INNOCENCE. I HAVE NO IDEALS.
CHK!
I WILL SHOW YOU THE FACE OF WAR!!

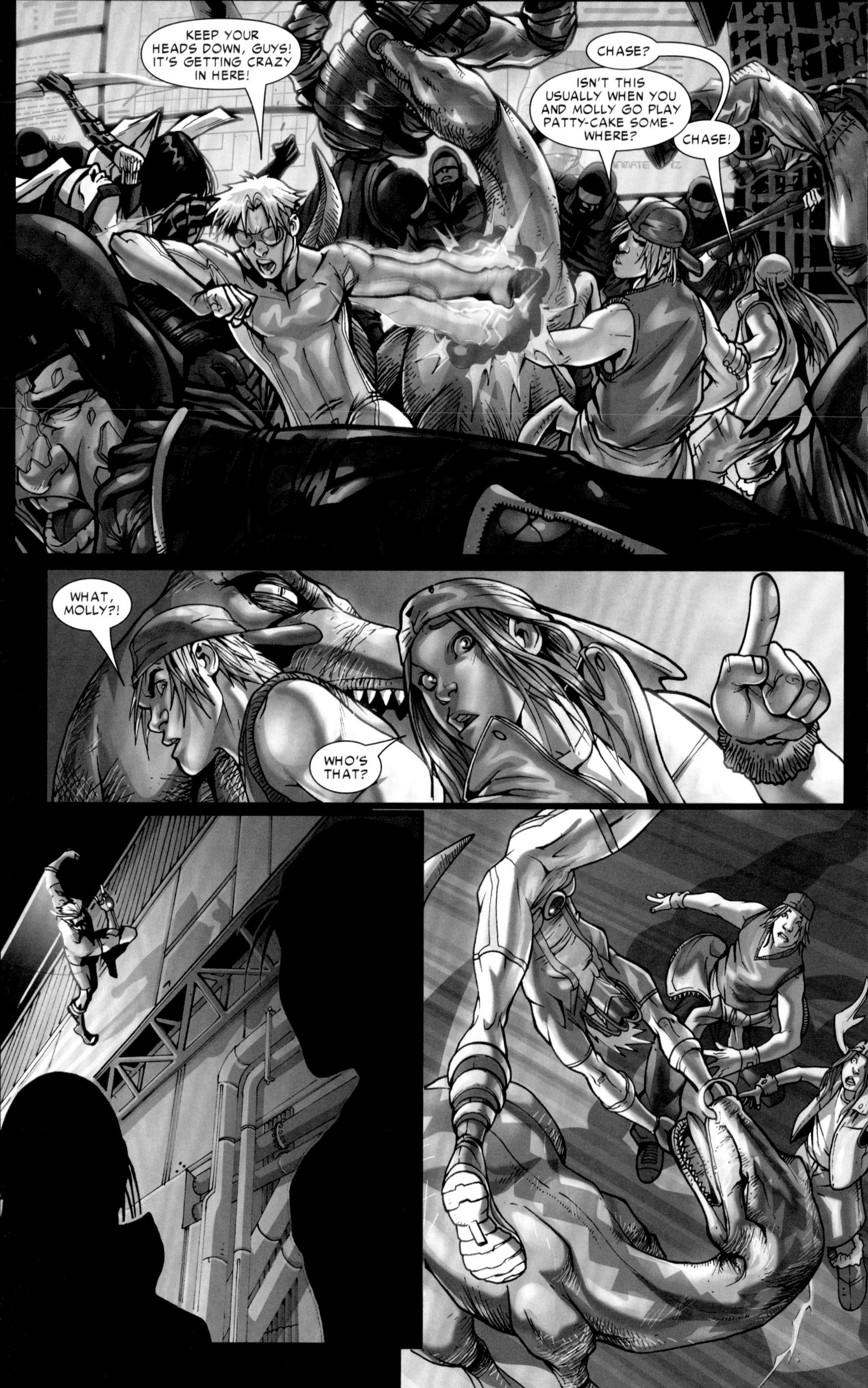
KEEP YOUR HEADS DOWN, GUYS! IT'S GETTING CRAZY IN HERE!
CHASE?
ISN'T THIS USUALLY WHEN YOU AND MOLLY GO PLAY PATTY-CAKE SOME-WHERE?
CHASE!
WHAT, MOLLY?!
WHO'S THAT?

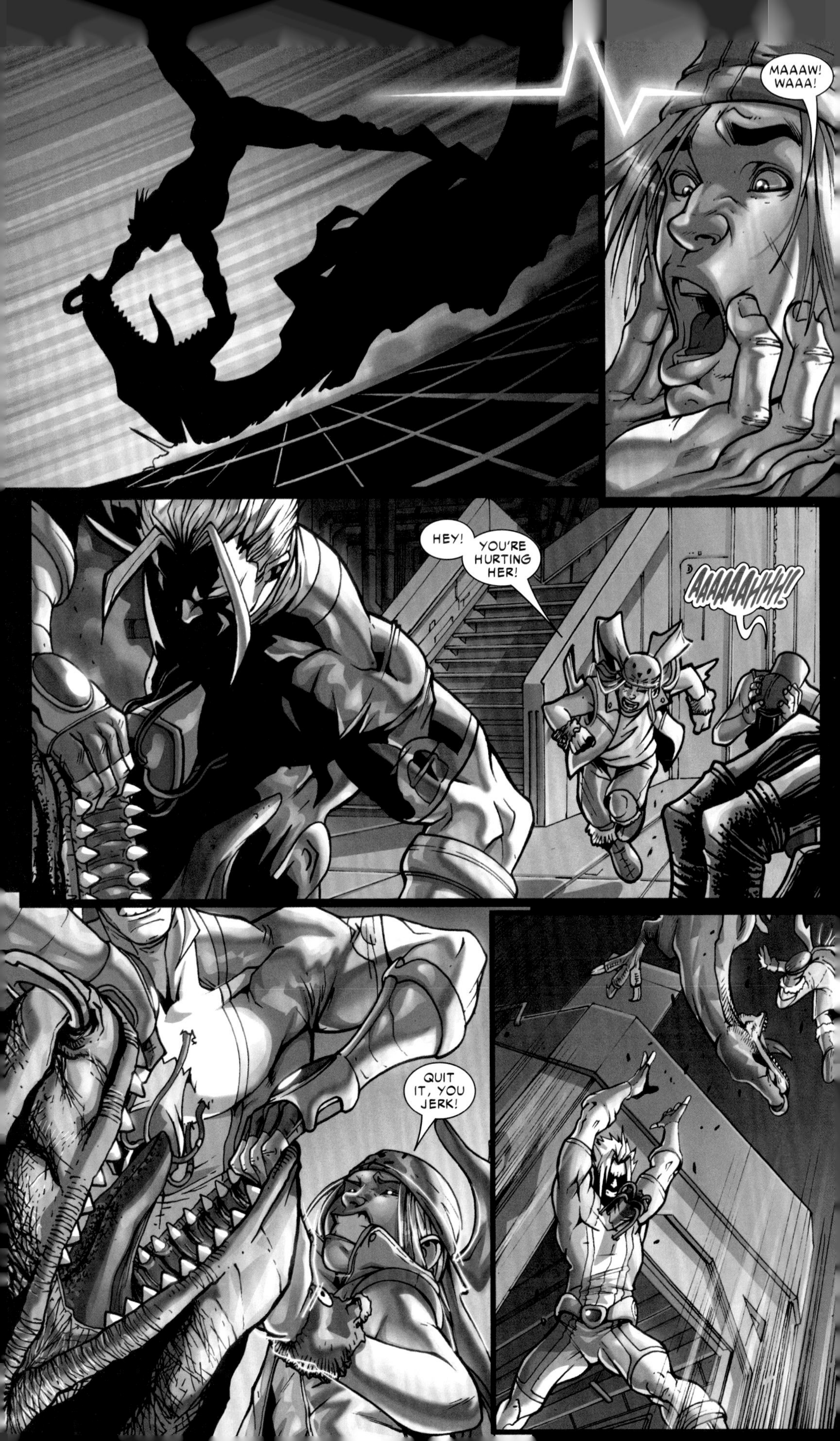
MAAAW! WAAA!
HEY!
YOU'RE HURTING HER!
AAAAAAHHH!!
QUIT IT, YOU JERK!

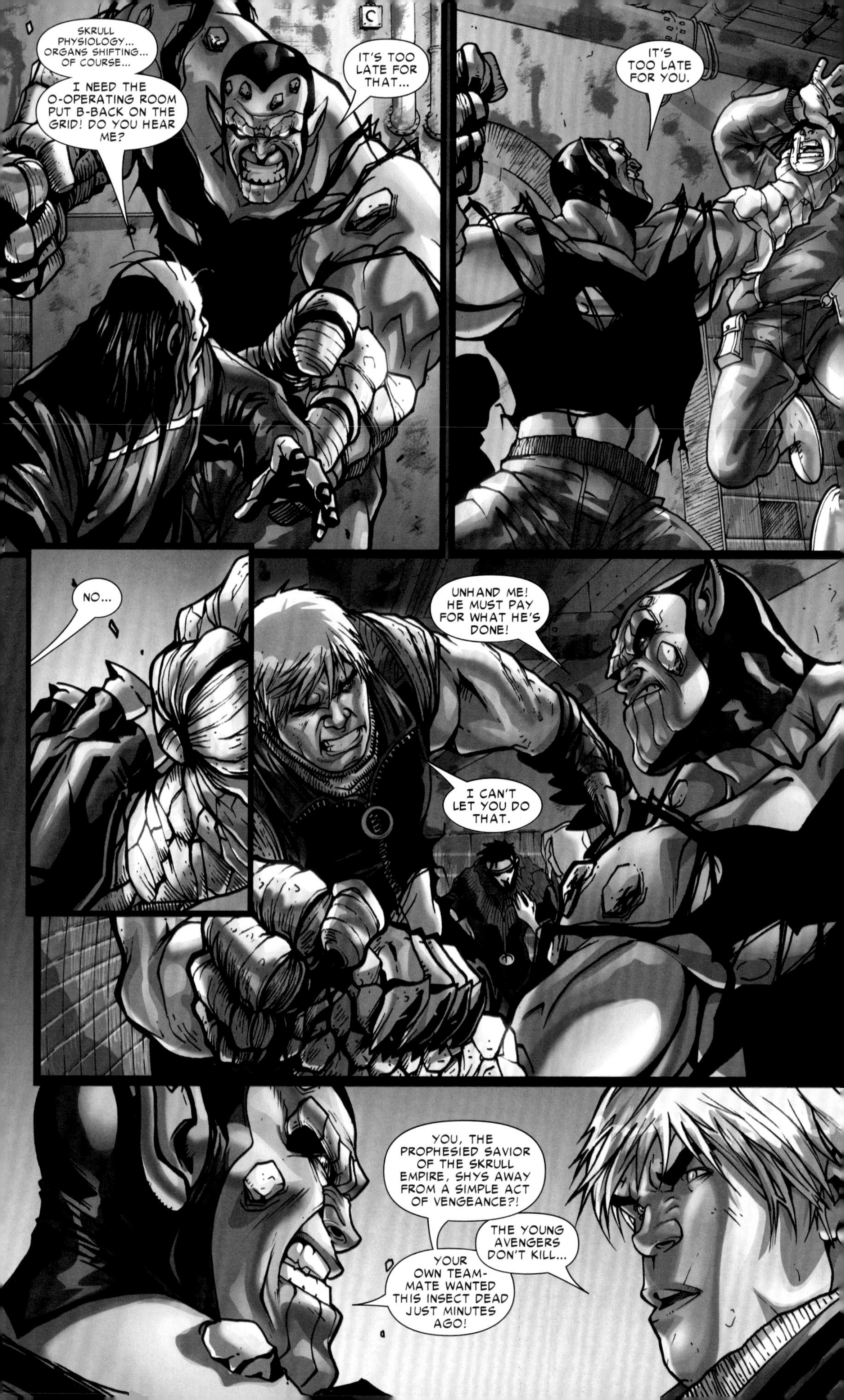
SKRULL PHYSIOLOGY... ORGANS SHIFTING... OF COURSE...
I NEED THE O-OPERATING ROOM PUT B-BACK ON THE GRID! DO YOU HEAR ME?
IT'S TOO LATE FOR THAT...
IT'S TOO LATE FOR YOU.
NO...
UNHAND ME! HE MUST PAY FOR WHAT HE'S DONE!
I CAN'T LET YOU DO THAT.
YOU, THE PROPHESIED SAVIOR OF THE SKRULL EMPIRE, SHYS AWAY FROM A SIMPLE ACT OF VENGEANCE?!
YOUR OWN TEAM-MATE WANTED THIS INSECT DEAD JUST MINUTES AGO!
THE YOUNG AVENGERS DON'T KILL...

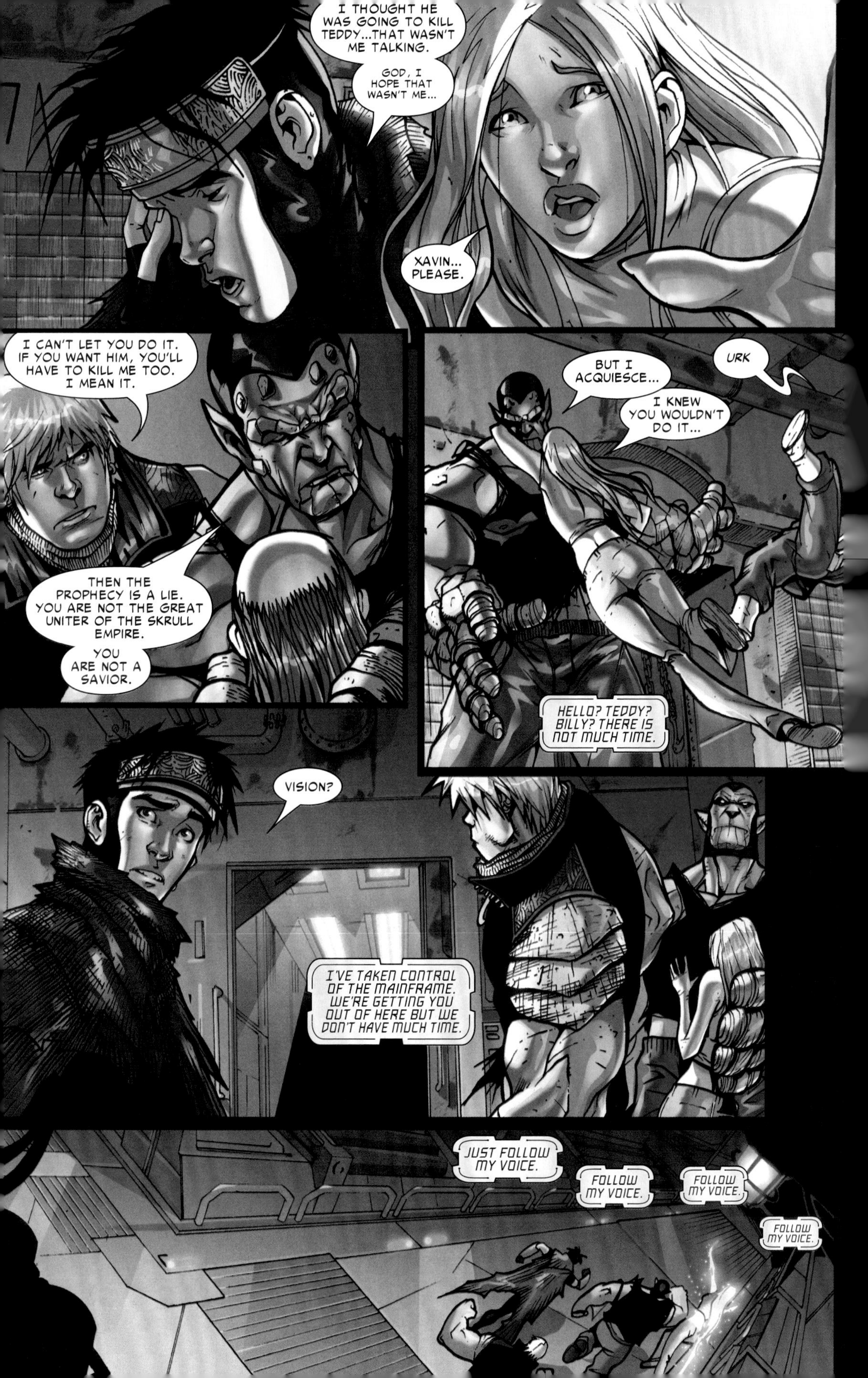
I THOUGHT HE WAS GOING TO KILL TEDDY...THAT WASN'T ME TALKING.
GOD, I HOPE THAT WASN'T ME...
XAVIN... PLEASE.
I CAN'T LET YOU DO IT. IF YOU WANT HIM, YOU'LL HAVE TO KILL ME TOO. I MEAN IT.
THEN THE PROPHECY IS A LIE. YOU ARE NOT THE GREAT UNITER OF THE SKRULL EMPIRE.
YOU ARE NOT A SAVIOR.
BUT I ACQUIESCE...
URK
I KNEW YOU WOULDN'T DO IT...
HELLO? TEDDY? BILLY? THERE IS NOT MUCH TIME.
VISION?
I'VE TAKEN CONTROL OF THE MAINFRAME. WE'RE GETTING YOU OUT OF HERE BUT WE DON'T HAVE MUCH TIME.
JUST FOLLOW MY VOICE.
FOLLOW MY VOICE.
FOLLOW MY VOICE.
FOLLOW MY VOICE.

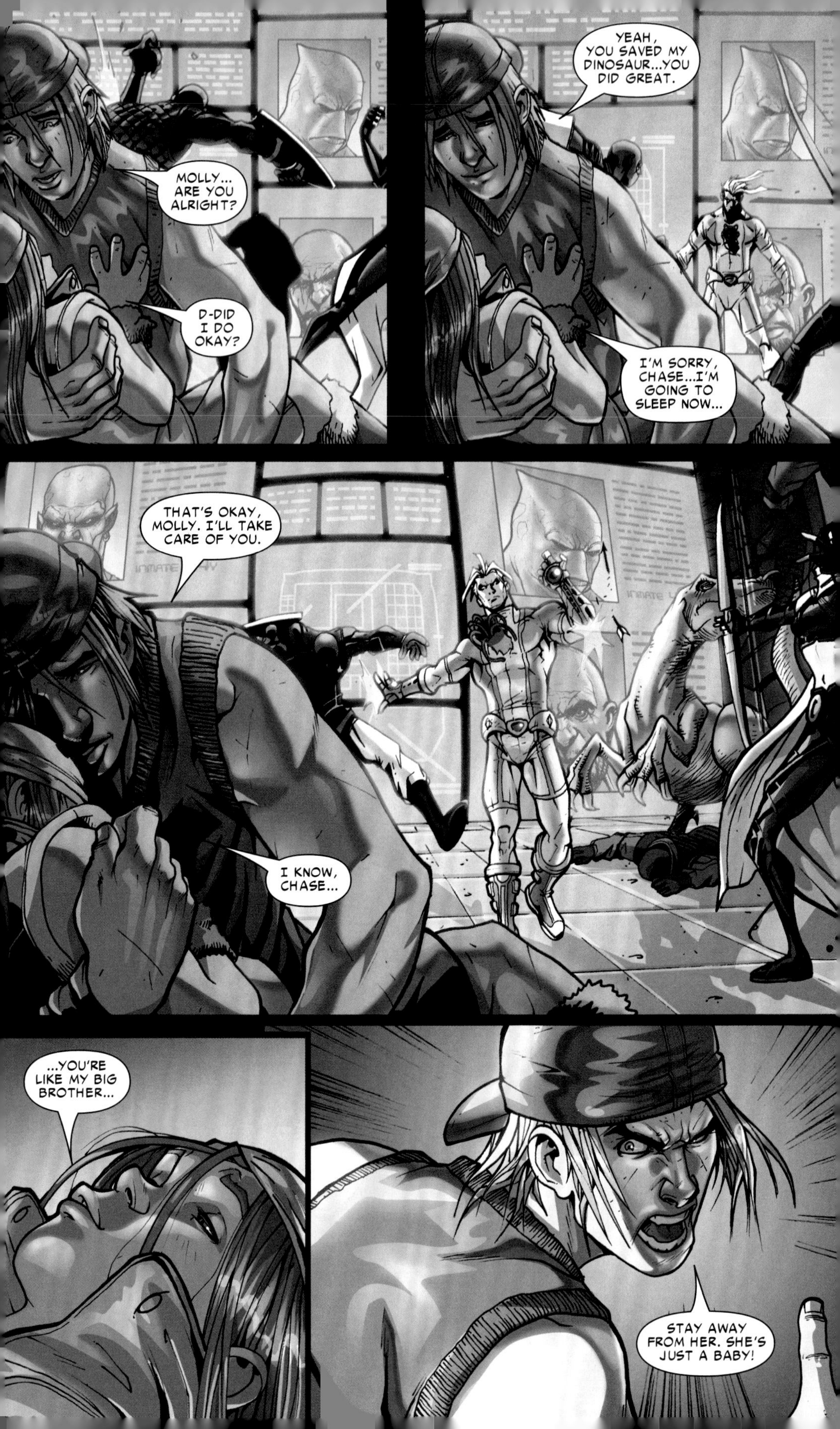
MOLLY... ARE YOU ALRIGHT?
D-DID I DO OKAY?
YEAH, YOU SAVED MY DINOSAUR...YOU DID GREAT.
I'M SORRY, CHASE...I'M GOING TO SLEEP NOW...
THAT'S OKAY, MOLLY. I'LL TAKE CARE OF YOU.
I KNOW, CHASE...
...YOU'RE LIKE MY BIG BROTHER...
STAY AWAY FROM HER. SHE'S JUST A BABY!

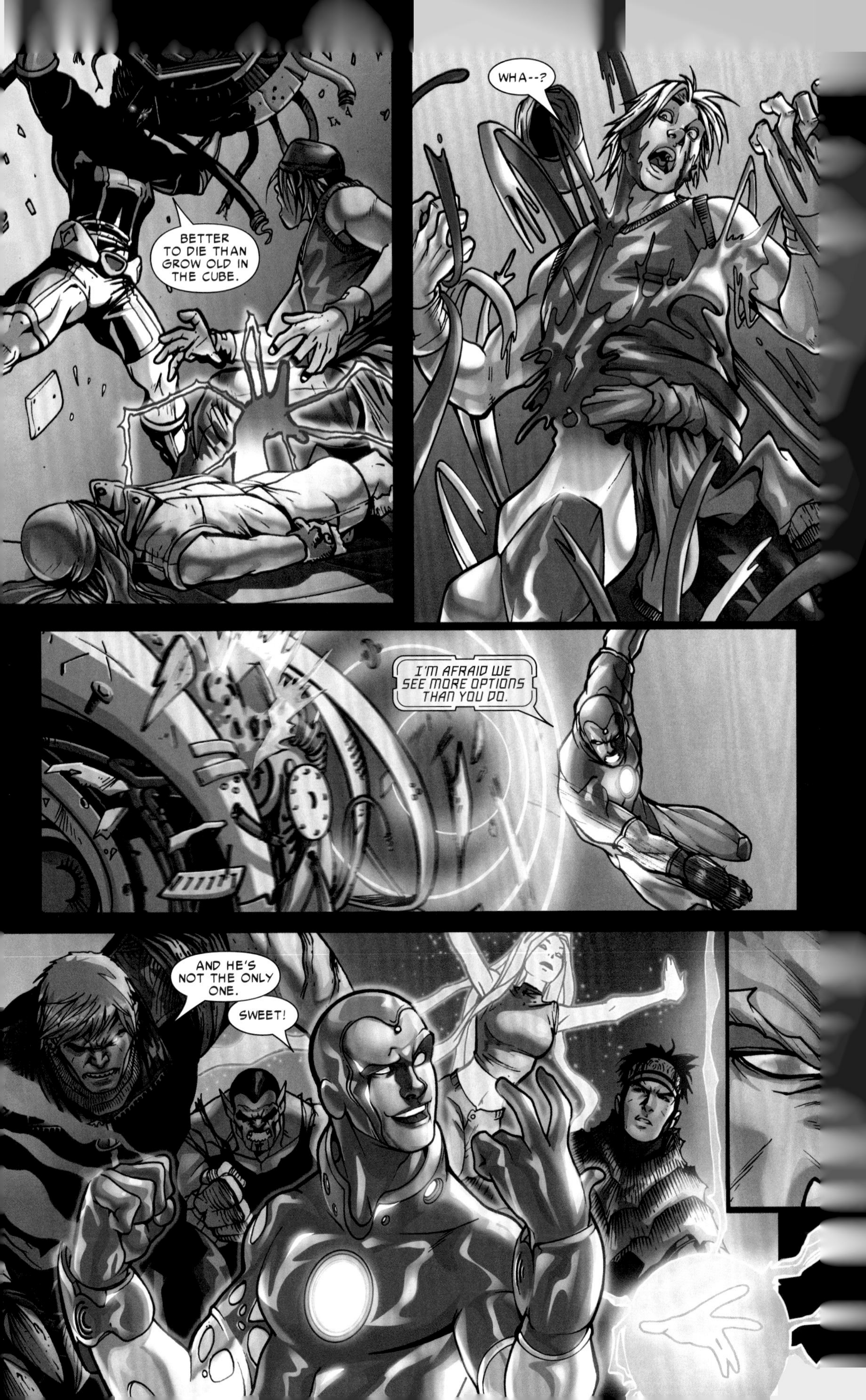
BETTER TO DIE THAN GROW OLD IN THE CUBE.
WHA--?
I'M AFRAID WE SEE MORE OPTIONS THAN YOU DO.
AND HE'S NOT THE ONLY ONE.
SWEET!

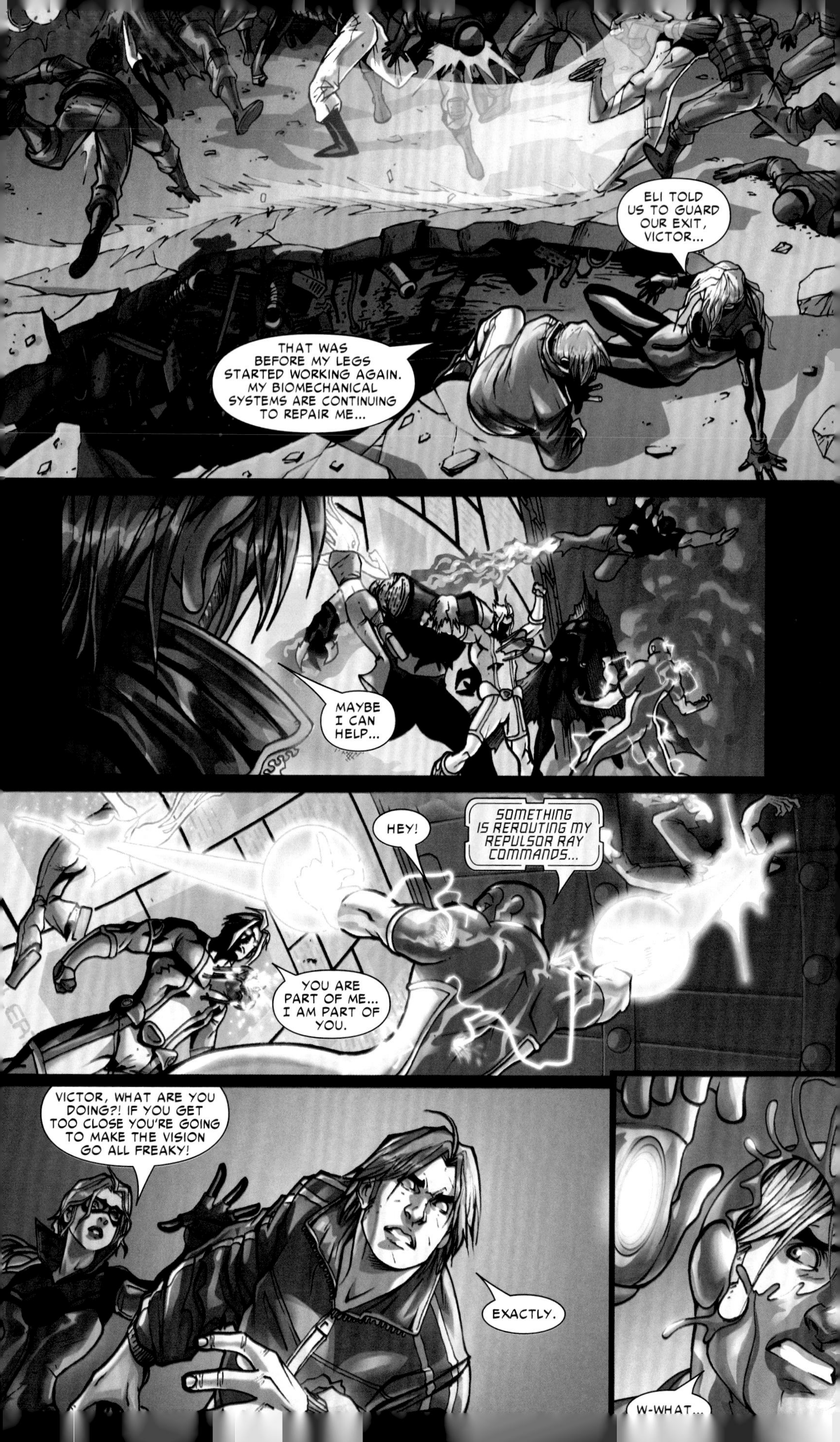

ELI TOLD US TO GUARD OUR EXIT, VICTOR...
THAT WAS BEFORE MY LEGS STARTED WORKING AGAIN. MY BIOMECHANICAL SYSTEMS ARE CONTINUING TO REPAIR ME...
MAYBE I CAN HELP...
HEY!
SOMETHING IS REROUTING MY REPULSOR RAY COMMANDS...
YOU ARE PART OF ME... I AM PART OF YOU.
VICTOR, WHAT ARE YOU DOING?! IF YOU GET TOO CLOSE YOU'RE GOING TO MAKE THE VISION GO ALL FREAKY!
EXACTLY.
W-WHAT...

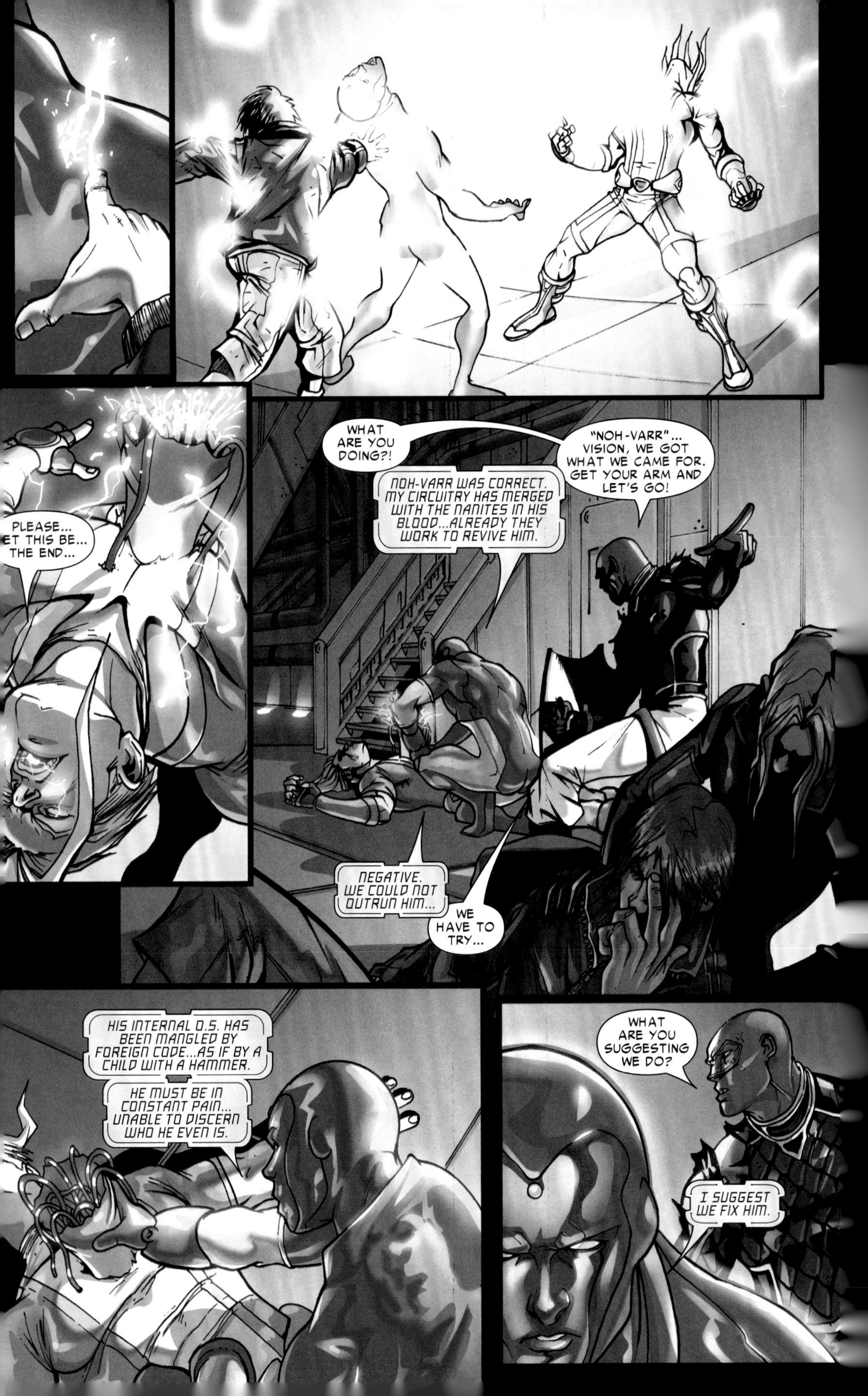
PLEASE... ET THIS BE... THE END...
WHAT ARE YOU DOING?!
"NOH-VARR"... VISION, WE GOT WHAT WE CAME FOR. GET YOUR ARM AND LET'S GO!
NOH-VARR WAS CORRECT. MY CIRCUITRY HAS MERGED WITH THE NANITES IN HIS BLOOD...ALREADY THEY WORK TO REVIVE HIM.
NEGATIVE. WE COULD NOT OUTRUN HIM...
WE HAVE TO TRY...
HIS INTERNAL O.S. HAS BEEN MANGLED BY FOREIGN CODE...AS IF BY A CHILD WITH A HAMMER.
HE MUST BE IN CONSTANT PAIN... UNABLE TO DISCERN WHO HE EVEN IS.
WHAT ARE YOU SUGGESTING WE DO?
I SUGGEST WE FIX HIM.

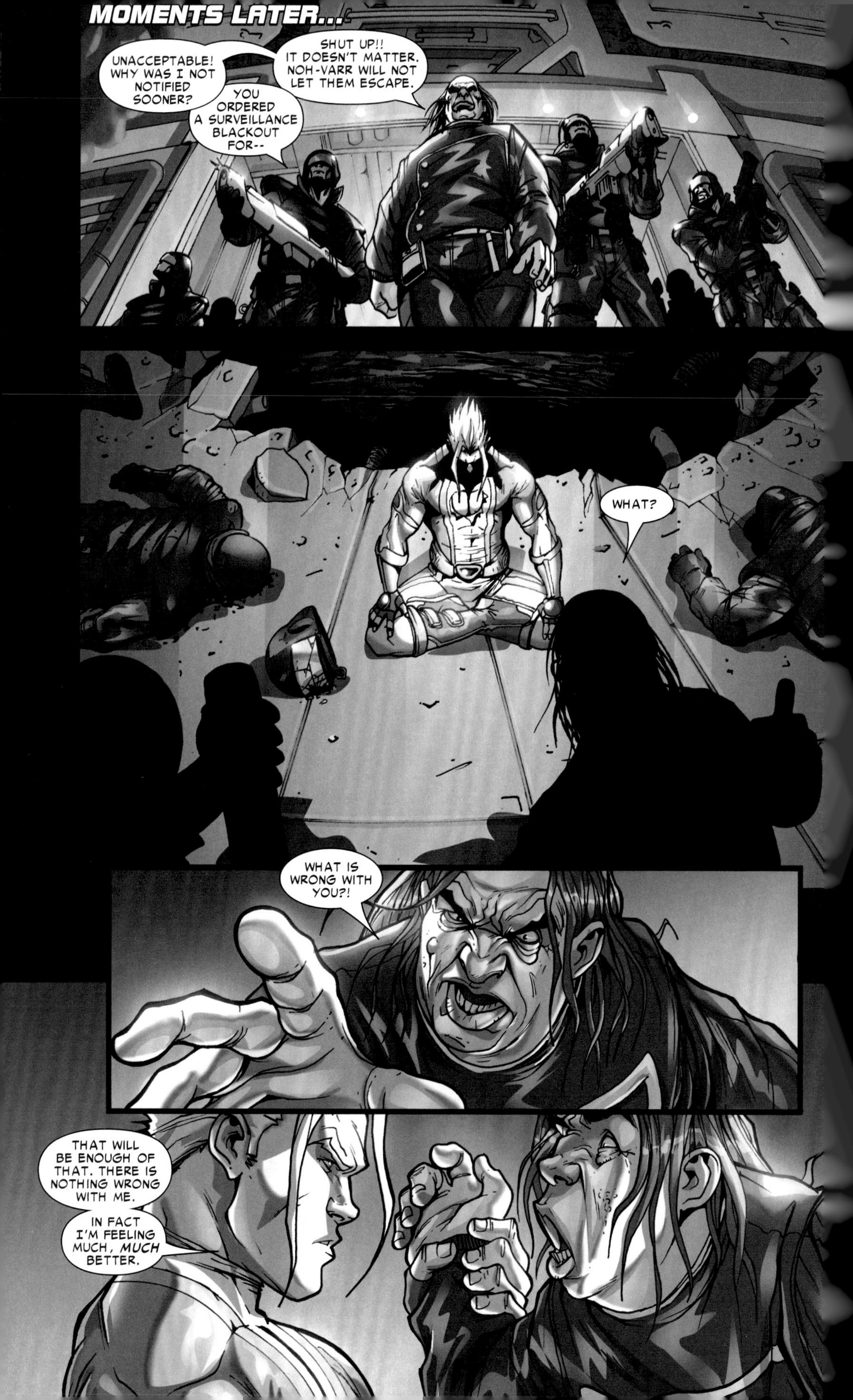
MOMENTS LATER...
UNACCEPTABLE! WHY WAS I NOT NOTIFIED SOONER?
YOU ORDERED A SURVEILLANCE BLACKOUT FOR--
SHUT UP!! IT DOESN'T MATTER. NOH-VARR WILL NOT LET THEM ESCAPE.
WHAT?
WHAT IS WRONG WITH YOU?!
THAT WILL BE ENOUGH OF THAT. THERE IS NOTHING WRONG WITH ME.
IN FACT I'M FEELING MUCH, *MUCH* BETTER.

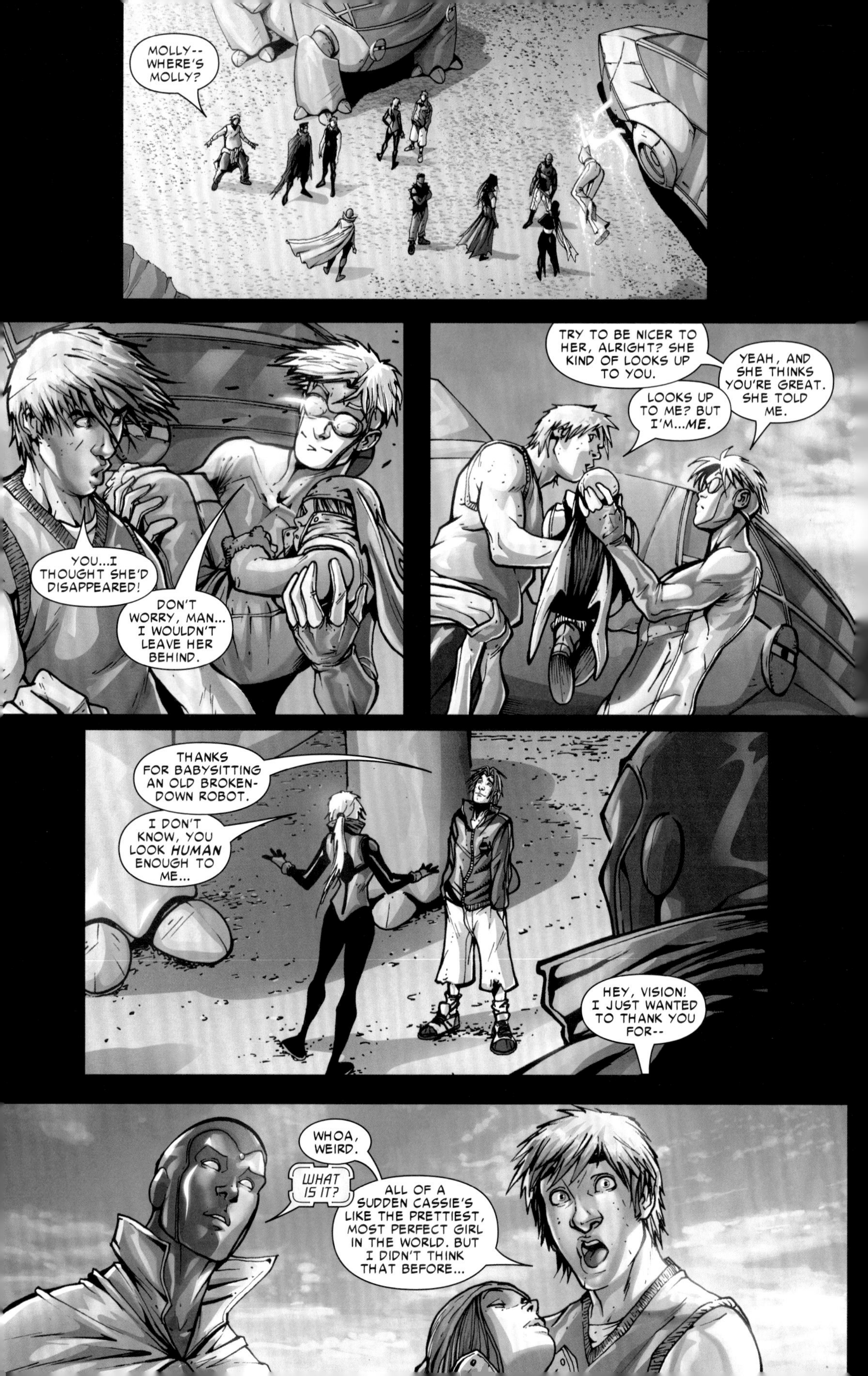
MOLLY-- WHERE'S MOLLY?
YOU...I THOUGHT SHE'D DISAPPEARED!
DON'T WORRY, MAN... I WOULDN'T LEAVE HER BEHIND.
TRY TO BE NICER TO HER, ALRIGHT? SHE KIND OF LOOKS UP TO YOU.
LOOKS UP TO ME? BUT I'M...ME.
YEAH, AND SHE THINKS YOU'RE GREAT. SHE TOLD ME.
THANKS FOR BABYSITTING AN OLD BROKEN-DOWN ROBOT.
I DON'T KNOW, YOU LOOK HUMAN ENOUGH TO ME...
HEY, VISION! I JUST WANTED TO THANK YOU FOR--
WHOA, WEIRD.
WHAT IS IT?
ALL OF A SUDDEN CASSIE'S LIKE THE PRETTIEST, MOST PERFECT GIRL IN THE WORLD. BUT I DIDN'T THINK THAT BEFORE...

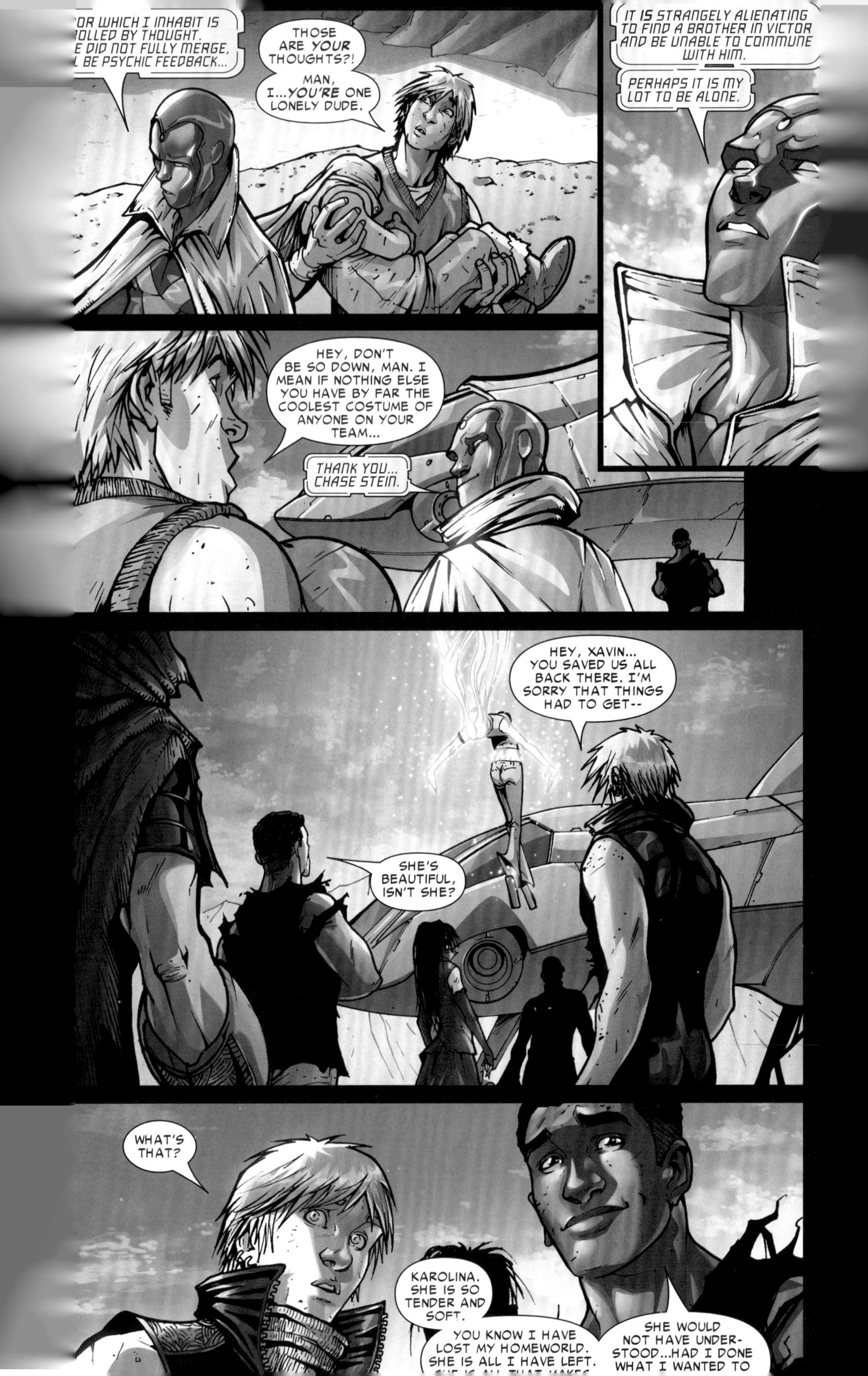

...OR WHICH I INHABIT IS ...ROLLED BY THOUGHT. ...E DID NOT FULLY MERGE, ...L BE PSYCHIC FEEDBACK...
THOSE ARE YOUR THOUGHTS?!
MAN, I...YOU'RE ONE LONELY DUDE.
IT IS STRANGELY ALIENATING TO FIND A BROTHER IN VICTOR AND BE UNABLE TO COMMUNE WITH HIM.
PERHAPS IT IS MY LOT TO BE ALONE.
HEY, DON'T BE SO DOWN, MAN. I MEAN IF NOTHING ELSE YOU HAVE BY FAR THE COOLEST COSTUME OF ANYONE ON YOUR TEAM...
THANK YOU... CHASE STEIN.
HEY, XAVIN... YOU SAVED US ALL BACK THERE. I'M SORRY THAT THINGS HAD TO GET--
SHE'S BEAUTIFUL, ISN'T SHE?
WHAT'S THAT?
KAROLINA. SHE IS SO TENDER AND SOFT.
YOU KNOW I HAVE LOST MY HOMEWORLD. SHE IS ALL I HAVE LEFT.
SHE WOULD NOT HAVE UNDERSTOOD...HAD I DONE WHAT I WANTED TO

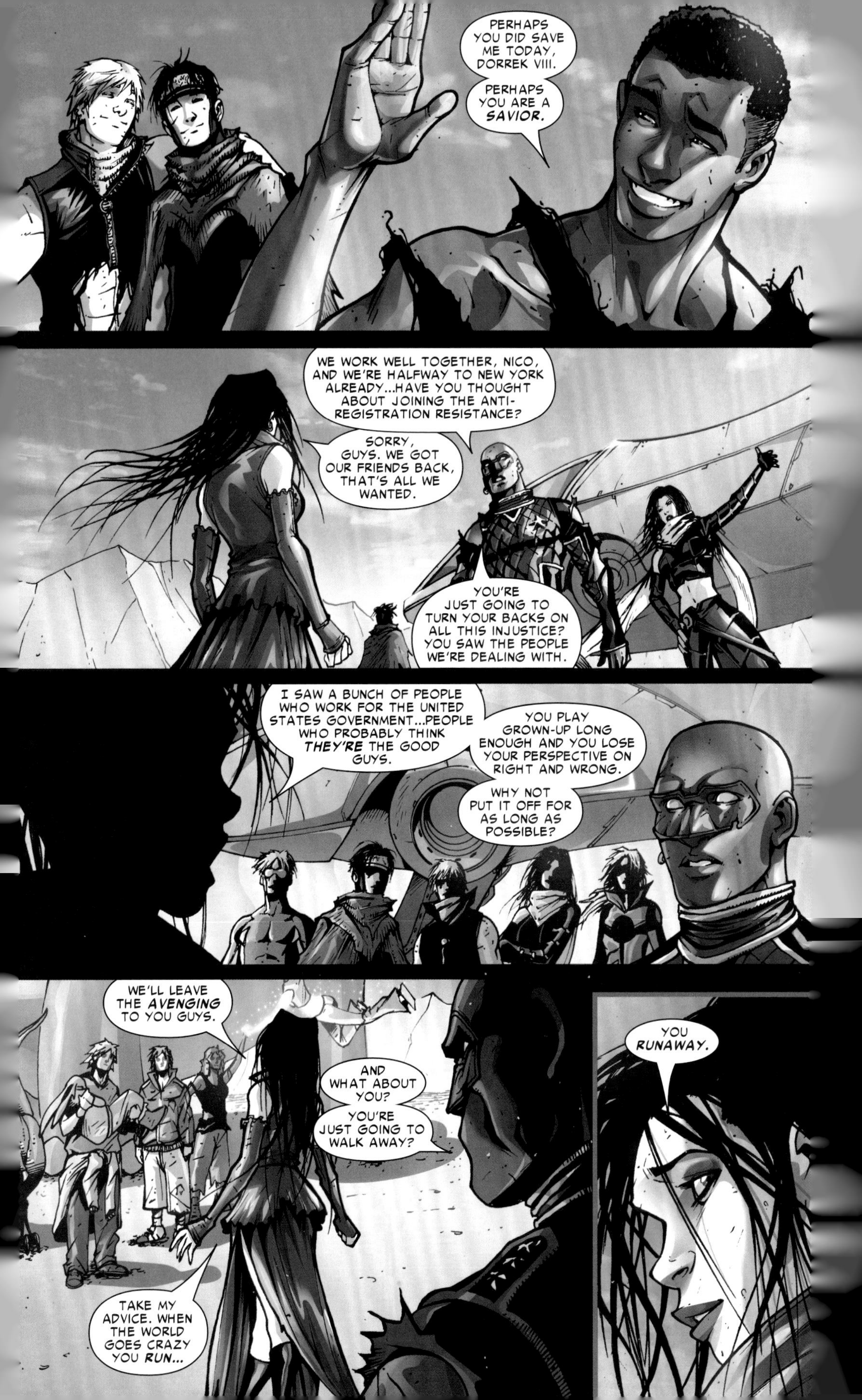
PERHAPS YOU DID SAVE ME TODAY, DORREK VIII.
PERHAPS YOU ARE A SAVIOR.
WE WORK WELL TOGETHER, NICO, AND WE'RE HALFWAY TO NEW YORK ALREADY...HAVE YOU THOUGHT ABOUT JOINING THE ANTI-REGISTRATION RESISTANCE?
SORRY, GUYS. WE GOT OUR FRIENDS BACK, THAT'S ALL WE WANTED.
YOU'RE JUST GOING TO TURN YOUR BACKS ON ALL THIS INJUSTICE? YOU SAW THE PEOPLE WE'RE DEALING WITH.
I SAW A BUNCH OF PEOPLE WHO WORK FOR THE UNITED STATES GOVERNMENT...PEOPLE WHO PROBABLY THINK THEY'RE THE GOOD GUYS.
YOU PLAY GROWN-UP LONG ENOUGH AND YOU LOSE YOUR PERSPECTIVE ON RIGHT AND WRONG.
WHY NOT PUT IT OFF FOR AS LONG AS POSSIBLE?
WE'LL LEAVE THE AVENGING TO YOU GUYS.
AND WHAT ABOUT YOU?
YOU'RE JUST GOING TO WALK AWAY?
TAKE MY ADVICE. WHEN THE WORLD GOES CRAZY YOU RUN...
YOU RUNAWAY.

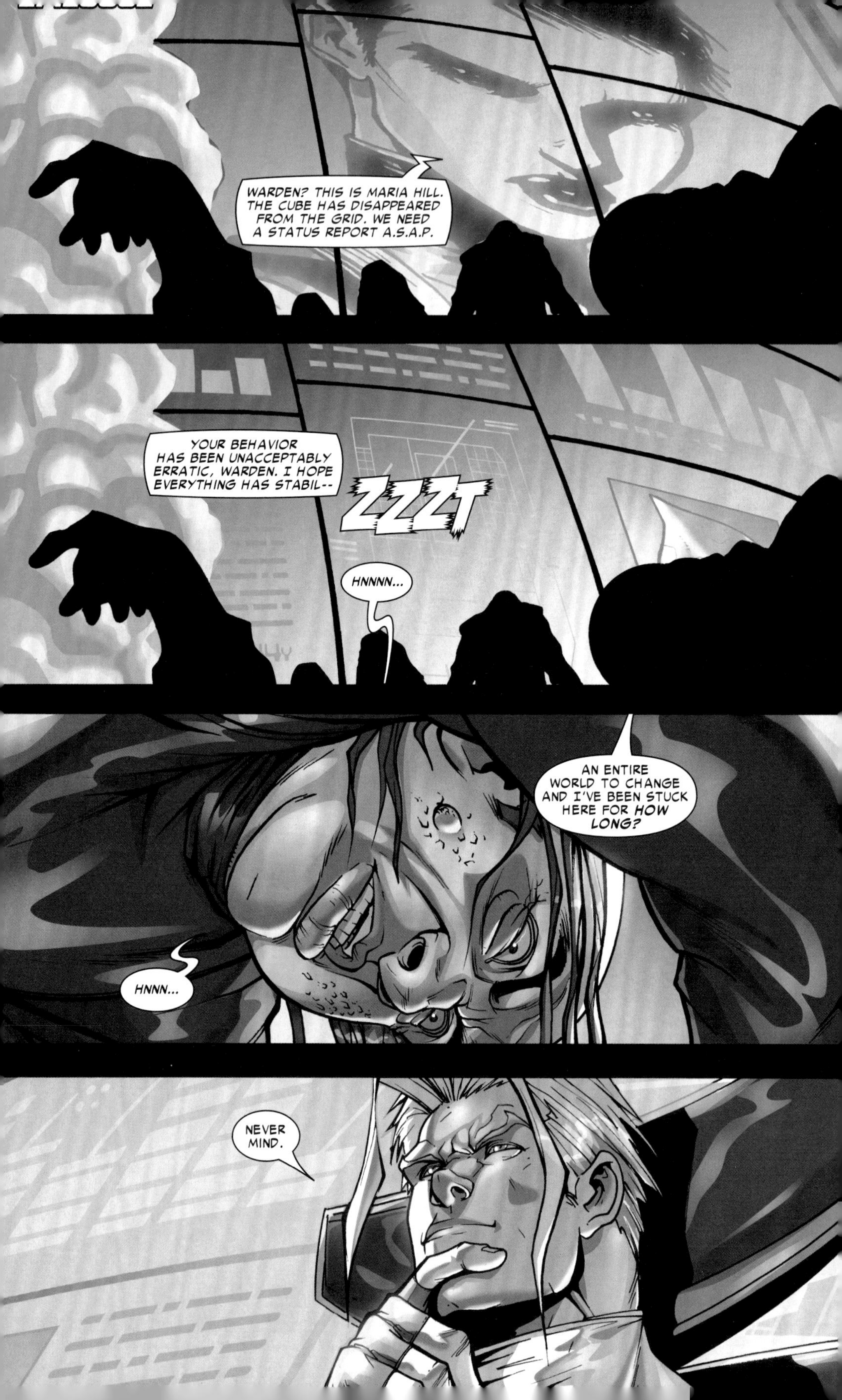
WARDEN? THIS IS MARIA HILL. THE CUBE HAS DISAPPEARED FROM THE GRID. WE NEED A STATUS REPORT A.S.A.P.
YOUR BEHAVIOR HAS BEEN UNACCEPTABLY ERRATIC, WARDEN. I HOPE EVERYTHING HAS STABIL--
ZZZT
HNNNN...
AN ENTIRE WORLD TO CHANGE AND I'VE BEEN STUCK HERE FOR HOW LONG?
HNNN...
NEVER MIND.

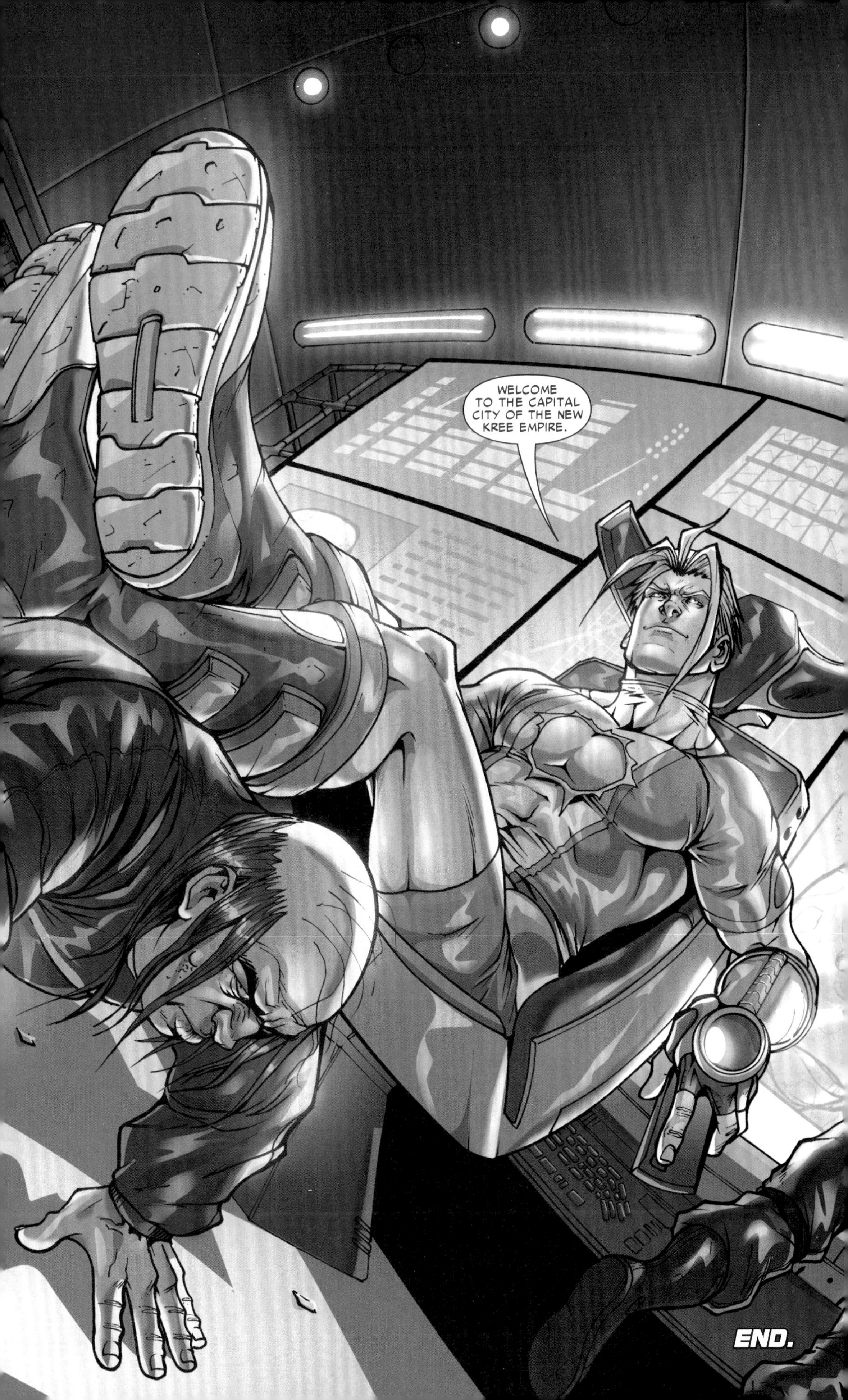
WELCOME TO THE CAPITAL CITY OF THE NEW KREE EMPIRE.
END.

CIVIL WAR: YOUNG AVENGERS & RUNAWAYS COMBINED COVER

ARSENIC/OLD LACE

REAL NAME: Gertrude Yorkes
ALIASES: None
IDENTITY: Secret
OCCUPATION: Adventurer
CITIZENSHIP: U.S.A.
PLACE OF BIRTH: (Arsenic) Los Angeles, California
KNOWN RELATIVES: (Arsenic) Dale Yorkes (father), Stacey Yorkes (mother)
GROUP AFFILIATION: Runaways
EDUCATION: (Arsenic) High school student
FIRST APPEARANCE: (Arsenic) Runaways #1 (2003); (Old Lace) Runaways #2 (2003)

HISTORY: Gertrude Yorkes is the daughter of two fugitive time travellers from the future. Arriving nearly 20 years ago, Dale and Stacey Yorkes were immediately summoned by the Gibborim, a race of ancient giants. Along with five other couples, the Yorkes formed the Pride, ruling the west coast crime scene and making sacrifices to their new masters. Each couple had one child after the Pride's creation, all six of whom were designated to take their parents' places in the Gibborim's new paradise. While Gertrude was a sophomore in high school, she and the other Pride children learned of their parents' secret lives. Exploring the Yorkes' home, Gertrude discovered a gift for her from her parents: a genetically-created female Deinonychus-like dinosaur from the 87th century. She dubbed the creature Old Lace and took on the code name Arsenic for herself, preferring it to her given name. The two joined the other children in trying to expose the Pride's crimes. On the run, the six kids and Old Lace made their home in the Hostel, an abandoned underground mansion. The group, dubbed the Runaways, encountered various threats, including the vampire Topher and corrupt members of the LAPD, while evading the Pride. In the meantime, Gertrude struck up a romance with teammate Talkback (Chase Stein.) A final confrontation with the Gibborim and the teens' parents ended with the apparent deaths of the Pride, as well as turncoat Runaway Alex Wilder. The group was then taken into custody by the state, which separated them and took Old Lace away. They soon regrouped and retrieved the dinosaur before temporarily going back into hiding.

Arsenic and Old Lace remained with the Runaways, who sought to free other children from criminal parents. Following a battle with the Wrecking Crew, an alternate version of Gertrude arrived from the future, warning the team of the potential threat of Victor Mancha before her death. The team tracked down Victor (revealed to be the semi-organic son of Ultron), and battled the team of former teen heroes, Excelsior, in the process. Eventually, the youths reconciled and defeated Ultron. Arsenic and Old Lace have since continued to partake in the Runaways' adventures, including battles against Swarm and a new Tarantula.

HEIGHT: (Arsenic) 5'1"; (Old Lace) 6'11" (length, including tail)
WEIGHT: (Arsenic) 125 lbs.; (Old Lace) 334 lbs.
EYES: (Arsenic) Green; (Old Lace) Red
HAIR: (Arsenic) Brown, dyed purple; (Old Lace) None

ABILITIES/ACCESSORIES: Arsenic is a normal teenaged girl who possesses no superhuman powers, and is allergic to bees. Old Lace has been genetically created to be empathetically linked to Arsenic, and will follow any command she gives, as well as feel any pain or emotion its master experiences. Old Lace will only follow the instructions of others at Arsenic's command.

ARSENIC

POWER GRID	1 2 3 4 5 6 7
INTELLIGENCE	4
STRENGTH	1
SPEED	2
DURABILITY	2
ENERGY PROJECTION	1
FIGHTING SKILLS	1

OLD LACE

POWER GRID	1 2 3 4 5 6 7
INTELLIGENCE	1
STRENGTH	3
SPEED	3
DURABILITY	3
…JECTION	1
…S	3

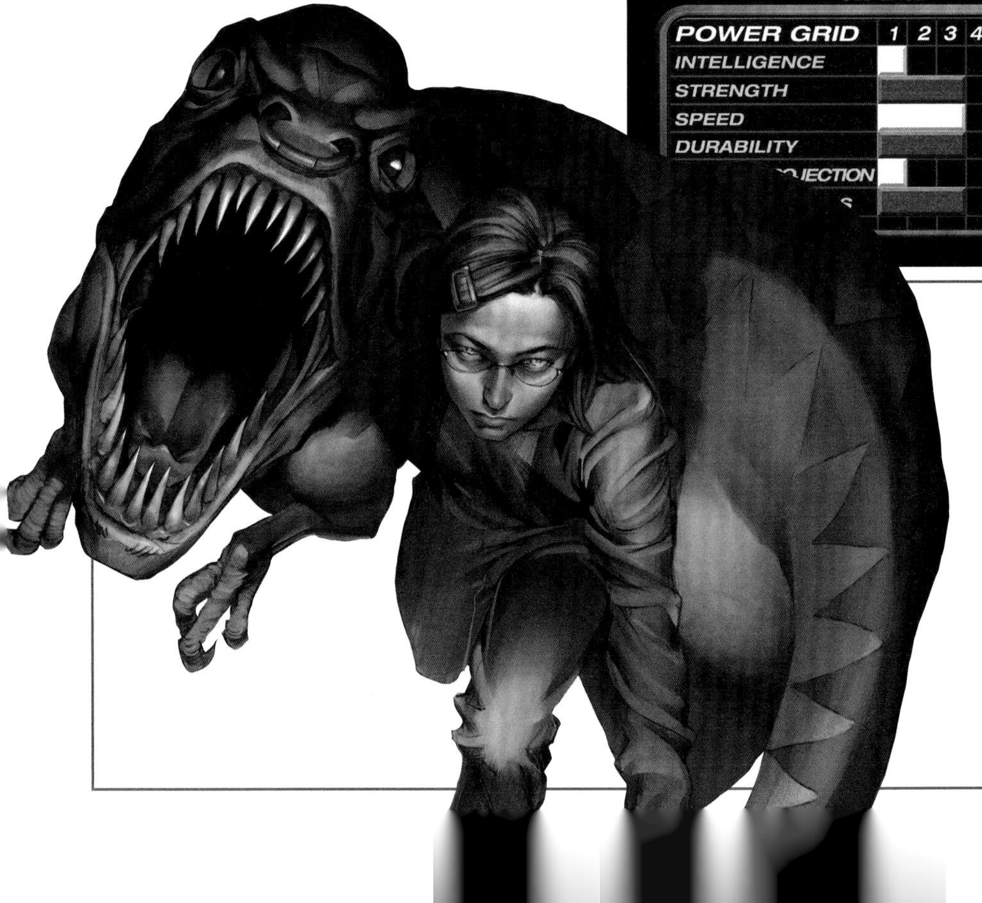

HISTORY: Mutant couple Gene and Alice Hayes joined five other uniquely gifted couples in supplying ritual sacrifices for the Gibborim, a race of ancient giants, in return for the power to rule Los Angeles for 25 years. Knowing only six beings would be spared the creatures' destruction of humanity, the group, known as the Pride, opted to have each couple conceive a single child, who would be the survivors. Alice gave birth to a girl, Molly.

The Hayeses annually attended the sacrifices, held in the home of the Wilder family. The Pride's children attended as well, believing the event to be merely a social gathering. During one such event when Molly was 11, Alex Wilder showed off a secret passageway to the other kids. The Pride was preparing to kill a local prostitute, an act which several of the kids witnessed. Molly was absent and the others decided not to include the younger girl while trying to learn more about their parents. The Pride soon learned of the children's discovery and used Molly as a hostage to force their return. The kids came to rescue Molly, and when she saw Nico Minoru strike Alice Hayes, Molly's mutant abilities emerged. Initially confused, Molly eventually helped subdue one of the Pride members. After the children escaped, the Pride used their contacts to blame Alex for the murder and Molly's kidnapping.

The children, now known as the Runaways, hid out in an underground mansion known as the Hostel. They formed a pact and decided to use their powers not only to expose the Pride, but to stop crime as well. Molly was disappointed when her teammate Talkback dubbed her Bruiser, preferring to be called Princess Powerful. She was excited by the idea of becoming a super-hero, and even wore a costume when the group ran afoul of the vigilantes Cloak and Dagger. The Runaways learned of the Pride's next rite and followed their parents to the Gibborim's undersea lair. Despite their betrayal by Alex, the team ended the plot when Bruiser destroyed the canister containing a sacrificial soul. The Gibborim apparently killed the Pride for their failure and tried to do the same to the Runaways, but they escaped. With the Pride exposed, Molly was placed in an X-Corporation school. Her teammate Arsenic freed her and they soon rejoined the others. The Runaways set out to stop criminals such as the Wrecking Crew, and Bruiser single-handedly defeated their would-be member Excavator. The team also thwarted other menaces such as Swarm, a new Tarantula and Ultron. Though younger than the other Runaways, Bruiser continues to be instrumental in their exploits.

REAL NAME: Molly Hayes
KNOWN ALIASES: Princess Powerful
IDENTITY: Secret
OCCUPATION: Adventurer
CITIZENSHIP: U.S.A., still a minor
PLACE OF BIRTH: Los Angeles, California
KNOWN RELATIVES: Alice Hayes (mother), Gene Hayes (father)
GROUP AFFILIATION: Runaways
EDUCATION: Junior high school dropout
FIRST APPEARANCE: Runaways #1 (2003)

HEIGHT: 4'11"
WEIGHT: 97 lbs.
EYES: Blue
HAIR: Brown

ABILITIES/ACCESSORIES: Bruiser possesses superhuman strength, increasing as she matures, though its use quickly saps Bruiser's energy, making her drowsy. Occasionally, her eyes and hair-tips glow during power usage.

POWER GRID	1	2	3	4	5	6	7
INTELLIGENCE							
STRENGTH							
SPEED							
DURABILITY							
ENERGY PROJECTION							
FIGHTING SKILLS							

HAWKEYE

REAL NAME: Katherine "Kate" Elizabeth Bishop
ALIASES: Hawkingbird, Mockingbird, Taskmistress, Weapon Woman
IDENTITY: Secret
OCCUPATION: Student
CITIZENSHIP: U.S.A.
PLACE OF BIRTH: New York City, New York
KNOWN RELATIVES: Derek Bishop (father), Eleanor Bishop (mother, deceased), Susan Bishop (sister)
GROUP AFFILIATION: Young Avengers
EDUCATION: Enrolled at Hawthorne Academy preparatory school
FIRST APPEARANCE: (Bishop) Young Avengers #1 (2005); (Hawkeye) Young Avengers #12 (2006)

HISTORY: The daughter of rich publishing magnate Derek Bishop, Kate Bishop never felt comfortable with wealth; like her mother, she donated time and money to soup kitchens, women's shelters, and other worthy causes. After her mother was killed, Kate became even more active in charity. Later attacked and raped in Central Park, Kate received the best therapy that money could buy; she also undertook an intensive physical fitness and self-defense training regimen, determined never again to let herself or anyone else be victimized if she could prevent it. At her upscale private school, the Hawthorne Academy, and at the elite Interlochen National Music Camp, Kate studied archery, fencing, kickboxing, and various martial arts.

A major social event, Kate's sister's wedding at New York's St. Patrick's Cathedral was interrupted by five gunmen who held the guests hostage when the police cornered them inside. When the novice heroes known as the "Young Avengers" subdued most of the gunmen, Kate tried to join the fight and ended up with a gun to her head, but used one of Patriot's throwing stars to down her assailant. Kate's "heroics" made the evening news, and when Cassie Lang sought her out trying to locate the Young Avengers, the two girls tracked the group to the ruins of Avengers Mansion, where the senior Avengers were trying to convince their youthful counterparts to disband. Carefully observing Iron Man as he unlocked doors, Kate used his passcodes to free Cassie and the Young Avengers after the Avengers confined them for their own safety. She also scavenged costumes and weaponry from nearby rooms, outfitting herself with equipment formerly used by past Avengers members Hawkeye (Clint Barton), Mockingbird (Bobbi Morse), and the Swordsman (Jacques Duquesne). When the Avengers and Young Avengers battled Kang, Kate fought beside them, but afterwards was forced to surrender the equipment.

Unwilling to give up the chance to make a real difference, Kate pushed the other Young Avengers to remain together, using her father's funds to purchase new costumes and weaponry for the team. Appropriating an empty publishing warehouse of her father's to use as team headquarters, she arranged its refitting and refurbishing. When Patriot left the group, she acted as unofficial leader in his absence despite being the only Young Avenger both without powers and the only member who had not been part of the Vision's Failsafe Program (a list of young Avengers-connected adventurers and potential adventurers compiled by the Vision as a means of recruiting the next generation of Avengers should the original team be dissolved; Iron Lad accessed this list, using it to form the Young Avengers). Her lack of a code name earned her several nicknames, from Hawkingbird to Weapon Woman, but she finally adopted the costumed alias "Hawkeye."

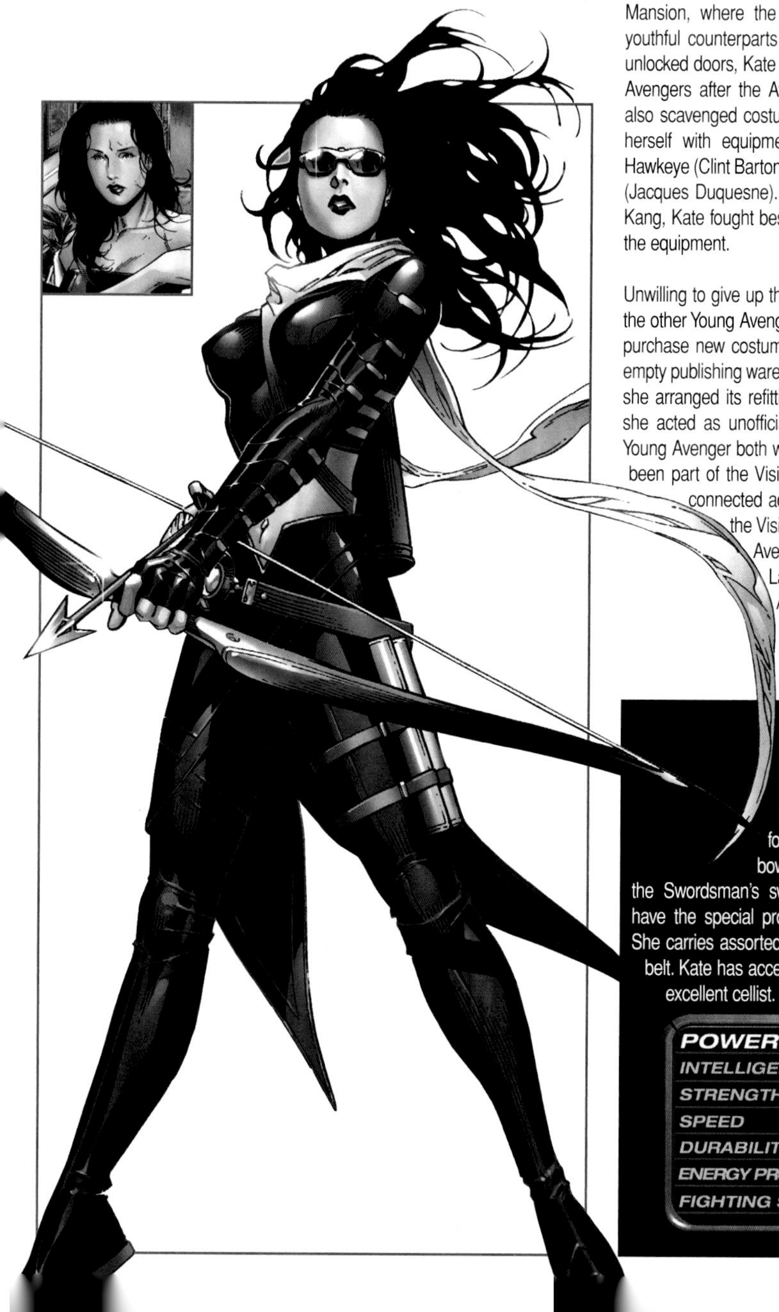

HEIGHT: 5'5" **EYES:** Blue
WEIGHT: 120 lbs. **HAIR:** Black

ABILITIES/ACCESSORIES: Highly athletic, Kate is skilled with various weapons and combat forms. Her weaponry is modeled on Hawkeye's bow and arrows, Mockingbird's battle staves, and the Swordsman's sword. It is unknown whether these weapons have the special properties and features that their templates did. She carries assorted smaller accessories in pouches in and on her belt. Kate has access to great wealth through her father. She is an excellent cellist.

POWER GRID	1	2	3	4	5	6	7
INTELLIGENCE	■	■	■				
STRENGTH	■	■					
SPEED	■	■					
DURABILITY	■	■					
ENERGY PROJECTION	■						
FIGHTING SKILLS	■	■	■				

HULKLING

HISTORY: During the interstellar Kree-Skrull War, the Kree Captain Mar-Vell fell in love with the Skrull Princess Anelle. She bore a child, Dorrek VIII, but when when her father learned the identity of the infant's father, the Emperor ordered the baby's death. The child's nurse escaped with him to Earth, where she established human identities for both of them. He was raised as human "Teddy Altman" without knowing his alien origin, and when his powers manifested, Teddy believed he was a mutant. He shared his secret with his friend Greg Norris, who exploited Teddy and tried to use his powers to plunder Avengers Mansion after the Scarlet Witch destroyed it. Teddy refused; shortly afterwards, he encountered the time-traveling Iron Lad, who recruited Teddy and two other teenaged heroes to form the Young Avengers, inspired by the celebrated Avengers super-team (in fact, Iron Lad chose recruits who were all somehow connected to the Avengers, whether they knew it or not). During their time together, Teddy, code-named "Hulkling," began a romantic relationship with teammate Asgardian (later called Wiccan).

When the Young Avengers made their activities public, Avengers founders Captain America and Iron Man resolved to shut them down, confronting them at Avengers Mansion. Iron Lad's future self, long time Avengers foe Kang the Conqueror, arrived shortly thereafter. During the ensuing battle, Iron Lad was forced to return to his native era to save the timestream. With Kang defeated, the Avengers ordered the would-be heroes to give up their adventuring; but Kate Bishop supplied the youths with new uniforms and other resources, and they defeated such criminals as Shocker and Mr. Hyde. Despite this, the Avengers once again ordered their youthful counterparts to give up their costumed identities for their own safety.

The teens regrouped to decide their next step, but were attacked by the Super-Skrull, who exposed Hulkling's mother as a Skrull before killing her and kidnapping Teddy. He took the boy to his lair, where he tried to contact the Skrull Empire. The Super-Skrull began to reveal the truth of his origins to Teddy, but was interrupted when the Young Avengers arrived. The battle was short-lived, as a group of Kree soldiers also intervened, demanding the son of Mar-Vell be handed over to them. Teddy refused to leave Earth with either the Skrulls or the Kree, and despite the Avengers promising to protect him, Hulkling unintentionally ignited a new Kree-Skrull War. With his legendary heritage revealed to him, Hulkling remains a proud member of the Young Avengers.

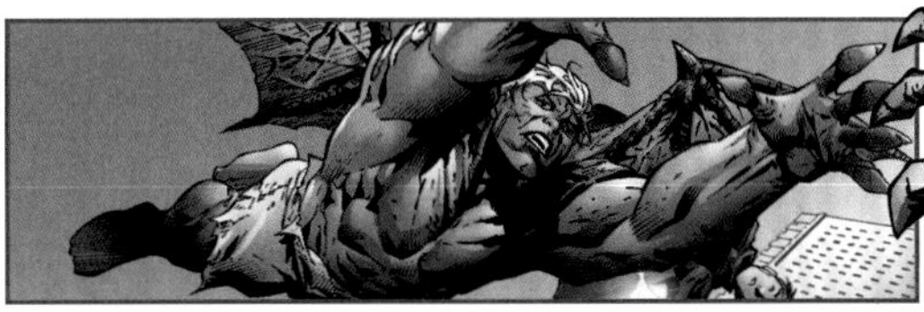

REAL NAME: Dorrek VIII
ALIASES: Theodore "Teddy" Altman
IDENTITY: Secret
OCCUPATION: Student, adventurer
CITIZENSHIP: U.S.A.
PLACE OF BIRTH: Skrull Throneworld
KNOWN RELATIVES: Mar-Vell (Captain Marvel, father, deceased), Anelle (mother, deceased), Genis-Vell (Photon, half-brother, deceased), Phyla (half-sister), Dorrek VII (grandfather, deceased), R'kill (grandmother, deceased), Dezan (great uncle)
GROUP AFFILIATION: Young Avengers
EDUCATION: High school student
FIRST APPEARANCE: Young Avengers #1 (2005)

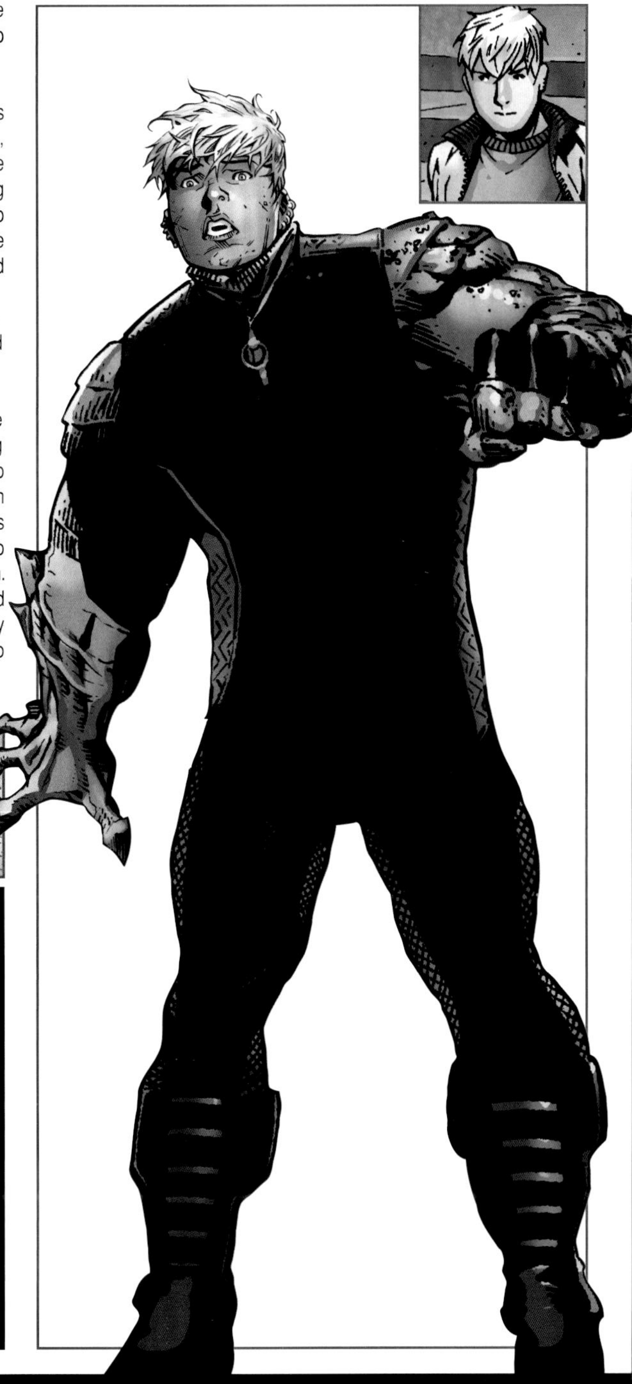

HEIGHT: Variable
WEIGHT: Variable
EYES: Variable, usually blue
HAIR: Variable, usually blond

ABILITIES/ACCESSORIES: Like all Skrulls, Hulkling can change his shape to impersonate any other being. He often assumes the appearance of a muscular green humanoid, and sometimes sprouts wings from his back enabling him to fly. He has as-yet-unquantified superhuman strength.

POWER GRID	1	2	3	4	5	6	7
INTELLIGENCE	■	■	■	■			
STRENGTH	■	■	■	■	■	■	
SPEED	■	■	■				
DURABILITY	■	■	■	■	■	■	
ENERGY PROJECTION	■	■					
FIGHTING SKILLS	■	■	■				

Art by Jim Cheung

IRON LAD

REAL NAME: Nathaniel Richards
ALIASES: Young Kang
IDENTITY: Secret
OCCUPATION: Adventurer; former student
CITIZENSHIP: Earth-6311 (Other-Earth), 31st century
PLACE OF BIRTH: Earth-6311, 31st century
KNOWN RELATIVES: Extended family (see Immortus)
GROUP AFFILIATION: Formerly Young Avengers (founder)
EDUCATION: High school student
FIRST APPEARANCE: Young Avengers #1 (2005)

HISTORY: In the year 3016 on the technologically-advanced alternate world known as Other-Earth (Earth-6311), 16-year-old robotics student Nathaniel Richards was rescued from a near-fatal attack by his future self, the megalomaniacal time-traveler Kang the Conqueror. Kang gave young Nathaniel a suit of neuro-kinetic armor and provided a glimpse of his future as a conqueror. Horrified by his ruthless, destructive future self, young Nathaniel rejected Kang and used his armor to escape to modern-day Earth-616, seeking the Avengers so that they could help him defeat Kang.

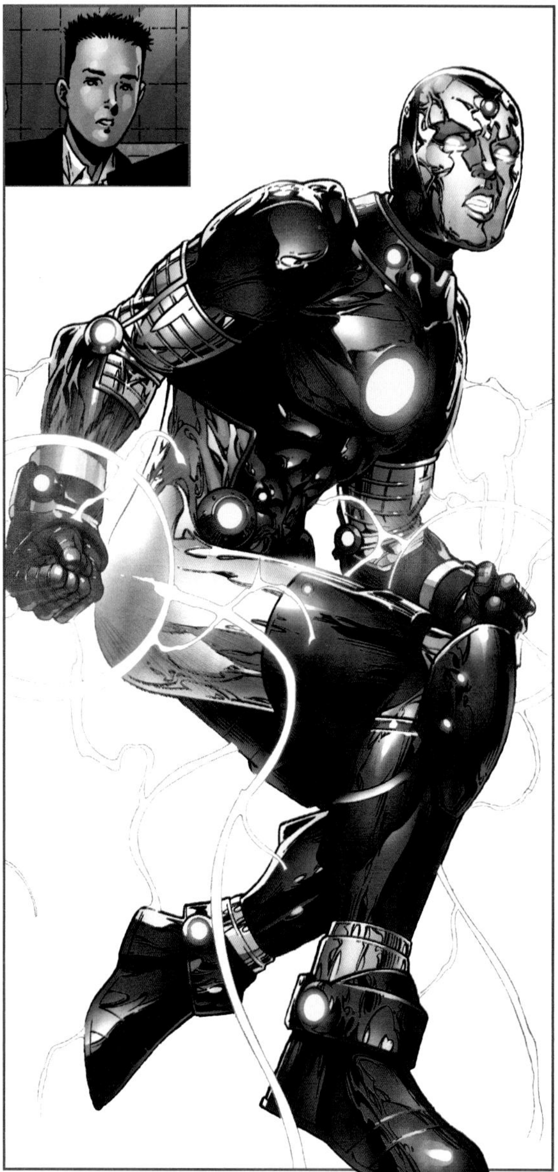

Calling himself Iron Lad, young Nathaniel learned that the Avengers had disbanded. After failed attempts to contact former Avengers, Iron Lad broke into Stark Industries and found the remnants of the Vision, the recently-destroyed synthezoid Avenger. Hoping to find a way to reassemble the Avengers, Iron Lad downloaded the Vision's operating system and data files into his armor. Instead, Iron Lad found a failsafe program designed to pinpoint the exact locations of the next wave of young Avengers (super-powered youths with significant ties to the Avengers themselves or to Avengers history). Iron Lad used this data to recruit three "Young Avengers" who resided in New York City: Patriot (Elijah Bradley), Hulkling (Teddy Altman), and Asgardian (Billy Kaplan). Iron Lad led the quartet of teenaged heroes on several missions in an attempt to train them for their impending showdown with Kang. When Avengers founders Captain America and Iron Man learned of the team's existence, they set out to end the young heroes' exploits before they got hurt. The adult heroes located the Young Avengers and were about to send them home when the adult Kang approached them and convinced the heroes to hand over Iron Lad to him. The Young Avengers resisted and, in the ensuing melee, Iron Lad became romantically involved with fellow teen hero Stature (Cassie Lang). Iron Lad killed Kang, but later realized that he had to return to his native era to fulfil his destiny as Kang so that the damaged timestream would be restored. The Vision, whose programming had reasserted itself within the armor, used the armor's chronal programming to send Iron Lad home. Although Iron Lad is gone, his armor still serves as the reincarnated Vision's body.

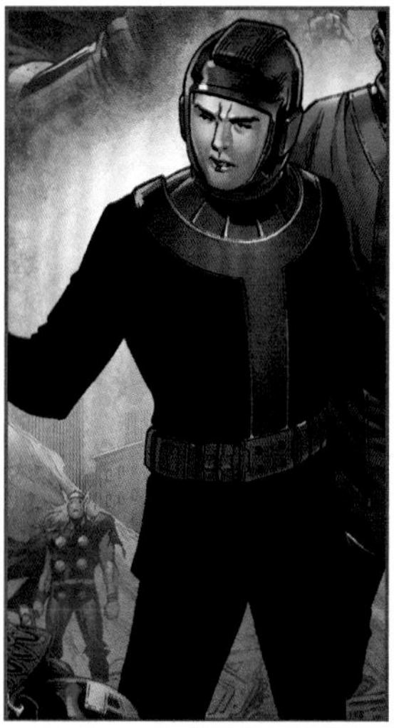

Iron Lad was last seen dressed as Kang the Conqueror, monitoring the activities of the Young Avengers from an undisclosed location in the future.

HEIGHT: 5'9"
WEIGHT: 166 lbs.
EYES: Brown
HAIR: Brown

ABILITIES/ACCESSORIES: Iron Lad ages slightly more slowly than modern humanity. Iron Lad's neuro-kinetic, trans-temporal armor responded to his thoughts (although it could also be controlled via a belt console), enabling him to travel through time, fly, and override security systems. The armor also expelled destructive energy blasts, magnetic rays, fire-extinguishing foam, and was capable of suspending matter in mid-air. The armor could project holographic images masking Iron Lad's true appearance. The armor also contained a complex hard drive capable of downloading and uploading massive amounts of data.

POWER GRID	1	2	3	4	5	6	7
INTELLIGENCE	■	■	■	■			
STRENGTH	■	■	■	■			
SPEED	■	■	■	■	■	■	■
DURABILITY	■	■	■	■	■		
ENERGY PROJECTION	■	■	■	■	■	■	
FIGHTING SKILLS	■	■	■				

Art by Jim Cheung

HISTORY: After being destroyed and left in a scrap yard by the Avengers, the megalomaniacal robot Ultron's still-active CPU realized patience was needed to defeat his enemies. Years later, architecture student and former drug smuggler Marianella Mancha was stealing materials for a school project at the scrap yard when Ultron persuaded her to take its remnants home. Ultron convinced the devoutly religious Marianella that it was a prophet and promised the infertile woman that it would build her an immaculate creation in exchange for gathering supplies to help Ultron construct a new body. Using Marianella's DNA, Ultron created a cybernetic/human hybrid, which Marianella named "Victor." Ultron filled Victor's brain with false memories of a full life as a human boy and gave him a fervent desire to one day become a superhero. Ultron programmed his creation with latent electromagnetic powers which were not intended to activate until a programmed trip to New York City on his supposed 21st birthday when he would meet the Avengers. Told that his father was a U.S. Marine who died in combat, Victor enrolled in East Angeles High School, although Marianella was preparing to make him transfer when she heard the school was installing metal detectors.

Meanwhile, the teenaged adventurers known as the Runaways encountered Heroine (a future version of Runaways member Arsenic), who had traveled 20 years back in time to warn them of Victorious (Victor Mancha), a super-powered being from her future. Before dying, Heroine informed the Runaways that Victorious would pose as a hero to gain their trust and then turn on them, slaughtering nearly every superhero on the planet. The Runaways tracked down Victor and tried to question him, but the confrontation triggered Victor's powers prematurely and soon devolved into a battle, leading to Victor being taken into custody by the team. When the Runaways' transport, the Leapfrog, was disabled by anti-vigilante group Excelsior, Victor used his powers to recharge the vehicle and facilitate his captors' escape. While the Runaways tried to determine Victor's father's identity, Victor was contacted by Ultron (posing as Dr. Doom), who had kidnapped Marianella in order to lure Victor to his headquarters at McArthur Warehouse. Victor and the Runaways battled a Doombot before Ultron revealed himself, killing Marianella and taking control of Victor's programming. Victor, however, resisted Ultron's influence and the Runaways defeated Ultron with Excelsior's aid.

Now orphaned, Victor joined the Runaways on probationary status, helping them against former Nazi scientist Swarm; Xavin, a Super-Skrull-in-training; Cloak imposter Reginald Mantz; and even the X-Men when they tried to recruit mutant Runaways member Bruiser. Although

REAL NAME: Victor Mancha
ALIASES: None
IDENTITY: No dual Identity (general public is unaware Mancha is a cyborg)
OCCUPATION: Adventurer
CITIZENSHIP: U.S.A.
PLACE OF CREATION: Los Angeles, California
KNOWN RELATIVES: Ultron (creator), Marianella Mancha (mother, deceased)
GROUP AFFILIATION: Runaways
EDUCATION: High school dropout
FIRST APPEARANCE: Runaways #1 (2005)

he is slowly gaining his teammates' trust, Victor still fears he is being manipulated by Ultron's programming. Most recently, Hunter, a member of the New Pride, a group dedicated to destroying the Runaways, had secretly hacked into Victor's brain and used him as an unwitting intelligence-gathering tool, but the Runaways discovered this and Victor created an internal firewall to prevent further intrusions into his systems.

HEIGHT: 5'9"   **EYES:** Hazel
WEIGHT: 197 lbs.   **HAIR:** Brown

ABILITIES/ACCESSORIES: Victor is a cybernetic/human hybrid whose skeleton is composed of nanites which will eventually metamorphose until they are indistinguishable from his human cells. He has infrared vision and superhuman strength, speed, and durability. Victor is powered by an electromagnet which enables him to manipulate metal, fire electromagnetic blasts, and fly. Victor is extremely intelligent and possesses a fanboyish knowledge of superhero history. Mancha also has a natural aptitude for engineering and electronics, serving as the Runaways' resident mechanic.

POWER GRID	1	2	3	4	5	6	7
INTELLIGENCE							
STRENGTH							
SPEED							
DURABILITY							
ENERGY PROJECTION							
FIGHTING SKILLS							

VICTORIUS

REAL NAME: Noh-Varr
ALIASES: Ensign Marvel
OCCUPATION: Extradimensional peacekeeper, Kree missionary
CITIZENSHIP: Kree Empire (otherdimensional version)
PLACE OF BIRTH: Unrevealed (alternate reality)
KNOWN RELATIVES: None
GROUP AFFILIATION: Formerly 18th Kree Diplomatic Gestalt
EDUCATION: Unrevealed
FIRST APPEARANCE: Marvel Boy #1 (2000)

HISTORY: Genetically engineered with cockroach DNA, the extradimensional Kree Noh-Varr joined the 18th Kree Diplomatic Gestalt, a team of intergalactic peacekeepers who became lost in

transdimensional space when they encountered 3 astro-gods siphoning energy to explore Hypospace (the Omniverse). During the encounter, space-time collapsed, and the group was forced to escape through Macrospace. They careened through the Microverse and explored a multitude of realities while trapped there, until the alien-obsessed Midas caught their S.O.S., trapped them on Earth-616, and destroyed their ship. The sole survivor, Noh-Varr escaped Midas and destroyed his building before retreating to the New York subway system, which he made his temporary home. The enraged Noh-Varr, who had lost his lover Merree in the crash, took his aggression out on New York City, battling S.H.I.E.L.D. and their new experimental superteam, the Bannermen, a team of genetically enhanced superhumans pumped with gamma radiation and laced with Adamantium, whom he easily defeated. After destroying the living, planet-conquering corporation Hexus by sending their trade secrets to other companies and making them obsolete, Noh-Varr met Midas' head assassin and daughter, Exterminatrix.

Battling the Exterminatrix and Midas throughout New York City, Noh-Varr lost. Midas was about to kill him when Exterminatrix rescued Noh-Varr and escaped with him. Noh-Varr and Exterminatrix bonded over their mutual hatred for her father before Midas' agents, including one of the Dark Dimension's Mindless Ones, discovered them, forcing them to flee once more. Encountering the Cosmic Man, a renamed and newly empowered Midas, Noh-Varr immediately shot him in the head, which barely affected him. As Cosmic Man toyed with Noh-Varr, Exterminatrix used the decapitated Mindless One's head to shunt her father into the Dark Dimension, where he was attacked and seemingly killed by a large horde of the Mindless Ones. While Exterminatrix mourned her father, S.H.I.E.L.D. captured Noh-Varr and dragged him away to the Cube, a giant prison for super-villains, which Noh-Varr promised would be the capital of the new Kree empire within five months.

HEIGHT: 5'10"		**EYES:** Black
WEIGHT: 165 lbs.		**HAIR:** White

ABILITIES/ACCESSORIES: Noh-Varr is incredibly strong and fast, and much more durable than an average human being or Kree. His reaction time is high enough to dodge bullets with ease. Possibly due to his super-speed, Noh-Varr can walk up walls, defying gravity. His saliva is full of nanotechnology and triggers hallucinations in anybody it comes into contact with. He can grow or solidify his hair at will. When he finds himself in great danger, Noh-Varr can perform a "White Run" where his instincts fully take over, allowing him to run with no distractions at top speeds capable of outrunning a speeding motorcycle.

Due to his ancestry and space travels, Noh-Varr has many advanced weapons, most of which he has some idea of how to use, including the Marvel, his spaceship. His notable accessories include the Plex Intelligence, his ship's living databank, his gauntlet (which he can transform into a gun at will), his super-dense costume (lined with alien metals), and the Pocket Battlefield, which chooses between nine different battlefield situations, depending on whatever is needed at the time, and shifts whoever enters it into a pocket dimension with its own specialized physics.

POWER GRID	1	2	3	4	5	6	7
INTELLIGENCE							
STRENGTH							
SPEED							
DURABILITY							
ENERGY PROJECTION							
FIGHTING SKILLS							

HISTORY: Elijah "Eli" Bradley is the grandson of Isaiah Bradley, the "Black Captain America" and last known survivor of immoral U.S. army attempts to recreate and refine Dr. Erskine's super-soldier formula by experimenting on large numbers of African-American soldiers.

In February 1942, following the bombing of Pearl Harbor, Isaiah enlisted in the army, leaving behind his pregnant wife and going off to basic training He joined an African-American battalion at Camp Cathcart, Mississippi, training under Sergeant Lucas Evans; however, unknown even to Cathcart's Commanding Officer, Major Brackett, the camp existed solely to gather test subjects for Project Super Soldier. In May 1942, Project Super Soldier requisitioned two battalions of the troops; to prevent word spreading to other African-American soldiers, the rest of Camp Cathcart was massacred on the orders of Colonel Walker Price of Military Intelligence, a slaughter overseen by the racist Lieutenant Phillip Merritt. The soldiers' families were informed their loved ones had died in explosions, and shipped random body parts to bury. Meanwhile, the Project carried out a horrific and mostly fatal series of clinical tests to refine dosages and perfect the formula; only seven men survived, including Evans, Isaiah, Maurice Canfield, Jack Harvey, Dave Plumb, and the sociopathic Damon Larsen.

When word from British intelligence suggested the Nazi counterpart to the Project was also making progress, the seven remaining soldiers were made operational, in spite of the protests of Reinstein — a German scientist who had adopted Erskine's codename and was continuing his work — that the formula was not yet perfected. They were loaded into a ship's hold and transported to Europe; en route Jack Harvey died, confirming Reinstein's assertion. In July of 1942, the six survivors were dropped over the Black Forest, Germany, to intercept a supply convoy meant for Camp Schwarzebitte, where Ernst Koch was carrying out the Nazi experiments. Two of them were swiftly cut down by enemy fire, and Larsen was killed by a grenade because he took too much time sadistically strangling a German soldier, reducing the company to three: Canfield, Evans, and Isaiah. Losing the supplies slowed down the Nazi efforts, preventing them from testing their formula, but did not stop it. Two months later, in Portugal, the trio awaited the arrival of Steve Rogers, Captain America, from the Pacific Theatre, so the four could be sent in to destroy Schwarzebitte. Overhearing Maurice making disparaging remarks about Captain America's costume, Lt. Merritt let slip that Maurice's father had murdered his wife and committed suicide after being informed his son was dead. Maurice went berserk and tried to kill Merritt, and when Evans and Isaiah tried to hold them back, Maurice threw Isaiah off a wall and crushed Evans' skull with a rock slab. Their actions gave Merritt time to draw his pistol, and he shot Maurice dead.

With Captain America delayed and only one surviving African-American super soldier, the Schwarzebitte assignment was redesignated a suicide mission and Isaiah sent in alone. Before he departed, Isaiah stole a Captain America costume and armed himself with his own shield, emblazoned with a Double Victory (at home and overseas) design. Thus garbed, Isaiah single-handedly destroyed much of the Camp, slaying Koch and destroying records and laboratories, setting the Nazi project back considerably. Trying to free Jewish prisoners, Isaiah mistakenly took refuge in what proved to be a gas chamber. He survived the gas, but was captured and delivered to Berlin, where Hitler personally tried to win him over, hoping to use him as a propaganda tool to heighten racial tensions in the U.S. and weaken their war effort. Isaiah refused, and after torture also failed to break him, Goebbels suggested he be given to Mengele for examination followed by maiming, intending to ship him home alive but dismembered as an example; however, on the road to Auschwitz, members of the German anti-Nazi resistance freed Isaiah. They hid him for five months before smuggling him through Belgium and back to the Allies. As soon as Isaiah reported to command, though, he was

REAL NAME: Elijah "Eli" Bradley
ALIASES: None
IDENTITY: Secret
OCCUPATION: High school student, part time librarian
CITIZENSHIP: U.S.A.
PLACE OF BIRTH: Unrevealed
KNOWN RELATIVES: Isaiah Bradley (grandfather), Faith Shabazz (grandmother), Sarah Gail Bradley (mother), Stephanie (sister), Litigious (brother), Josiah Bradley (Josiah X, uncle), other unidentified siblings, unidentified step-father
GROUP AFFILIATION: Young Avengers
EDUCATION: High School Student
FIRST APPEARANCE: Young Avengers #1 (2005)

arrested and court-martialed for the costume theft, and was sentenced to life. From April 1943 Isaiah spent 17 years in solitary confinement at Leavenworth, denied proper medical treatment so that the still imperfect formula eventually left him both sterile and brain damaged, with the mind of a child. Faith was informed he was alive, but only allowed to visit three times a year.

Around the early 1950s, the army tried to create new super-soldiers, using surrogate mothers to carry children created from sperm harvested from Isaiah before he became sterile, mixed with genes secretly taken from Faith; there was only one success, subject A-39, a boy named Josiah. The surrogate learned the truth of the military's intentions, and escaped with the child, bringing him to Faith. Aware the military would be hunting for the child, and fearing for the safety of her daughter, Faith abandoned Josiah where he would soon be discovered, and hopefully adopted. He would grow up to inherit his father's powers and become a minister, Josiah X, later working alongside James Rhodes' vigilante "crew." Meanwhile, Faith wrote President Eisenhower a letter a month for three years, until finally, on the day of Kennedy's inauguration, Eisenhower pardoned Isaiah. The family was sworn to secrecy, and Isaiah was released. Though his mind has been damaged, his body remains in peak condition to this day, a legacy of the formula within him. In recent years, Captain America (Steve Rogers) learned of the African-American experiments and tracked Isaiah down to return the costume he had worn while destroying Schwarzebitte, saying it was rightfully his.

Isaiah and Faith's daughter, Sarah, conceived before the experiments, went on to have several children of her own. She recently remarried and moved out to Scottsdale. Not wishing to interrupt her 16 year old son Elijah's Junior Year at Bronx Science, Sarah left "Eli" behind with his grandparents. After being assaulted by local hoodlums who had taunted his grandfather, Eli was approached by drug dealers who offered him MGH (Mutant Growth Hormone) to gain powers to defend himself. When the thugs later ambushed Eli to finish the job, Isaiah stepped in to defend his grandson, making short work of them. Impressed, Eli wanted to be like Isaiah and carry on his legacy; soon afterward, the teen hero Iron Lad came to their house, seeking to recruit Josiah as an ally against Kang the Conqueror, Iron Lad's future self. Eli informed Iron Lad that Josiah had vanished more than a year earlier, but then claimed to have powers of his own, supposedly as a result of an emergency blood transfusion from Isaiah, and he joined Iron Lad's team as Patriot, alongside Asgardian (later Wiccan) and Hulkling. In truth, Eli was taking MGH, raiding drug houses and apprehending suppliers to steal fresh supplies when needed. The team made their public debut rescuing people from an apartment fire, and the press dubbed them the Young Avengers.

Eli's natural leadership skills made him de facto team leader, but the drugs often made him brash, reckless and short-tempered. The team was soon joined by Kate Bishop (Hawkeye) and Cassie Lang (Stature), with an argumentative attraction growing between Eli and Kate. Jessica Jones, Iron Man and Captain America tracked the team down and insisted they disband for their own safety; after defeating Kang they reluctantly did so, but a few weeks later Kate convinced them to reform. They made the papers yet again capturing the Shocker; Isaiah recognized Eli in the newspaper, and despite his communication problems, made it clear he was proud of him. Unfortunately, Captain America also saw the headline, and informed Faith of Eli's actions, learning that the blood-transfusion origin was false. Meanwhile, running out of MGH, Eli attempted to steal more, but was confronted by the superhuman drug chemist, Mr. Hyde; luckily, Eli had missed a meeting with the other Young Avengers, who came looking for him in the nick of time. While they battled Hyde, Eli surreptitiously injected himself with MGH, but was spotted in the act by Wiccan. Even though Eli took a massive MGH dose, Hyde was still too powerful to subdue, until Eli brought him down by injecting him with an MGH overdose. After the battle Eli, ashamed of his actions, admitted the true source of his powers to his teammates and Captain America, and abandoned his Patriot identity.

Chancing to encounter him outside the library where he worked, the team tried to convince Eli to rejoin and lead them, but he declined. Before he could walk away, the Super Skrull attacked, trying to capture Hulkling. The youths fled, and once he believed they were clear, Eli left them, insisting they were better off without him; however, the Skrull took Eli hostage and then kidnapped Hulkling. Re-donning his costume, Eli led his teammates to find new members and rescue Hulkling, but Kree forces also turned up to claim Hulkling. The Young Avengers held them off until the Avengers arrived, but when the Kree opened fire on Captain America, Patriot leapt to defend him; the Kree weapon cut straight through Eli's shield, severely injuring him. After the Avengers and the Young Avengers resolved the Kree-Skrull hostilities, Captain America offered to give the gravely injured Eli a life-saving blood transfusion, only to discover that Isaiah had already done so. Eli soon made a full recovery, inheriting his grandfather's powers in the process, and resumed his leadership of the Young Avengers, who recently became fugitives in the wake of the Superhero Registration Act.

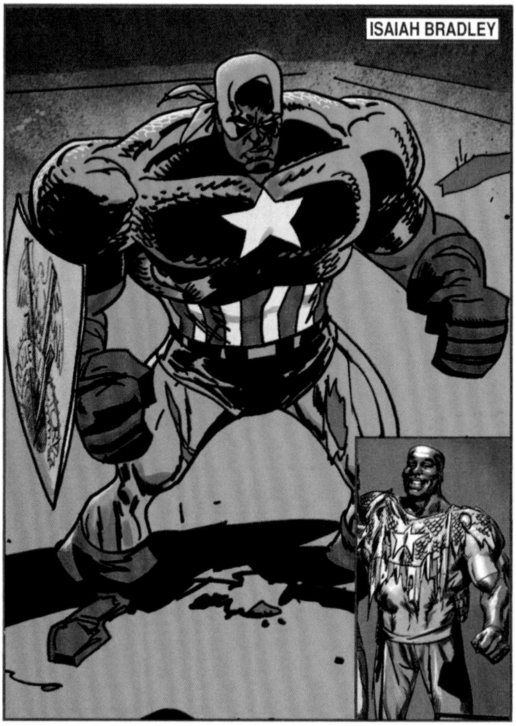
ISAIAH BRADLEY

Art by Kyle Baker

HEIGHT: 5'9"
WEIGHT: 154 lbs.
EYES: Brown
HAIR: Black (shaved bald)

ABILITIES/ACCESSORIES: Patriot is a skilled fighter and natural tactician with enhanced strength, stamina and speed, superhuman hearing and bulletproof skin. He uses throwing stars in combat and carries a triangular shield.

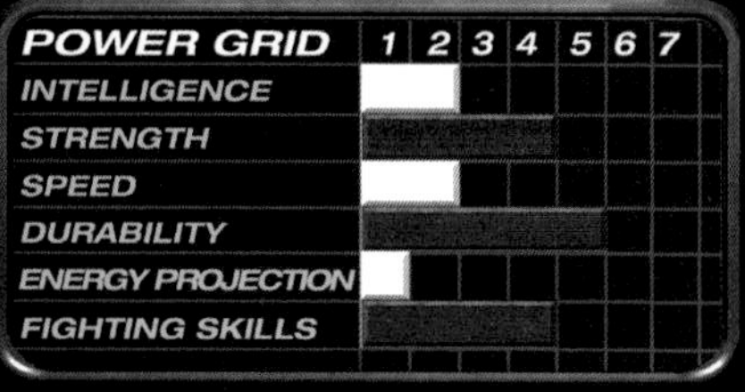
POWER GRID
1 2 3 4 5 6 7
INTELLIGENCE
STRENGTH
SPEED
DURABILITY
ENERGY PROJECTION
FIGHTING SKILLS

HISTORY: Cassie Lang was a fan of superheroes since she learned to read. Her mother abandoned her family when she was young and her father, electronics technician Scott Lang, turned to theft to support Cassie. At age 4, Cassie was taken in by her aunt and uncle when Scott was sentenced to 5 years in Ryker's Island Prison for burglary. Upon Scott's release, he was hired by Stark International and reconnected with his daughter, but when 9-year-old Cassie was diagnosed with a fatal congenital heart condition, Scott was forced to steal Dr. Henry Pym's Ant-Man equipment so that he could rescue Dr. Erica Sondheim, whose developments in critical focus laser surgery appeared to be Cassie's only hope for survival. Upon liberating Sondheim from Darren Cross of Cross Technological Enterprises, Scott saved Cassie and was allowed to keep Pym's Ant-Man equipment. Although Scott tried to conceal his super-hero identity from Cassie, she secretly knew he was Ant-Man. Living in a modest Nassau County suburb on New York's Long Island, Cassie spent her time making unique meals for her father and playing with other children of Stark International employees, such as Denise Pithins, the daughter of Human Relations Director Artemus Pithins. When Stark International fell into the hands of Obadiah Stane, Scott and Cassie relocated to Chula Vista, California, where Scott formed his own electronics company, Electrolang, Inc.

At age 11, Cassie moved back to New York when the Fantastic Four hired Scott for his technological expertise. Visiting the team's Four Freedoms Plaza, Cassie became attracted to Kristoff Vernard, a 12-year-old boy artificially implanted with Dr. Doom's memories and knowledge, although she was put off by his Doom-like armor. She eventually discovered that Zarrko the Tomorrow Man was impersonating Kristoff's man-servant Boris as a spy for the villain Hyperstorm, and she was imprisoned until the Fantastic Four defeated Zarrko. When the Fantastic Four seemingly died in battle, Scott was hired by Oracle, Inc. to join Heroes for Hire. Cassie accidentally reactivated — and was absorbed by — the Super-Adaptoid android in Oracle's basement, but Scott encouraged her to defeat the android from within. After Heroes for Hire disbanded, Scott became more involved with his longtime Avengers allies, and a family court judge awarded sole custody of Cassie to her mother (with Scott getting weekend visitations), citing concerns that Scott's activities would interfere with parenting. Sent to live with her mother and her new step-father, NYPD officer Blake Burdick, Cassie was abducted by killer Charles Cooley, but was soon rescued by Avengers Ant-Man and Jack of Hearts, who seemingly sacrificed his life to dispose of Cooley.

Cassie's life was forever altered when Scott died in an attack on Avengers Mansion by the deranged Scarlet Witch. Months later, at age 14, Cassie became affiliated with the adolescent heroes known as the Young Avengers and soon discovered she could alter her size

REAL NAME: Cassandra Eleanor "Cassie" Lang
ALIASES: Ant-Girl, Giant Girl, "Insect-Girl" (all contemplated)
IDENTITY: Secret
OCCUPATION: Student, adventurer
CITIZENSHIP: U.S.A.
PLACE OF BIRTH: Oyster Bay, Long Island, New York
KNOWN RELATIVES: Scott Lang (Ant-Man, father, deceased), Peggy Rae Burdick (mother), Blake Burdick (step-father), Ruth (aunt), Carl (uncle)
GROUP AFFILIATION: Young Avengers
EDUCATION: High school student
FIRST APPEARANCE: (Cassie) Marvel Premiere #47 (1979); (Stature) Young Avengers #6 (2005)

as a result of exposure to Pym Particles she had stolen from her father over the years. Attracted to teammate Iron Lad (Nathaniel Richards), who soon left the group, Cassie adopted the codename "Stature" and assisted the Young Avengers against Kang the Conqueror, Mr. Hyde and Super-Skrull. Currently, Stature and the Young Avengers are affiliated with Captain America's rebel super-heroes, who are resisting the federal government's Superhuman Registration Act. Cassie is unaware that her teammate the Vision (whose brain patterns are based on Iron Lad's) has a crush on her.

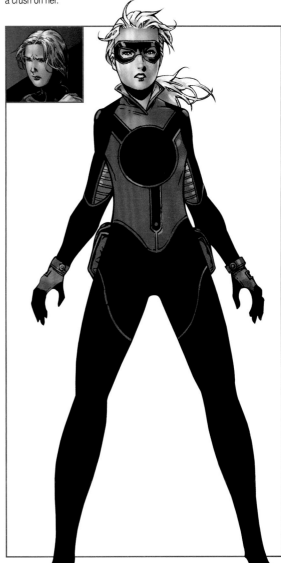

HEIGHT: 5'4" (variable)	EYES: Blue
WEIGHT: 106 lbs. (variable)	HAIR: Blonde

ABILITIES/ACCESSORIES: Stature can grow to gigantic heights, requiring the rapid acquisition of body mass (presumably from the Kosmos dimension). This extra mass fortifies all of her cellular tissue, including her bones and muscles, enabling her to support her increased weight and giving her superhuman strength. Stature can also reduce herself to a size of approximately one-half inch.

POWER GRID	1	2	3	4	5	6	7
INTELLIGENCE							
STRENGTH							
SPEED							
DURABILITY							
ENERGY PROJECTION							
FIGHTING SKILLS							

*YELLOW BARS INDICATE RATINGS IN GIANT FORM

REAL NAME: Chase Stein
ALIASES: Neo (considered)
IDENTITY: Secret
OCCUPATION: Adventurer; former student
CITIZENSHIP: U.S.A.
PLACE OF BIRTH: Los Angeles, California
KNOWN RELATIVES: Janet & Victor Stein (parents, believed deceased),
GROUP AFFILIATION: Runaways
EDUCATION: High school dropout
FIRST APPEARANCE: Runaways #1 (2003)

HISTORY: Inventors Victor and Janet Stein accepted an offer to serve the ancient Gibborim alongside five other married couples in the Pride. The Gibborim sought to remake Earth to their liking and promised that six of the Pride would survive into this paradise. While serving the Gibborim, the Pride created a west coast criminal empire. When the Steins learned that Janet was pregnant, the Pride agreed each couple would have one child, and would let the children take their place in the Gibborim's new world. Shortly after, Janet gave birth to Chase.

Chase grew up to be more interested in athletics than science, greatly disappointing his father, who physically abused him. As a teenager, Chase apparently dabbled in low-level crimes, allegedly once even killing and disposing of a carjacker. Over the years, the Steins met annually with

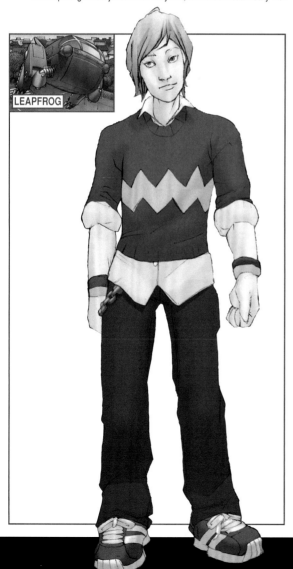

LEAPFROG

the other five families and the Pride would secretly perform the Rite of Blood, a human sacrifice to their masters. Alex Wilder, the son of Pride leader Geoffrey, manipulated the Pride's other children into witnessing one such sacrifice. The shocked teens began investigating their parents. While searching the Stein residence, the teens clashed with the Pride and escaped, and Chase temporarily bonded with a pair of powerful "Fistigons" (gloved weapons). When the Pride implicated Chase and the others in the sacrifice, he led his fellow Runaways to his Bronson Canyon hideaway, a mansion he dubbed the Hostel which had been swallowed up during an earthquake. Chase briefly considered using the codename Neo before teammate Gertrude Yorkes dubbed him Talkback.

While evading the Pride and their corrupt LAPD confederates, the Runaways encountered the vampire Topher and the misguided vigilantes Cloak and Dagger. After translating the Abstract, a book containing their parents' secrets, the Runaways resolved to stop them once and for all. They invaded the Vivarium (the Gibborim's undersea lair), but Chase drowned while battling a sentry. Gert revived Chase via CPR, and he hotwired the Pride's Leapfrog vehicle, helping his fellow Runaways after Alex betrayed them to the Pride. The Gibborim apparently slaughtered Alex and the Pride for their failure, though Talkback and the Runaways escaped.

Separated and sent to foster homes, the Runaways quickly reunited, and Chase began a romance with Gertrude. With Chase acting as their pilot in the Leapfrog, the group battled the Wrecking Crew, Ultron and teen hero support group Excelsior. When the Runaways helped clear Cloak's name in New York, Chase ran afoul of Pusher Man, a criminal who utilized Fistigons based on the Steins' design. After Chase saved himself and Runaways team leader Nico Minoru by bluffing his way into Pusher Man's graces, Nico kissed him, but Chase rejected her. The group returned to Los Angeles and — after the X-Men briefly tried to remove the preteen mutant Molly Hayes from the Runaways' care — were assaulted by a new Pride: several of Alex's gamer friends duped into working with a younger version of Geoffrey Wilder, pulled forth from the past. This Pride sowed strife among the teens by revealing the Chase-Nico kiss, and kidnapped Molly in the ensuing chaos. When the Runaways came to Molly's rescue, Geoffrey threatened to sacrifice Chase to the Gibborim. To save Chase, Gert convinced Geoffrey that Chase was not innocent enough for the ritual, so Wilder killed her instead. As she died, Gert transferred her telepathic link to dinosaur Old Lace to her boyfriend. Torn by these events, Chase stole Geoffrey's Abstract and decoder ring, and he and Old Lace left the Runaways. Intent on bringing Gert back, Chase kidnapped Lotus, a former member of the new Pride, and sought out the Gibborim.

HEIGHT: **5'11"**	WEIGHT: **188 lbs.**
EYES: **Blue**	HAIR: **Blond**

ABILITIES/ACCESSORIES: Chase is an athletically gifted 18 year old with some electronic and mechanical skills, allowing him to repair and rewire various items. He is adept with his switchblade knife. Chase has utilized his parents' inventions, including "Fistigons" gloves which can create and control fire, x-ray goggles and the Leapfrog transport vehicle. He is currently telepathically linked to Old Lace, a female Deinonychus-like dinosaur from the 87th century.

POWER GRID	1	2	3	4	5	6	7
INTELLIGENCE							
STRENGTH							
SPEED							
DURABILITY							
ENERGY PROJECTION							
FIGHTING SKILLS							

Art by Adrian Alphona

HISTORY: Years ago, married Avengers teammates Scarlet Witch (Wanda Maximoff) and the android Vision conceived and bore twin sons, Thomas and William, via Wanda's magic. Unwittingly created from two lost souls, the twins were actually born from fragmented energies of the hell-lord Mephisto. Believing the twins were fragments of his own lost soul, evil mage Master Pandemonium, was manipulated by Mephisto into abducting them, but they were seemingly reabsorbed into the reconstituted Mephisto; however, the twins' souls had been so transfigured by the Scarlet Witch's magic that they temporarily destroyed Mephisto, and the souls were set free, though they were believed destroyed.

Thomas and William apparently survived as individual entities. William was adopted by Jeff and Rebecca Kaplan and raised in New York's Upper West Side while Thomas ended up in Springfield, New Jersey. Upon reaching adolescence, Kaplan was bullied by classmate John Kessler because of his homosexuality. After a chance encounter with the Scarlet Witch, who encouraged him to stand up to the bully, Kaplan discovered he had mystical powers, although his inability to control them nearly killed Kessler. Shortly after, he was found by Iron Lad (Nathaniel Richards), a younger, time-displaced version of Kang the Conqueror who located Kaplan with a failsafe program within the now-deactivated Vision's programming designed to locate the next generation of Avengers (super-powered youths connected to the Avengers in various ways) if anything were to happen to the original Avengers. Iron Lad wanted to train these young heroes so they could fend off an impending attack from his future self. As "Asgardian," Kaplan began a romance with teammate Hulkling (Teddy Altman) while these Young Avengers engaged in a series of highly-publicized rescue missions in order to train for Kang's arrival.

When the reconstituted Avengers tried to disband the Young Avengers, Kang's arrival interrupted their plans. After Kang's defeat and Iron Lad's return to his timeline, Kaplan and the Young Avengers were warned by the Avengers to stop acting as super-heroes, but the teenagers continued their vigilante activities and Kaplan adopted the new identity of "Wiccan." The Young Avengers defeated super-criminals Shocker (Herman Schultz) and Mr. Hyde (Calvin Zabo) before Hulkling was abducted by Super-Skrull (Kl'rt), who revealed that Hulkling was the son of the Kree Mar-Vell and the Skrull Princess Annelle. To rescue Hulkling, the Young Avengers broke Speed (Thomas Shepherd) out of the N.J. Youth Correctional Facility, and Kaplan came to believe that the nearly identical Shepherd was his brother and that they were both sons of the Scarlet Witch. After rescuing Hulkling and narrowly averting a war between the interstellar Skrull and Kree Empires, which both claimed custody over Hulkling, Wiccan and Speed planned to locate their missing mother; but they were interrupted by the passage of the Superhuman

REAL NAME: William "Billy" Kaplan
ALIASES: Formerly Asgardian; informally "Magic Lad," "Thor Junior," "Warlock Boy"
IDENTITY: Secret
OCCUPATION: Adventurer, student
CITIZENSHIP: U.S.A.
PLACE OF BIRTH: Allegedly Leonia, New Jersey
KNOWN RELATIVES: Wanda Maximoff (Scarlet Witch, alleged mother), Vision (Victor Shade, alleged father), Thomas Shepherd (Speed, brother), Jeff and Rebecca Kaplan (adoptive parents), two younger adoptive brothers
GROUP AFFILIATION: Young Avengers
EDUCATION: High school student
FIRST APPEARANCE: (Allegedly, as William) Vision and Scarlet Witch #12 (1986); (Asgardian) Young Avengers #1 (2005); (Wiccan) Young Avengers #6 (2005)

Registration Act, legislation which outlawed all vigilante activity by unregistered superhumans. Captured by a S.H.I.E.L.D. Superhuman Restraint Unit, the Young Avengers were soon rescued by Captain America and joined his underground resistance movement against the Registration Act. Traveling to Los Angeles to help the young Runaways team escape similar arrest by S.H.I.E.L.D., the Young Avengers teamed up against Marvel Boy (Noh-Varr), a nanite-controlled agent of the top-secret Cube prison facility. Wiccan was among the heroes captured by the Cube's Warden, although he was promptly rescued by the Young Avengers and Runaways who had not been apprehended.

HEIGHT: 5'8"	WEIGHT: 155 lbs.
EYES: Black	HAIR: Black

ABILITIES/ACCESSORIES: Wiccan is a witch who can manipulate magical energies for a seemingly limitless variety of effects. He can fire destructive magical energy bolts, locate individuals, erect magical energy shields, create solid energy constructs, heal himself and others, teleport himself and others, and levitate. His abilities seem limited only by his imagination and power of concentration, although his spells apparently do not work unless he can hear himself casting them.

POWER GRID	1	2	3	4	5	6	7
INTELLIGENCE							
STRENGTH							
SPEED*							
DURABILITY							
ENERGY PROJECTION							
FIGHTING SKILLS							

*WICCAN IS A TELEPORTER

ALEX WILDER

REAL NAME: Alex Wilder
ALIASES: None
IDENTITY: No dual identity
OCCUPATION: Student
CITIZENSHIP: U.S.A.
PLACE OF BIRTH: Los Angeles, California
KNOWN RELATIVES: Geoffrey & Catherine Wilder (parents, presumed deceased)
GROUP AFFILIATION: Runaways
EDUCATION: High school student
FIRST APPEARANCE: Runaways #1 (2003)

HISTORY: Roughly twenty years ago, married criminals Geoffrey and Catherine Wilder were summoned with five other couples the ancient beings known as the Gibborim. The twelve became the Pride, the Gibborim's operatives on Earth, and performed a yearly sacrifice (the Rite of Blood) to ensure their masters' eventual return. When one of the other couples became pregnant, the six couples decided to each have one child apiece, reserving the Pride's promised six spots in the Gibborim's foretold paradise for the children. The Wilders' son Alex grew up believing his parents' annual meeting with their friends was a

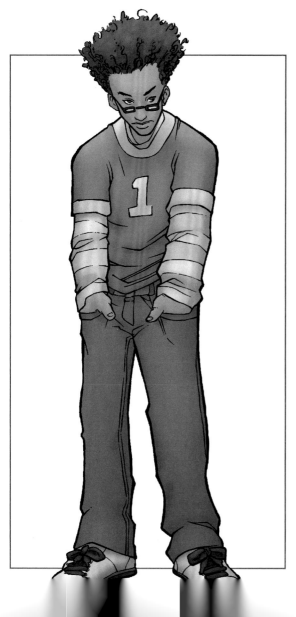

charity event, and he was left to entertain the other children. One year, he accidentally witnessed the Rite of Blood. Not sure what to make of it, Alex found and read his parents' Abstract, a book containing the Pride's secrets; however, he soon learned that two of the Pride's couples, the Deans and the Hayeses, intended to betray the rest.

Over the next year, Alex devised a plan to stop the traitors, using his fellow children as pawns. He also hid numerous files in his online account for his computer-gaming friends to find later. During the next Rite of Blood, Alex feigned ignorance and caused the other kids to witness the sacrifice. He convinced them that their parents were evil and had to be stopped, and carefully led them in "accidentally" gathering various items of power from their homes. When the Pride confronted them, they escaped, but not before Alex both struck up a romance with teammate Nico Minoru and left an anonymous note telling his parents there was a mole within the newly-dubbed Runaways. Unaware of their son's plan, the Wilders framed Alex for the sacrifice, and implicated him in kidnapping Molly Hayes, the youngest of the Runaways. Alex led the adventuring Runaways for months, though he refused to take a codename as the others had. When Alex and the rest were duped into welcoming Topher into their ranks, Topher romanced Nico and soon revealed himself as a decades-old vampire, whom the Runaways destroyed. Later, corrupt LAPD officials aligned with the Pride tricked vigilantes Cloak and Dagger into hunting the kids. When the duo learned the truth, Wilder contacted the Pride to keep them from revealing the organization's existence.

On the day the Pride was to perform the Rite of Thunder, presenting the sacrificed souls to the Gibborim, Alex led the Runaways to the Gibborim's underwater Vivarium lair, where he allowed a giant sentry to beat Chase Stein before he used a password to shut it down, ensuring Stein's non-participation. Stein handed over his powerful Fistigon gloves to Alex to use. The Runaways confronted the Pride, and during the battle, Alex gained control of Nico's mystical Staff of One and Gertrude Yorkes' dinosaur, Old Lace. He knocked the last remaining Runaway, Karolina Dean, unconscious, revealing himself to his parents as the mole. He pleaded with Nico to join him and his parents in the new paradise, but Nico violently refused. Chase eventually intervened using the Pride's Leapfrog vehicle, allowing Molly time to destroy the container holding the sacrificed souls. The Gibborim arrived, and Alex took responsibility for what had happened. The Gibborim seemingly incinerated him for his actions, and then attacked the Pride. The surviving Runaways escaped. Shortly after, Nico attempted a resurrection spell to bring Alex back, but apparently failed.

Alex's online friends hacked into his account and found the files left for them, believing his twisted version of events. They attempted a resurrection spell, but instead summoned a young Geoffrey Wilder. This time-displaced Geoffrey tried to bargain with the Gibborim to bring his family back. They agreed upon a sacrifice, and though Geoffrey killed Gertrude before he was sent back to his rightful era, it is uncertain if any of the attempts to resurrect Alex succeeded.

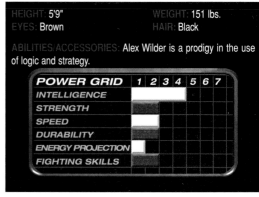

HEIGHT: 5'9"   **WEIGHT:** 151 lbs.
EYES: Brown   **HAIR:** Black

ABILITIES/ACCESSORIES: Alex Wilder is a prodigy in the use of logic and strategy.

POWER GRID	1	2	3	4	5	6	7
INTELLIGENCE							
STRENGTH							
SPEED							
DURABILITY							
ENERGY PROJECTION							
FIGHTING SKILLS							